SUPERNATURAL SECURITY CLEARANCES

BY

VINCE BAKER

Scripture quotations are taken from the Holy Bible, King James Version. The King James Version is public domain in the United States of America. All bolding and emphasis are added by the author.

Cover Illustration and Design by: Guy Manzur

Formatting by: Deborah Ling and Emmanuel Okpeniku

Printed in the United States of America

DEDICATION

I dedicate this book to God the Father, Jesus His Son, and the Holy Spirit. I attribute all that I am and anything I have accomplished to the Godhead. All three of the Godhead have played an integral part in my life. You revealed yourselves to me when I was young and have always been there for me throughout my whole life. I love you with all my heart, mind, soul, body, and strength. I will never forget what you have done for me. I THANK YOU from the bottom of my heart!

I also dedicate this book to my wonderful wife, Eunice. The way you love me and take care of me does not go unnoticed. You also played a significant role in getting this book out. Thank you for always supporting me, my walk with God, and the ministry God has given me. You are not only my wife, but you are my companion and friend.

TABLE OF CONTENTS

INTRODUCTION

The Lord revealed to me that this book is historical. What He meant by historical is that this book was written in a pioneering way with the concept of *Supernatural Security Clearances*. The term *Supernatural Security Clearance* was given to me by the Holy Spirit and is a term I have never heard before. The Holy Spirit then walked me through the stories of the Bible and showed me how there are *Supernatural Security Clearances* throughout the Scriptures and the requirements to gain one.

The whole Bible opened up to me, and I started to view it differently once I fully understood the concept of what He was revealing to me about *Supernatural Security Clearances*. Once you understand what it takes to get a security clearance in the natural and that God's kingdom is no different, the Bible will also open up to you. Stories like Elijah having to take Elisha to four locations and what those four locations spiritually represented before he was taken up into a whirlwind started to make sense. Or how Samson lost his strength when his hair was cut. People in the Bible had to meet requirements and be fully committed to God to be able to walk in His power and maintain their *Supernatural Security Clearance.*

I believe anyone who picks up this book and reads the truth about *Supernatural Security Clearances* will be changed. This book was written with many Biblical examples of people who gave up everything to serve God. The Bible is filled with clues on how to tap into the *High Calling* of God. If you follow the clues revealed in the Bible, it will lead you to the requirements of fulfilling the *High Calling* of God and how to receive your own *Supernatural Security Clearance.*

God led me to write this book for those who want more out of this life. There is a voice inside of you calling you to something deeper than what this world has to offer. You know there must be more than what you see in the local Church. Your heart tells you there must be more to Christianity than making a confession of Christ and going to Church once a week to hear a nice sermon while living a mundane life with no power. What you are sensing is the voice of God calling you to come up higher.

If you are reading this book, then the voice of God is speaking to you. God is revealing Himself to you in His own special way. God is talking to you by His Spirit. If you follow the leading of His Spirit and His voice, He will lead you on a spiritual journey that will last a lifetime and bring you into fellowship with God throughout all of eternity.

Many are called, but few are chosen in God's kingdom. God puts out His offer to the world, but few accept God's offer of abundant life. The kingdom of God and the *High Calling* of God are more valuable than anything this world offers. Far too many people put all their hope in this life and what it has to offer. Even if you become a billionaire, it still wouldn't compare to what God has for you.

There is a *High Calling* in God that most Churches of our day do not walk in or talk about. They don't walk in or reveal the *High Calling*

2

because of the work and price you must pay to enter all that God has for you. No one can expect something of value or to accomplish something great that costs you nothing. What I mean by *cost you* is in reference to your commitment level and what you will do to achieve something great. The Gospel is free, and by the free grace of God, we are saved by the sacrifice of Jesus, but to gain a *Supernatural Security Clearance* will cost a total commitment to God.

This book is written for those who want to know what Jesus expects of His disciples to walk in the *High Calling* of God and receive a *Supernatural Security Clearance.* In the parable of the sower sows the Word, Jesus revealed that we could either reap thirtyfold, sixtyfold, or a hundredfold of His kingdom, based upon how we heard and responded to the Word of God sown in our hearts. This book was written for those who want to understand and do what it takes to reach the one-hundredfold harvest of the kingdom of God. You are tired of the lies trying to keep you down and back from all that God has to offer you.

You know in your heart there is no way that Abraham, Moses, Joshua, Samuel, King David, Elijah, Elisha, the Old Testament Prophets, John the Baptist, and the apostles of Jesus did what they did without making an all-in commitment to God. These men were 100% devoted to God, His kingdom, and His will. They loved God with all of their hearts, minds, souls, bodies, and strength. God is now looking for those who will be like these anointed men, fulfill their *High Calling*, and receive a *Supernatural Security Clearance.*

Even Jesus Himself, revealed through His life, teaching, and death on the cross that He was all-in. God is not asking more of us than what was asked and revealed in Jesus our Lord. Jesus was the perfect

3

example of how to live and be committed to God. Jesus passed every temptation the devil threw at Him and was granted a *Supernatural Security Clearance* to walk in the power of the Holy Spirit.

God is speaking to a rare breed of Christians in this generation who will not settle for less than God's best. They know God has a *High Calling* and are willing to pay the price to gain the rite of passage. In this Divine rite of passage, you leave complacency, lack of commitment, lack of love for God, fear, doubt, and unbelief behind. You are willing to pay the same price the early followers of Christ paid to take up their cross daily and follow Him.

So, if you are ready to come into your *High Calling* and fulfill the perfect will of God, this book is for you. The Spirit of the Lord has been speaking to your heart for years, and now you are ready to do what it takes to take up your mantle, walk in the power of God's kingdom and obtain a **Supernatural Security Clearance.** The stakes could not be higher, and the rewards could not be greater!

CHAPTER 1
SUPERNATURAL SECURITY CLEARANCE

The Bible is filled with examples of people who gained and lost their *Supernatural Security Clearance*. The term *Supernatural Security Clearance* may be a new term to some people, but after reading this book, you will see from the Word of God that God has *Supernatural Security Clearances,* and they play an essential role in His kingdom. God has many secrets, places, and anointings to guard and protect. Therefore, God needs people He can trust to manage and run His kingdom. The kingdom of God is no different than any other kingdom or nation on earth in that it needs to protect its interests. This book will discover the importance of a **Supernatural Security Clearance** required for any believer seeking greater access to God's kingdom and the ability to operate in a powerful high dimension of the anointing.

Before I go into detail about *Supernatural Security Clearances,* let us talk about natural security clearances and how an individual can obtain one. Every nation has secrets to protect and therefore needs trusted citizens to be granted a security clearance before being trusted with their nation's top-secret information. Security clearances are vital for every sovereign nation's ongoing protection and stability to protect their people and interests.

To be granted a security clearance in this world, a citizen must pass a background check to confirm they are trustworthy, honest, dependable, and free from any conflicting foreign allegiances that have the potential for coercion or betrayal. A security clearance can take up to a year before someone is approved. During this time, there are specific criteria governmental agencies are looking for. They must also go through a selection process to determine if they are fit and committed to what it takes to be granted a security clearance.

The main requirement is if someone is patriotic to their country. They must be free from any influence of outside governments so they cannot be pressured to give up national secrets. They must not be able to be influenced by family members or friendships whereby the enemy can pressure them to betray their country. They must also be free from sexual addictions, money problems, alcohol abuse, drug involvement, and criminal activity.

In general, the government granting access to a security clearance requires an assessment that includes all factors of a person's life. This involves looking at the applicant's entire life, not just some specific items or incidents that may have been listed as being of concern. They are looking to see if the person in consideration of the security clearance can be trusted and not be tempted by the enemy in any area of their life. For example, if they have financial problems, someone might be open to accepting money from the enemy in exchange for secret information. Another example could be a relationship they are in with a friend, family member, or spouse tied to a foreign government, and where that family member could put pressure on them to give up secrets.

The background check needs to be thorough to know how loyal one will be to their country. It also ensures they have the ability and aptitude to perform their job. The person given the security clearance must be trusted and relied upon to exercise the responsibility necessary for working in a secure environment where protecting classified top-secret information is paramount.

Once someone is granted a security clearance, they can access the following items.

1. **SECRET LOCATIONS** – Bases, Underground Facilities, Top Secret Locations

2. **POWERFUL WEAPONS** – Secret Weapons, Nuclear Bombs, Chemical Warfare, and Fire Power

3. **CONFIDENTIAL INFORMATION** – Private Information, Technical Data, and National Interests

Now that we understand security clearances in the natural and the background check required to obtain one, let's explore what a *Supernatural Security Clearance* is. A *Supernatural Security Clearance* is when God authorizes someone access to the following:

1. Entrance Into the Kingdom of God

2. Ability to See into the Future

3. Heavenly Visions and Dreams

4. Access to the Mysteries of the Kingdom of God

5. Entrance into God's Throne Room

6. Granted the Ability to Operate in a Powerful Anointing

7. Graced with a Five-Fold Calling to Be an Apostle, Prophet, Evangelist, Pastor, or Teacher

8. Endowed with One of the Nine Gifts of the Holy Spirit

9. Prophetic Insight into People's Destinies

10. Given the Responsibility to Bring Judgment Upon the Enemies of God

In many ways, security clearances in the natural are like *Supernatural Security Clearances*. Both require trusted individuals who pass a background check to access confidential information, powerful weapons, and secret locations. However, this is managed differently when discussing a background check and God giving a *Supernatural Security Clearance.* It is handled differently because God takes sinners and turns them into saints. God is forgiving, and if someone allows Him to do a work in them by writing His Laws upon their heart, He can change them into a very trusted Heavenly citizen. They may have done terrible acts in their past, but if they allow God to change them, they can still be granted a *Supernatural Security Clearance*.

Once someone repents of their sins, a transformation begins in their character; then, God can grant them a *Supernatural Security Clearance*. At this point, they can be entrusted with His secrets, anointed weaponry, and access to Heavenly places. Governments of this world may not forgive people's past and grant them a security clearance, and these governments are not there to make you a better person. However, God can take the worst of people and the greatest of sinners and change them into glorious saints of God.

When it comes to God and a *Supernatural Security Clearance,* it is about allowing God to change someone by the power of the Holy Spirit on the inside to where they come to a place of maturity and can be trusted to walk in an anointing. Once the Holy Spirit sanctifies them, they become a person who can be trusted with the secrets of God. Trust is the main attribute God is looking for before granting someone access to His Divine secrets, anointed power, and entrance into Heavenly places. God must know that you will not betray Him like Judas Iscariot betrayed Jesus.

The Apostle Paul said he was the chiefest of sinners, but we can see that he became one of the most influential apostles of the New Testament. Before he was saved, he persecuted Christians, but Jesus still had mercy on him and changed him into a saint. His salvation experience was used as a pattern of what God would do for others.

> **1 Timothy 1:15-16 (KJV)**
> 15 This is a faithful saying, and worthy of all acceptation, **that Christ Jesus came into the world to save sinners; of whom I am chief.**
> 16 Howbeit for this cause I obtained mercy, that in me first Jesus Christ might shew forth all longsuffering, **for a pattern to them which should hereafter believe on him to life everlasting.**

The Apostle Paul was granted a *Supernatural Security Clearance*. With this *Supernatural Security Clearance*, he was given access to go before the Throne of God in the third Heaven and hear unspeakable Words that he could not utter. He was also granted access to the mysteries of God and a powerful five-fold anointing as an apostle.

2 Corinthians 12:1-5 (KJV)
> 1 It is not expedient for me doubtless to glory. **I will come to visions and revelations of the Lord.**
> 2 I knew a man in Christ above fourteen years ago, (whether in the body, I cannot tell; or whether out of the body, I cannot tell: God knoweth;) **such an one caught up to the third heaven.**
> 3 And I knew such a man, (whether in the body, or out of the body, I cannot tell: God knoweth;)
> 4 **How that he was caught up into paradise, and heard unspeakable words, which it is not lawful for a man to utter.**
> 5 Of such an one will I glory: yet of myself I will not glory, but in mine infirmities.

When Jesus was on the earth, He told His disciples they were being given access to know the mysteries of the kingdom of God, but others were not granted access to these secrets but only heard parables.

Luke 8:10 (KJV)
> 10 **And he said, Unto you it is given to know the mysteries of the kingdom of God: but to others in parables;** that seeing they might not see, and hearing they might not understand.

Jesus rejoiced in His spirit when the seventy disciples He sent out returned saying the devils were subject to them. He said that the Father hid these secrets from the wise and prudent and revealed them to babes.

Luke 10:17-24 (KJV)
> 17 And the seventy returned again with joy, saying, Lord, even the devils are subject unto us through thy name.
> 18 And he said unto them, I beheld Satan as lightning fall from heaven.

19 Behold, I give unto you power to tread on serpents and scorpions, and over all the power of the enemy: and nothing shall by any means hurt you.

20 Notwithstanding in this rejoice not, that the spirits are subject unto you; but rather rejoice, because your names are written in heaven.

21 In that hour Jesus rejoiced in spirit, and said, I thank thee, O Father, Lord of heaven and earth, that thou hast hid these things from the wise and prudent, and hast revealed them unto babes: even so, Father; for so it seemed good in thy sight.

22 All things are delivered to me of my Father: and no man knoweth who the Son is, but the Father; and who the Father is, but the Son, and he to whom the Son will reveal him.

23 And he turned him unto his disciples, and said privately, **Blessed are the eyes which see the things that ye see:**

24 For I tell you, that many prophets and kings have desired to see those things which ye see, and have not seen them; and to hear those things which ye hear, and have not heard them.

The ultimate *Supernatural Security Clearance* is granted to those who accept Jesus Christ as their Lord and are given the privilege to live forever in Heaven. They believed in their heart that God raised Jesus from the dead and confessed Him as their Lord. These sanctified believing Christians will be given the privilege of living with God forever in a new glorified body and having access to the Throne of God. Let us read what the Scripture says about those who will be granted eternal access and those who will not be granted access in the Book of Revelation.

Revelation 21:1-8 (KJV)

1 And I saw a new heaven and a new earth: for the first heaven and the first earth were passed away; and there was no more sea.

 2 And I John saw the holy city, new Jerusalem, coming down from God out of heaven, prepared as a bride adorned for her husband.

3 And I heard a great voice out of heaven saying, Behold, the tabernacle of God is with men, and he will dwell with them, and they shall be his people, and God himself shall be with them, and be their God.

4 And God shall wipe away all tears from their eyes; and there shall be no more death, neither sorrow, nor crying, neither shall there be any more pain: for the former things are passed away.

5 And he that sat upon the throne said, Behold, I make all things new. And he said unto me, Write: for these words are true and faithful.

6 And he said unto me, It is done. I am Alpha and Omega, the beginning and the end. **I will give unto him that is athirst of the fountain of the water of life freely.**

7 **He that overcometh shall inherit all things; and I will be his God, and he shall be my son.**

8 **But the fearful, and unbelieving, and the abominable, and murderers, and whoremongers, and sorcerers, and idolaters, and all liars, shall have their part in the lake which burneth with fire and brimstone: which is the second death.**

We can see that God does a background check on anyone wanting to live with Him forever. If people do not repent of their sins and accept Jesus as their Lord and Savior, they will not inherit the kingdom of God. God's kingdom is no different than any other kingdom in that it has ***Top Secrets and Holy Places*** to protect. If you want to drink the water of life freely, you must repent and become like God. If you repent and overcome, you will inherit all things, and God will be your God, and you will be His son. If you do not repent of your sins, you will suffer the consequence of eternal damnation.

I will reveal in this book people who were granted *Supernatural Security Clearances* in both the Old and New Testaments and how some people lost their God-given security clearance. I will also reveal what Jesus went through before He was granted His Anointing and *Supernatural Security Clearance* before His earthly ministry began. You will discover what God is looking for and what requirements must be met before He gives someone a *Supernatural Security Clearance.* Finally, I will reveal how you can be granted a *Supernatural Security Clearance* from God and fulfill your *High Calling.*

CHAPTER 2
THE GRACE OF GOD THAT BRINGS SALVATION

Before we go deeper into the subject of *Supernatural Security Clearances* and what it takes to be granted one, we have to clearly understand God's grace and the free gift of salvation. There is nothing we can do to earn the right to be saved by God and given the opportunity to go to Heaven. Salvation is a free gift from God paid for by the death, burial, and resurrection of Jesus Christ. Grace has everything to do with how we respond in faith to God's free gift. Once God's grace freely saves us through faith, what we do or do not do can determine our level of authority and access to the deeper things of God. It also determines what type of rewards, crowns, and position of authority you will be granted in God's eternal kingdom.

To understand this truth deeper, let us start by looking at what the Bible has to say about the grace of God. What is the grace of God? The word grace comes from the Greek word *charis,* which means undeserved favor, gift, blessing, and kindness. Grace has to do with showing favor to an undeserving person without expecting anything in return. However, when the word grace is used in connection with God, it takes on a deeper meaning. When God shows grace to someone, He chooses to bless them rather than curse them as their sin deserves. God's grace is free, and when bestowed upon someone, it allows them to be freely blessed in this life and go to Heaven. All of this is possible because of what Jesus paid for when He went to the cross.

> **Ephesians 2:4-9 (KJV)**
> 4 But God, who is rich in mercy, **for his great love wherewith he loved us,**
> 5 Even when we were dead in sins, hath quickened us together with Christ, **(by grace ye are saved;)**
> 6 And hath raised us up together, and made us sit together in heavenly places in Christ Jesus:
> 7 That in the ages to come he might shew the exceeding riches of his grace in his kindness toward us through Christ Jesus.
> 8 **For by grace are ye saved through faith; and that not of yourselves: it is the gift of God:**
> 9 **Not of works, lest any man should boast.**

When a sinner experiences the grace of God and the forgiveness of God, it transforms their sinful heart and changes them into a new creation in Christ. A repentant sinner experiencing the grace of God is no longer the same person. The repentant sinner no longer desires to sin but to serve God because of the favor of grace bestowed upon them. The grace of God not only forgives the undeserving sinner but teaches the sinner not to sin anymore. Once God's grace changes someone, they can be entrusted with a *Supernatural Security Clearance.* This is the true grace of God that brings salvation.

Titus 2:11-12 (KJV)

11 **For the grace of God that bringeth salvation hath appeared to all men,**

12 **Teaching us that, denying ungodliness and worldly lusts, we should live soberly, righteously, and godly, in this present world;**

The grace of God that brings salvation teaches us to deny ungodliness and worldly lust. Someone saved by grace learns to serve and obey God because they were forgiven and not so they can be forgiven. There is nothing we can do on our own accord to enter Heaven or buy our salvation. Nothing can be given or done to earn God's grace; it is free and undeserved. However, we must respond to the grace of God by faith and back that faith with works of faith.

Jesus told people when He forgave them to go and sin no more. Meaning, they were granted the undeserved favor of God, but now they were to walk as a new person and not sin. Let us look at the woman caught in adultery to see the grace of God in action.

John 8:1-11 (KJV)

1 Jesus went unto the mount of Olives.

2 And early in the morning he came again into the temple, and all the people came unto him; and he sat down, and taught them.

3 **And the scribes and Pharisees brought unto him a woman taken in adultery;** and when they had set her in the midst,

4 They say unto him, Master, this woman was taken in adultery, in the very act.

5 Now Moses in the law commanded us, that such should be stoned: but what sayest thou?

6 This they said, tempting him, that they might have to accuse him. But Jesus stooped down, and with his finger wrote on the ground, as though he heard them not.

7 So when they continued asking him, he lifted up himself, and said unto them, He that is without sin among you, let him first cast a stone at her.

8 And again he stooped down, and wrote on the ground.

9 And they which heard it, being convicted by their own conscience, went out one by one, beginning at the eldest, even unto the last: and Jesus was left alone, and the woman standing in the midst.

10 When Jesus had lifted up himself, and saw none but the woman, he said unto her, Woman, where are those thine accusers? hath no man condemned thee?

11 She said, No man, Lord. **And Jesus said unto her, Neither do I condemn thee: go, and sin no more.**

From this story, we can see the woman caught in adultery deserved to be stoned according to the Law of Moses. However, Jesus showed mercy upon her and was gracious to her. But at the exact moment He shows her grace; He tells her to go and sin no more. So, when God shows mercy and grace to someone, we can see that He expects them to go and sin no more. When someone accepts Jesus as their Lord, they are baptized into His death, and from then on, they are expected not to sin anymore and walk in newness of life. The grace of God frees you from living a sinful life because your old nature is crucified with Christ.

Romans 6:1-7 (KJV)

1 **What shall we say then? Shall we continue in sin, that grace may abound?**

2 God forbid. How shall we, that are dead to sin, live any longer therein?

18

3 Know ye not, that so many of us as were baptized into Jesus Christ were baptized into his death?

4 Therefore we are buried with him by baptism into death: **that like as Christ was raised up from the dead by the glory of the Father, even so we also should walk in newness of life.**

5 For if we have been planted together in the likeness of his death, we shall be also in the likeness of his resurrection:

6 Knowing this, that our old man is crucified with him, that the body of sin might be destroyed, that henceforth we should not serve sin.

7 For he that is dead is freed from sin.

From these Scriptures, we can see two powerful truths. One, God's grace is a free gift and undeserved. Two, it is important how we respond to God's grace being bestowed upon us. When God bestows His undeserved grace upon someone, He expects them to walk in newness of life. The true grace of God bestows favors and blessings upon undeserving people. The grace of God also influences and changes these undeserving people's hearts where they want to serve and obey His Commandments. Once God's grace has changed you, you can be trusted and thus be granted a *Supernatural Security Clearance.*

I want to denote the difference in the word *works*. God's grace freely saves us by faith outside of the works of the flesh, but we must still accompany our faith with what the Bible calls the work of faith. The Apostle Paul mentions the work of faith in the Book of 1 Thessalonians chapter 1.

1 Thessalonians 1:2-3 (KJV)

2 We give thanks to God always for you all, making mention of you in our prayers;

3 Remembering without ceasing your **work of faith**, and labour of love, and patience of hope in our Lord Jesus Christ, in the sight of God and our Father;

The Book of James says it this way. Faith without works is dead being alone. James goes on to say that faith without works is dead.

James 2:17-20 (KJV)

17 **Even so faith, if it hath not works, is dead, being alone.**
18 **Yea, a man may say, Thou hast faith, and I have works: shew me thy faith without thy works, and I will shew thee my faith by my works.**
19 Thou believest that there is one God; thou doest well: the devils also believe, and tremble.
20 But wilt thou know, O vain man, **that faith without works is dead?**

Works of faith must back someone's faith, but the works of the Law will never give you access into God's kingdom or a *Supernatural Security Clearance*. So, we can see the Bible is talking about a different type of work regarding our faith than when it speaks about the works of the Law. The work of faith has more to do with how we respond to God and His grace. Works of the flesh are man's attempt to please God outside of His grace on their own merit.

Galatians 2:16 (KJV)

16 **Knowing that a man is not justified by the works of the law, but by the faith of Jesus Christ,** even we have believed in Jesus Christ, **that we might be justified by the faith of Christ, and not by the works of the law: for by the works of the law shall no flesh be justified.**

The grace of God plays a vital role in the believer's life, and the Bible says we should be careful not to fail the grace of God. This can be done by having a root of bitterness, being a fornicator, or being a profane person. A profane person acts in an unholy way and is hateful towards God.

> **Hebrews 12:14-16 (KJV)**
> 14 Follow peace with all men, and holiness, without which no man shall see the Lord:
> 15 **Looking diligently lest any man fail of the grace of God; lest any root of bitterness springing up trouble you, and thereby many be defiled;**
> 16 **Lest there be any fornicator, or profane person, as Esau,** who for one morsel of meat sold his birthright.

We are also to come to God's Throne of Grace when we need help. God's grace is there to help us in our time of need.

> **Hebrews 4:16 (KJV)**
> 16 **Let us therefore come boldly unto the Throne of Grace, that we may obtain mercy, and find grace to help in time of need.**

We are justified by faith and granted peace with God through our Lord Jesus Christ. But we only have access to God's grace by faith. We must believe in God to activate the grace of God in our lives.

> **Romans 5:1-2 (KJV)**
> 1 **Therefore being justified by faith, we have peace with God through our Lord Jesus Christ:**
> 2 **By whom also we have access by faith into this grace wherein we stand,** and rejoice in hope of the glory of God.

The Book of Romans says where sin abounded; grace did much more abound. Someone may have been a terrible sinner, but God's amazing grace can abound in such a way to change the terrible sinner into a saint.

Romans 5:20 (KJV)
20 Moreover the law entered, that the offence might abound. **But where sin abounded, grace did much more abound:**

It is only by knowing the true grace of God that we can stand.

1 Peter 5:12 (KJV)
12 By Silvanus, a faithful brother unto you, as I suppose, I have written briefly, exhorting, and testifying that **this is the true grace of God wherein ye stand.**

The Apostle Paul taught a solid foundation of the Gospel by the grace of God given to him as a wise masterbuilder of the Church at Corinth. He said different ministers would build upon his foundation, but it must be gold, silver, and precious stones. The gold, silver, and precious stones had to do with the truth of God's Word and the work of grace by the Holy Spirit. Paul revealed that some ministers would build upon his work of grace with wood, hay, and stubble. On judgment day, the fire of God is going to reveal how someone ministered and built upon God's foundation of grace.

1 Corinthians 3:9-15 (KJV)
9 For we are labourers together with God: ye are God's husbandry, ye are God's building.
10 **According to the grace of God which is given unto me, as a wise masterbuilder,** I have laid the foundation, and

another buildeth thereon. But let every man take heed how he buildeth thereupon.

11 For other foundation can no man lay than that is laid, which is Jesus Christ.

12 **Now if any man build upon this foundation gold, silver, precious stones, wood, hay, stubble;**

13 Every man's work shall be made manifest: for the day shall declare it, because it shall be revealed by fire; and the fire shall try every man's work of what sort it is.

14 If any man's work abide which he hath built thereupon, he shall receive a reward.

15 If any man's work shall be burned, he shall suffer loss: but he himself shall be saved; yet so as by fire.

This passage reveals that someone could be saved by grace, become a minister, and their works are burned up on Judgment Day. This is an excellent example of someone being saved, but their works are burned up. Works that are considered wood, hay, and stubble refer to selfish works of the flesh. It also could refer to works done with wrong motives and not for the glory of God. So, you could say they received the grace of God to be saved, but on Judgment Day, their works could be burned up, which could determine positions of authority lost or gained in the future kingdom of God.

When you understand this truth, you can start to understand many of the parables that Jesus taught about faithful servants and their rewards in Heaven. God will reward people based upon their works, and He will also judge people by their works. So, the grace of God can save you, but that does not mean everyone will have the same rewards in Heaven. God is looking for faithful people that He has saved by grace through faith to rule and reign with Him throughout all eternity.

I went into detail about the grace of God that brings salvation because I do not want anyone to be confused about the requirements to obtain a *Supernatural Security Clearance* and the salvation of God. When Jesus died on the cross, He fully paid the requirement for everyone to be saved. With this being said, there are requirements for how we respond to the grace of God and the death, burial, and resurrection of Jesus. God's grace freely saves you through faith, but there are still many requirements to access the deeper levels of God and His kingdom.

This book will go through the many requirements different men and women of God had to do to access what I am calling a *Supernatural Security Clearance*. *Supernatural Security Clearances* are granted to people called to walk in powerful anointings on this earth. It takes a *Supernatural Security Clearance* to have access to the gates of Heaven. Not all *Supernatural Security Clearances* are the same. Some will be granted a greater level of security clearance based on what they did on this earth and how they responded to God's grace.

As I go through examples in the Scriptures, you will see that God freely gave Jesus as a sacrifice on the cross to save people, but that does not mean they did not have to respond and act accordingly when the grace of God was revealed to them. You must respond to God's grace and what He has done for you to be granted greater levels of anointing and authority in God. *Supernatural Security Clearances* are not freely handed out to just anyone. If someone does get a *Supernatural Security Clearance,* there are requirements to keeping it. We will see that some people lost their *Supernatural Security Clearance* through failure to obey God's Word, while others were faithful to fulfill their high calling and keep their *Supernatural Security Clearance.*

CHAPTER 3
KINGDOM OF GOD TOP SECRETS

Jesus had a lot to say about the secrets of God's kingdom during His earthly ministry. The kingdom of God was one of Jesus' main messages. The kingdom of God was also a new message that most people did not know much about or understand when Jesus taught about it. To protect the secrets of the kingdom of God, Jesus primarily taught in parables when teaching the multitudes, but He expounded more deeply on what the parables meant to His disciples. This chapter will get into whom and why someone would be allowed access into the more profound secret mysteries of the kingdom of God and be granted a *Supernatural Security Clearance*.

The phrase *Kingdom of God* appears 53 times in the Gospels and is mainly mentioned by Jesus. Another closely related term, *Kingdom of Heaven*, is mentioned 32 times in the Gospel of Matthew. So, you can see how important this term was to Jesus. No one up to this point in history expounded on the message of the kingdom of God like Jesus did. The *kingdom of God* message was Jesus' central and main message.

So, what does the term *kingdom of God* mean? Many people have come up with different ideas about what the term *kingdom of God* means. I have discovered from my deep study of the Scriptures is the term *kingdom of God* mainly has to do with the **Rule and Reign of God through His Spirit.** God is a Spirit, and everything is ruled and governed by His Spirit. Therefore, you must know how to respond and work with the Holy Spirit to access the kingdom of God. Jesus did not begin His ministry until the Holy Spirit came upon Him at the age of thirty when John baptized Him.

As much as Jesus taught about the kingdom of God, He only expounded the more profound mystery of the message of the kingdom of God to His closest disciples. Not everyone was granted access to the deeper meaning behind the message of the kingdom of God. Jesus taught in parables to conceal the deeper meaning of His message. People needed a *Supernatural Security Clearance* to access the mysteries of the kingdom of God.

Jesus gave us clues to whom and why someone could receive this deeper access into the mysteries of His kingdom. We must go to the 13th chapter of the Book of Matthew to understand who would gain this Heavenly access to the very secrets of God's kingdom. This message was hidden throughout time until Jesus started teaching during His earthly ministry.

Matthew 13 starts with Jesus teaching the sower sowing the Word to the multitudes. His disciples came to Him after and asked why He spoke in parables?

> **Matthew 13:10-11 (KJV)**
> 10 And the disciples came, and said unto him, **Why speakest thou unto them in parables?**

11 He answered and said unto them, **Because it is given unto you to know the mysteries of the kingdom of heaven, but to them it is not given.**

Jesus' disciples were given access to the mysteries of God. But you must ask, "Why were they granted access and others were not?" You have to go to the parable of the sower sows the Word to find the answer. Jesus said if you could not understand this parable, how would you understand all parables? This parable was the foundation for establishing how you could access the extraordinary secrets to the mysteries of God's kingdom.

Mark 4:13 (KJV)

13 **And he said unto them, Know ye not this parable? and how then will ye know all parables?**

Let's dig deep into this parable and see who and how one can access the hidden secrets of the mysteries of God's kingdom.

Matthew 13:18-23 (KJV)

18 Hear ye therefore the parable of the sower.

19 When any one heareth the word of the kingdom, **and understandeth it not, then cometh the wicked one, and catcheth away that which was sown in his heart.** This is he which received seed by the way side.

20 But he that received the seed into stony places, the same is he that heareth the word, and anon with joy receiveth it;

21 Yet hath he not root in himself, but dureth for a while: **for when tribulation or persecution ariseth because of the word, by and by he is offended.**

22 He also that received seed among the thorns is he that heareth the word; **and the care of this world, and the**

deceitfulness of riches, choke the word, and he becometh unfruitful.
23 But he that received seed into the good ground is he that heareth the word**, and understandeth it;** which also beareth fruit, **and bringeth forth, some an hundredfold, some sixty, some thirty.**

This parable talks about a sower sowing seed into four different types of soil. The seed represents the Word of God, and the soil represents the heart of humankind. There are four different responses to the Word of God, which determine the outcome of what is sown in their hearts. This outcome would make all the difference in the world as to who and why someone could access God's secret mysteries to the kingdom of God and be granted a *Supernatural Security Clearance.* Let us look at these four different responses to the sower sowing the Word to understand why some access the mysteries of God's kingdom while others do not.

1. **LACK OF UNDERSTANDING** - The first person does not understand the Word of the kingdom, and the devil (wicked one) steals what was sown in their heart.

2. **LACK OF COMMITMENT** – The second person receives the Word of God with joy, but when tribulation or persecution arises because of the Word of God sown in their heart, they are offended and fall away. They are not committed to the Word of God's kingdom when trials come their way.

3. **DISTRACTIONS** – The third person understands the Word, receives the Word, and starts to produce a harvest. However, they get distracted by the cares of the world, the deceitfulness of riches, the Word is choked out, and they become unfruitful. They lack the focus to bring forth a harvest.

4. **UNDERSTANDING, PERSEVERANCE, & FOCUS –** The fourth person receives the seed on a good heart, understands what is sowed, joyfully receives the Word, and pushes past persecution or tribulation for the Word. Finally, they do not allow themselves to get distracted by the cares of this world, the deceitfulness of riches, and they produce a harvest for the kingdom of God.

This parable of the sower sows the Word reveals who can access the more profound mysteries of God and be granted a *Supernatural Security Clearance*. First, they must understand what is preached; secondly, they must push past persecution for the Word; and lastly, they must stay focused on the Word of the kingdom by clearing out all distractions of this life. Jesus revealed how to obtain a *Supernatural Security Clearance* in this one powerful parable. He also revealed why people did not receive access to God's deeper secrets. They did not receive access to the secret mysteries of God's kingdom because of a lack of understanding, lack of commitment, and lack of focus.

Before Jesus expounded on this parable, He said whoever had would be given more, and whoever did not have, what they did have would be taken away. In this statement, Jesus is referring to the knowledge of the kingdom as to what they would have. If someone had some knowledge of the mysteries of the kingdom of God, they would be given more, and if they did not have any knowledge of God's kingdom, whatever they had would be taken from them.

Matthew 13:12 (KJV)

12 **For whosoever hath, to him shall be given, and he shall have more abundance: but whosoever hath not, from him shall be taken away even that he hath.**

It is also important to note that there were three levels for those who produced a harvest of God's kingdom when it was sown in their heart. This reveals there are deeper levels to God's kingdom and mysteries, even if you are granted a *Supernatural Security Clearance*. The three levels are thirty, sixty, and a hundredfold. It takes focus, perseverance, dedication, understanding, and commitment to receive a hundredfold harvest of God's kingdom message.

> **Matthew 13:23 (KJV)**
> 23 But he that received seed into the good ground is he that heareth the word, and understandeth it; which also beareth fruit, and bringeth forth, **some an hundredfold, some sixty, some thirty.**

Jesus was revealing mysteries of the kingdom of God that had been kept secret since the foundation of the world. Many prophets and righteous men desired to see and hear the mysteries of the kingdom of God but did not have access to them.

> **Matthew 13:17 (KJV)**
> 17 For verily I say unto you, **That many prophets and righteous men have desired to see those things which ye see, and have not seen them; and to hear those things which ye hear, and have not heard them.**

I want to turn your attention to the Apostle Peter, who was one of the prominent disciples of Jesus, and why he was granted access to the secret mysteries of God's kingdom. Peter was granted greater access to God's kingdom than most other apostles. Peter walked on water with Jesus and was granted access to the Mount of Transfiguration. On the Mount of Transfiguration, Jesus appeared in all His glory with Moses and Elijah while the Father spoke out of Heaven. Peter was also one of the first disciples to acknowledge that Jesus was the Christ. When Peter made this confession, he was granted the keys to the kingdom of God.

Matthew 16:13-19 (KJV)

13 When Jesus came into the coasts of Caesarea Philippi, he asked his disciples, saying, Whom do men say that I the Son of man am?

14 And they said, Some say that thou art John the Baptist: some, Elias; and others, Jeremias, or one of the prophets.

15 He saith unto them, But whom say ye that I am?

16 **And Simon Peter answered and said, Thou art the Christ, the Son of the living God.**

17 And Jesus answered and said unto him, Blessed art thou, Simon Barjona: **for flesh and blood hath not revealed it unto thee, but my Father which is in heaven.**

18 And I say also unto thee, That thou art Peter, and upon this rock I will build my church; and the gates of hell shall not prevail against it.

19 **And I will give unto thee the keys of the kingdom of heaven:** and whatsoever thou shalt bind on earth shall be bound in heaven: and whatsoever thou shalt loose on earth shall be loosed in heaven.

What set Peter apart where God would grant him such access and privilege to be given a *Supernatural Security Clearance?* We can discover what set him apart by looking at the story of the rich young ruler. A rich young ruler came to Jesus and asked what he must do to inherit eternal life. Jesus asked the rich young ruler if he knew the Commandments, referring to the Ten Commandments of Moses. The rich young ruler replied that he had kept all the Ten Commandments from his youth. Jesus then reveals to him that he lacks one thing. He tells the rich young ruler to sell everything he has, give to the poor, take up his cross and follow Him.

The rich young ruler was saddened at this offer and walked away grieved because he had great possessions. Jesus went on to tell His disciples that it was easier for a camel to go through an eye of a needle than for a rich man to enter the kingdom of God. The disciples of Jesus were astonished at this statement and said, "Who then can be saved?" At this point, Peter reveals what he has done by leaving everything and following Jesus. Let us look at what Jesus has to say in response to Peter.

> **Mark 10:28-30 (KJV)**
> 28 **Then Peter began to say unto him, Lo, we have left all, and have followed thee.**
> 29 **And Jesus answered and said, Verily I say unto you, There is no man that hath left house, or brethren, or sisters, or father, or mother, or wife, or children, or lands, for my sake, and the Gospel's,**
> 30 But he shall receive an hundredfold now in this time, houses, and brethren, and sisters, and mothers, and children, and lands, with persecutions; and in the world to come eternal life.

Peter and many apostles had left their professions and families to follow Jesus. They soon found out that Jesus was the Christ. Jesus was teaching and preaching God's high calling and for people to take up their cross, which meant to die to themselves and everything this life has to offer. They were also called to leave their family members and preach the Gospel to the lost. *Supernatural Security Clearances* were only given to those who sacrificed and committed to being a follower of Christ at this level. The Apostle Peter had made all those sacrifices, and therefore he was granted one of the highest *Supernatural Security Clearances* given by God!

> ### Luke 14:25-33 (KJV)
> 25 And there went great multitudes with him: and he turned, and said unto them,
> **26 If any man come to me, and hate not his father, and mother, and wife, and children, and brethren, and sisters, yea, and his own life also, he cannot be my disciple.**
> **And whosoever doth not bear his cross, and come after me, cannot be my disciple.**
> 28 For which of you, intending to build a tower, sitteth not down first, and counteth the cost, whether he have sufficient to finish it?
> 29 Lest haply, after he hath laid the foundation, and is not able to finish it, all that behold it begin to mock him,
> 30 Saying, This man began to build, and was not able to finish.
> 31 Or what king, going to make war against another king, sitteth not down first, and consulteth whether he be able with ten thousand to meet him that cometh against him with twenty thousand?
> 32 Or else, while the other is yet a great way off, he sendeth an ambassage, and desireth conditions of peace.
> **33 So likewise, whosoever he be of you that forsaketh not all that he hath, he cannot be my disciple.**

Jesus placed a heavy requirement for people to be His disciples and receive a *Supernatural Security Clearance.* There was a selection process, and not everyone made the cut. Jesus did not preach a weak Gospel with a weak commitment. On the contrary, people had to be willing to give up and forsake everything to be His disciple. Many were called, but few were chosen to take up this *High Calling.*

Peter was one of the first people to announce that Jesus was the Christ. Peter made this confession when you could be persecuted by the religious leaders of his day for making this confession. When he made this confession, Jesus told him he was going to be given the keys to the Kingdom of Heaven. Keys are used for accessing *Secret Places*. He was granted greater access to a *Supernatural Security Clearance* to the kingdom of God for making this confession.

Matthew 16:18-19 (KJV)
18 And I say also unto thee, That thou art Peter, and upon this rock I will build my church; and the gates of hell shall not prevail against it.
19 **And I will give unto thee the keys of the kingdom of heaven:** and whatsoever thou shalt bind on earth shall be bound in heaven: and whatsoever thou shalt loose on earth shall be loosed in heaven.

Jesus went on to talk about the commitment it was going to take to be a true follower of Christ. It is interesting to note that after Peter makes this great confession, he tries to rebuke Jesus, but Jesus ends up rebuking him. Jesus rebukes Peter because he tries to tell Jesus He should not die on a cross. At this point, Jesus reveals that all His disciples need to take up their cross and follow Him. Let us read what He spoke to Peter and the other disciples when Peter tried to rebuke Him.

Matthew 16:20-27 (KJV)
20 Then charged he his disciples that they should tell no man that he was Jesus the Christ.
21 From that time forth began Jesus to shew unto his disciples, how that he must go unto Jerusalem, and suffer many things of the elders and chief priests and scribes, and be killed, and be raised again the third day.

22 Then Peter took him, and began to rebuke him, saying, Be it far from thee, Lord: this shall not be unto thee.

23 But he turned, and said unto Peter, Get thee behind me, Satan: thou art an offence unto me: for thou savourest not the things that be of God, but those that be of men.

24 **Then said Jesus unto his disciples, If any man will come after me, let him deny himself, and take up his cross, and follow me.**

25 **For whosoever will save his life shall lose it: and whosoever will lose his life for my sake shall find it.**

26 For what is a man profited, if he shall gain the whole world, and lose his own soul? or what shall a man give in exchange for his soul?

27 For the Son of man shall come in the glory of his Father with his angels; and then he shall reward every man according to his works.

From all these Scriptures, we can see that Jesus did have His system of background checks for anyone who wanted to be His true disciple. They had to be willing to take up the cross, which meant dying to everything in this life by forsaking family, friends, and careers. They also had to keep all of Jesus' Commandments and call Him the Lord of their lives. Calling Jesus Lord meant that you kept all His Commandments and did what He told you to do. Many of Jesus' disciples were willing to do this, and they obtained some of the greatest *Supernatural Security Clearances* ever given to humanity.

On a side note, we need to maintain what we are doing in this life and wait for the calling of the Holy Spirit. Remember, Jesus was thirty when He entered His *High Calling*. Jesus was working as a carpenter up to that point. However, when it came time to fulfill His mission and answer the call of God, He dropped everything to follow His Father.

You may be called to be at a job for a time, but don't leave that job or the people around you until God places a *High Call* upon you. You will know by God's Spirit when this happens. Do not miss out on your opportunity to sacrifice everything for God at that moment. Until then, keep doing what you are doing faithfully before God.

In conclusion, *Supernatural Security Clearances* are extremely hard to come by in the kingdom of God. You must be willing to take up your cross daily, follow Christ and give your whole life in dedication to the kingdom of God. This message has not always been taught throughout the ages, but it is the message of commitment that Jesus taught. If we are going to access a *Supernatural Security Clearance* from God, we must get back to the original message of commitment that Jesus taught and preached to His disciples. Those who make this commitment to Christ will be granted a *Supernatural Security Clearance*, which will give them access to understanding the secret mysteries of the kingdom of God.

CHAPTER 4
THE SELECTION PROCESS

In this chapter, I will be using Elite Special Forces as an example of their selection process and how this can apply to the kingdom of God and God's selection process. Elite Special Forces are the most powerful warriors globally and are known for having the most challenging selection processes. Elite Special Forces of any earthly military establishment is an excellent example because they are highly trained and dedicated warriors. God has called all His disciples into the army of the Lord as soldiers. So, if you are going to be a soldier in the army of the Lord, you might as well aim at becoming an *Elite Spiritual Warrior* and endure hardness as a good soldier of Jesus Christ.

> **2 Timothy 2:3-4 (KJV)**
> 3 **Thou therefore endure hardness, as a good soldier of Jesus Christ.**
> 4 **No man that warreth entangleth himself with the affairs of this life; that he may please him who hath chosen him to be a soldier.**

If you are going to be chosen as a part of an Elite Special Forces unit or top-secret governmental organization, you will have to pass a selection process. The selection process is the key to finding the best candidates for certain top-secret and highly classified positions. God's government is no different from the natural governments of the earth. God and governments of this world need to qualify people and put them through tests before giving them a security clearance to operate in top-secret and highly classified powerful positions.

Every Christian, at one level, is granted a *Supernatural Security Clearance,* but this does not mean they tapped into their *High Calling.* What I mean by *High Calling* is the hundredfold fulfillment of their Divine destiny. The Bible reveals that some people may be called by God and enter a portion of what God has called them to. But just because you entered into a portion of what God had called you to do, does not mean you came into the perfect will of God and accomplished your Divine destiny.

For example, Elisha may have been able to live out his normal life as a Jew and go to Heaven. However, when Elijah threw his mantle on him, he had the choice of entering into a higher calling of God. Elisha made that choice and left everything to enter his *High Calling.* He passed the selection process of every test thrown at him and was granted the opportunity to take up Elijah's mantle and inherit a double portion of his spirit.

When I am talking about the selection process, I am talking about those who want more of God and want to play a big part in God's army. These people understand they must be tested like Peter and the other apostles before they could walk in the same power that Jesus walked in. These apostles gave up everything to walk with Jesus while He was on the earth and helped Him in preaching the Gospel.

These apostles of Jesus were granted a deeper level of a *Supernatural Security Clearance* when the Holy Spirit came upon them on the day of

Pentecost. They operated in one level of authority while Jesus was on the earth, and after Jesus left the earth, they walked in a high anointing. They passed their tests, God anointed them, and they went on to evangelize the world. These men stood up to the whole Roman society and won. Rome went from a pagan society to a Christian society, because of the preaching of the Gospel.

I am using many examples in the natural to help better understand *Supernatural Security Clearances*. You can learn a lot about how God operates His kingdom and the requirements He places for people to access His top secrets by using examples from the natural. In many ways, governments of this world operate like God in His kingdom when selecting and granting security clearances to their chosen citizens.

As soldiers of the Lord, we are called to fight the good fight of faith and put on the whole armor of God so we can stand against evil demonic forces. God is a Warrior, and He equips His Christian soldiers with His armor and weaponry, whereby they can victoriously fight demonic forces and defend themselves.

Ephesians 6:10-17 (KJV)
> 10 Finally, my brethren, be strong in the Lord, and in the power of his might.
> 11 **Put on the whole armour of God,** that ye may be able to stand against the wiles of the devil.
> 12 For we wrestle not against flesh and blood, but against principalities, against powers, against the rulers of the darkness of this world, against spiritual wickedness in high places.
> 13 **Wherefore take unto you the whole armour of God, that ye may be able to withstand in the evil day, and having done all, to stand.**

14 **Stand therefore, having your loins girt about with truth, and having on the breastplate of righteousness;**
15 **And your feet shod with the preparation of the Gospel of peace;**
16 **Above all, taking the shield of faith, wherewith ye shall be able to quench all the fiery darts of the wicked.**
17 **And take the helmet of salvation, and the sword of the Spirit, which is the word of God:**

As Christians, the battle we face is not in the natural. We are in a spiritual battle, which requires spiritual weapons and spiritual armor. These spiritual weapons are not carnal but mighty through God to the pulling down of strongholds.

2 Corinthians 10:3-6 (KJV)
3 **For though we walk in the flesh, we do not war after the flesh:**
4 **(For the weapons of our warfare are not carnal, but mighty through God to the pulling down of strong holds;)**
5 Casting down imaginations, and every high thing that exalteth itself against the knowledge of God, and bringing into captivity every thought to the obedience of Christ;
6 And having in a readiness to revenge all disobedience, when your obedience is fulfilled.

Now that you understand you are chosen to be a soldier in a spiritual battle as a Christian, let's study the Elite Special Forces and the selection process they go through to find the best candidates for their programs. To start with, let's define what the selection process is. The selection process refers to the steps and tests involved in choosing candidates with the right qualifications and skillsets to fill a position. The goal of the selection process is to funnel candidates through a rigid structure of tests to see who is qualified and who is not qualified to handle the demands of a highly classified position. In the case of Christians, God is looking for believers who will remain faithful under persecution or spiritual attacks to complete the mission of preaching the Gospel and being a part of His Heavenly Kingdom.

To become an Elite Special Warrior, they must complete months of hands-on training and testing. If they do not qualify or fail to pass these tests, they can be dropped from this kind of specialized training. Unfortunately, some candidates drop out and quit on their own accord because they cannot handle the pressure or stress of becoming an Elite Warrior. Thousands of candidates join these programs yearly, but many drop out before completion because they cannot handle the demands placed upon them.

The first phase of the Elite Special Forces selection process starts with increasing physical and mental conditions. Future potential Elite Warriors are placed in multiple scenarios where they are physically and mentally challenged beyond what is thought capable. The whole time they are being tested to see if they can meet the qualifications and demands of becoming an Elite Warrior. They must be able to endure hardness as a good soldier.

During all these strenuous tests, they are reminded that they can quit at any time. Every trial they are going through during this selection process is of their own will. All Elite Special Forces Units are optional to join; candidates choose of their own free will to partake in these programs. Military units are looking for qualified soldiers who have a no-quit attitude and have a mindset that they can overcome any obstacle. These elite soldiers will keep fighting and pressing through no matter what they face or what the enemy might throw at them. They are dedicated to winning the war and accomplishing their mission at all costs. They don't allow anything to stop them or get in their way of accomplishing their mission.

If a military trainer sees a weak candidate, they will attack their weakness through a series of beat downs. A beat down is where the trainer adds extra stressful physical trials and mental pressure to get the potential Elite Warrior to quit and give up. If they quit and give up on their own accord, they are out of the program and selection process. Beat downs can go on for hours and even days. The whole idea is to see if the soldier will not quit no matter what is thrown at them. Once the trainer sees they have a no-quit attitude, they back off. The future Elite Warrior who passed the test of the beat downs can move on to the next series of tests.

A true Spiritual Elite Warrior has learned to live a disciplined life. The disciplined Christian life includes hours of studying and meditating on God's Word, memorizing Scriptures, praying without ceasing, giving to the poor, serving others, being led by God's Spirit, preaching and teaching the Gospel to others, saying no to all temptations, keeping their mind on God, and keeping focused on God's kingdom. A disciplined soldier for Christ resists the pleasures of this world to please God. They also never allow themselves to become complacent about the things of God.

God is also looking for spiritual soldiers who will not quit or give up under pressure. The early Church faced tremendous persecution and even death by becoming a Christian. God is looking for soldiers who will not give up and have that victorious warrior spirit. When the battle gets entirely out of hand, these Elite Spiritual Warriors kick into high gear and take the battle to the enemy. They know how to keep the upper hand against the enemy and stay in the fight until they win. A true spiritual warrior will never give up but will remain faithful to the end.

Jesus did not quit or give up in whatever trial He faced. Even when faced with going to the cross, He maintained a faithful attitude toward His Heavenly Father that He would be raised from the dead. Before Jesus went to the cross, He sweated drops of blood because of the pressure and stress He was facing about dying a torturous crucifixion. Jesus had a victorious spirit and defeated the devil in every spiritual combat the devil engaged Him in. Jesus is the most powerful spiritual warrior this world has ever witnessed.

Luke 22:41-44 (KJV)
41 And he was withdrawn from them about a stone's cast, and kneeled down, and prayed,
42 Saying, Father, if thou be willing, remove this cup from me: nevertheless not my will, but thine, be done.
43 And there appeared an angel unto him from heaven, strengthening him.
44 And being in an agony he prayed more earnestly: **and his sweat was as it were great drops of blood falling down to the ground.**

Hebrews 12:1-4 (KJV)
1 Wherefore seeing we also are compassed about with so great a cloud of witnesses, let us lay aside every weight, and the sin which doth so easily beset us, and let us run with patience the race that is set before us,
2 **Looking unto Jesus the author and finisher of our faith;** who for the joy that was set before him endured the cross, despising the shame, and is set down at the right hand of the Throne of God.

3 For consider him that endured such contradiction of sinners against himself, lest ye be wearied and faint in your minds.
4 Ye have not yet resisted unto blood, striving against sin.

Governmental militaries are looking for mentally tough soldiers, and so is God. A mentally tough soldier can control their thoughts and stay positive when under extreme pressure and heavy warfare. Only the mentally strong thrive, survive, and conquer during intense battles. Your mind will come under heavy warfare during a spiritual attack, but you must stay focused and mentally strong. You must have spiritual fortitude and a strong mind to win during these times. The devil can easily defeat mentally weak Christians. One of the main tactics of the devil is to throw thoughts at believers and try to get them to be discouraged or give up when they are engaged in a spiritual battle.

2 Corinthians 10:4-5 (KJV)

4 (For the weapons of our warfare are not carnal, but mighty through God to the pulling down of strong holds;)
5 **Casting down imaginations, and every high thing that exalteth itself against the knowledge of God, and bringing into captivity every thought to the obedience of Christ;**

The devil attacks the mind, and if you are not mentally strong, you could succumb to one of his spiritual attacks on the mind. This spiritual attack is like darts hitting the mind. Mental weakness is one of the main reasons some Christians fail to become Elite Spiritual Warriors. Mental weakness can stop a Christian from accomplishing their God-given mission in life. Christians must become mentally tough to defeat the devil in their lives and fulfill their high calling.

Ephesians 6:16 (KJV)
16 Above all, taking the shield of faith, **wherewith ye shall be able to quench all the fiery darts of the wicked.**

Future Elite Warriors are put in mock warfare situations to see how they perform. Many potential Elite Warriors are unprepared for combat simulation, let alone real warfare. Real warfare is no joke, and much is at stake when under attack. However, military units are looking for those who can dominate the battlefield with a strong and overcoming spirit. This is called having the upper hand. A tested Elite Warrior can dominate the battlefield through strict training and an overcoming warrior spirit.

God is also looking for Elite Spiritual Warriors who can dominate the spiritual battlefield and maintain the upper hand against the devil. Those who can pass His selection process will be granted a *Supernatural Security Clearance* in which they can engage and defeat the enemies of God. When someone becomes a Christian, they must understand they are entering into an eternal war that has been raging from the beginning of time. This war is God versus the devil, and humankind is caught in the middle. To win this war, you must be committed to God at all costs and be prepared to fight demonic forces to the very end.

God already defeated the devil when Jesus died on the cross and rose from the dead. The war we are in is enforcing God's judgment on the devil, demons, and fallen angels while preaching that people must repent of their sins to be saved. A New Testament believer's war is over their faith. Faith has to do with what you believe in your heart and speak out of your mouth. The New Testament refers to this as the good fight of faith. The devil is seeking those who are weak and will not believe God. A believer fights the good fight of faith because they know that God has already won the battle.

1 Timothy 6:12 (KJV)

12 **Fight the good fight of faith,** lay hold on eternal life, whereunto thou art also called, and hast professed a good profession before many witnesses.

God has already won the victory, and if we believe, we can come out victorious every time we enter a spiritual battle. We are more than conquerors through Him that loved us. Jesus already defeated the devil; we must believe it, receive, and walk in this victory.

Romans 8:37 (KJV)

37 **Nay, in all these things we are more than conquerors through him that loved us.**

However, just because Jesus has won the war does not mean we do not still have warfare. Our warfare is all about battling the enemy's deception and renegade demonic spirits who need the judgment of God declared to them by the Church. After Jesus died and rose again, He gave the responsibility to the Church to carry out the enforcing of God's judgment on demonic forces to the enlisted soldiers of the Lord. These enlisted soldiers of the Lord were also entrusted with the good news of the Gospel to proclaim liberty to all those oppressed by the devil.

Jesus spoiled and triumphed over principalities and powers.

Colossians 2:15 (KJV)

15 **And having spoiled principalities and powers, he made a shew of them openly, triumphing over them in it.**

When Jesus died and rose again, all authority was given to Him in Heaven and in earth. The Church is called to proclaim this victory to the world through preaching the good news of the Gospel.

Matthew 28:18-20 (KJV)
18 And Jesus came and spake unto them, saying, **All power is given unto me in heaven and in earth.**
19 **Go ye therefore,** and teach all nations, baptizing them in the Name of the Father, and of the Son, and of the Holy Ghost:
20 Teaching them to observe all things whatsoever I have commanded you: and, lo, I am with you always, even unto the end of the world. Amen.

When Jesus sent the seventy out before He went to the cross, they returned, saying that even the devils were subject to them through His Name. Jesus responded by saying that He saw Satan fall like lightning. When the Gospel is preached, and people respond by repenting, the devil falls like lighting because he is defeated.

Luke 10:17-22 (KJV)
17 **And the seventy returned again with joy, saying, Lord, even the devils are subject unto us through thy name.**
18 **And he said unto them, I beheld Satan as lightning fall from heaven.**
19 **Behold, I give unto you power to tread on serpents and scorpions, and over all the power of the enemy: and nothing shall by any means hurt you.**
20 Notwithstanding in this rejoice not, that the spirits are subject unto you; but rather rejoice, because your names are written in heaven.
21 In that hour Jesus rejoiced in spirit, and said, I thank thee, O Father, Lord of heaven and earth, that thou hast hid these things from the wise and prudent, and hast revealed them

unto babes: even so, Father; for so it seemed good in thy sight.

22 All things are delivered to me of my Father: and no man knoweth who the Son is, but the Father; and who the Father is, but the Son, and he to whom the Son will reveal him.

As we can see, Jesus is looking for Elite Spiritual Warriors who will fight and defeat the devil and his demons. God needs committed spiritual warriors who can pass the selection process. These Elite Spiritual Warriors are not afraid to fight and take on the devil and his demonic forces. People's souls are at stake, and God needs Elite Warriors who can pass the selection process to fight His battles and defeat the devil.

One thing to note about the Elite Warriors is that their first phase of the selection process is not training, and they are not given a weapon at this time. An Elite Warrior must pass the selection process before being given access to a weapon. Elite Warriors have access to some of the best military weapons, but they are not given access to these weapons until they meet all qualifications. They must first complete and pass the selection process before being entrusted with a powerful weapon.

God also has qualifications and a selection process before He hands out His spiritual weaponry. You must be a committed Christian who has been tested and proven that you will not deny or betray the Lord under intense spiritual warfare. Jesus said to His disciples that the harvest was plenteous, but the laborers were few. There is a great harvest, but few people qualified to help harvest. God needs more Christians to become qualified soldiers to reap the harvest. God cannot just send anyone out who is not prepared or qualified to meet the demands that will be placed upon them.

Matthew 9:37-38 (KJV)

> 37 Then saith he unto his disciples, **The harvest truly is plenteous, but the labourers are few;**
> 38 **Pray ye therefore the Lord of the harvest, that he will send forth labourers into his harvest.**

The weapons of God come in the form of the nine gifts of the Holy Spirit. A fully equipped Elite Spiritual warrior will be empowered with one or more gifts of the Spirit.

1 Corinthians 12:7-11 (KJV)

> **7 But the manifestation of the Spirit is given to every man to profit withal.**
> 8 For to one is given by the Spirit the word of wisdom; to another the word of knowledge by the same Spirit;
> 9 To another faith by the same Spirit; to another the gifts of healing by the same Spirit;
> 10 To another the working of miracles; to another prophecy; to another discerning of spirits; to another divers kinds of tongues; to another the interpretation of tongues:
> 11 But all these worketh that one and the selfsame Spirit, dividing to every man severally as he will.

These spiritual warriors take the fight against the enemy by preaching the Gospel, casting out demons, raising the dead, and healing the sick. They are called to free people from demonic oppression as they set the captives free.

Mark 16:15-20 (KJV)

> 15 And he said unto them, **Go ye into all the world, and preach the Gospel to every creature.**
> 16 He that believeth and is baptized shall be saved; but he that believeth not shall be damned.

17 And these signs shall follow them that believe; In my name shall they cast out devils; they shall speak with new tongues; **18 They shall take up serpents; and if they drink any deadly thing, it shall not hurt them; they shall lay hands on the sick, and they shall recover.**
19 So then after the Lord had spoken unto them, he was received up into heaven, and sat on the right hand of God.
20 And they went forth, and preached every where, the Lord working with them, and confirming the word with signs following. Amen.

These Elite Spiritual Warriors fight with the Word of God, which is the sword of the Spirit.

Ephesians 6:17 (KJV)
17 And take the helmet of salvation, **and the sword of the Spirit, which is the word of God:**

Hebrews 4:12 (KJV)
12 **For the word of God is quick, and powerful, and sharper than any twoedged sword,** piercing even to the dividing asunder of soul and spirit, and of the joints and marrow, and is a discerner of the thoughts and intents of the heart.

Elite Warriors are equipped for battle and dedicated to whatever mission they are sent on. Even if a disaster strikes, this special breed of highly trained, equipped, and committed Elite Spiritual Soldiers will press on even when the odds are stacked against them. Elite Spiritual Warriors have an unwavering belief in their mission and ability to win against any odds on the battlefield. This is precisely the same attitude God requires from those who were granted a *Supernatural Security Clearance* and the opportunity of the Divine mission of preaching the Gospel. God is looking for those with a never-quit attitude and domineering spiritual warfare mentality that will not accept defeat. They take the fight against the enemy and are never out of the fight because they are more than conquerors through Christ Jesus.

It is important to understand that God calls many people, but few are chosen. Few are chosen because only certain people are committed to God's *High Calling.* Not everyone is willing to take up their cross and give themselves to God as the early Church did. A weak Gospel message produces weak non-committed Christians. God is looking for those who will respond with their whole life to the Gospel of the kingdom of God. These are the ones who have been granted a *Supernatural Security Clearance* and fight the good fight of faith as an Elite Spiritual Warrior.

Matthew 22:14 (KJV)
14 **For many are called, but few are chosen.**

In conclusion, we can see that God is looking for a specially chosen select group of Elite Spiritual Warriors who are willing to fight the devil and his hordes from hell. To do this, you must be ready to go through the selection process of commitment to gain and maintain a *Supernatural Security Clearance.* Elite Spiritual Warriors are a great example because they reveal what natural warriors are willing to go through to become Elite Warriors. We can learn to become Elite Spiritual Warriors by following the spiritual truths they display in the natural. The days we live in are evil, and it will take a special breed of Elite Christian Warriors to take on the devil and walk away from the battlefield victorious. We are that chosen generation!

CHAPTER 5
SECRET LOCATIONS

God has always had numerous secret locations that are not accessible to everyone. Just as in the natural, governments have secret locations such as bases, throne rooms, or hideouts from their enemies; God has His top-secret locations. It takes a security clearance to access secret locations in both God's kingdom and the governments of this world. This chapter will reveal some of God's secret locations and what it takes to gain a *Supernatural Security Clearance* to access these highly classified protected areas.

Secret locations allow governments to protect high-ranking government officials, powerful weaponry, and top secrets. Some governments build bases and bunkers inside mountains or underground, so no enemy can see what they are protecting. They are also built for governments to protect themselves from a nuclear attack. These underground facilities play an essential role in the security, safety, and protection of governments and sovereign nations.

God has secret locations to protect, just like governments on the earth. God only allows certain people who have been granted a *Supernatural*

Security Clearance to enter His secret locations. Not everyone is qualified or welcomed into these high-valued and protected locations.

Below is a list of some of God's secret locations in the Bible:

1. The Garden of Eden

2. Mount Sinai, the Mountain of God

3. The Tabernacle and Temple of God

4. The Holy of Holies

5. The Throne of God

6. The Secret Place of the Most High

7. Heavenly Jerusalem; the Eternal City of God

The Garden of Eden

To start with, let us go back to the first revealed secret location in the Bible, the Garden of Eden. The Garden of Eden was a special garden God created for Adam and Eve to live in after He created the world. God created this special Garden for Adam and Eve to enjoy, and it was also a place where God would meet with Adam and Eve in the cool of the day. Adam was to dwell in, dress, and keep the Garden of Eden as his assignment from God. God also placed the Tree of Life and the Tree of the Knowledge of Good and Evil in this secret Garden. These two trees later became a test for Adam and Eve to see if they would obey God's Word.

> **Genesis 2:8-14 (KJV)**
> **8 And the Lord God planted a garden eastward in Eden; and there he put the man whom he had formed.**

9 And out of the ground made the Lord God to grow every tree that is pleasant to the sight, and good for food; **the tree of life also in the midst of the garden, and the tree of knowledge of good and evil.**

10 And a river went out of Eden to water the garden; and from thence it was parted, and became into four heads.

11 The name of the first is Pison: that is it which compasseth the whole land of Havilah, where there is gold;

12 And the gold of that land is good: there is bdellium and the onyx stone.

13 And the name of the second river is Gihon: the same is it that compasseth the whole land of Ethiopia.

14 And the name of the third river is Hiddekel: that is it which goeth toward the east of Assyria. And the fourth river is Euphrates.

After God created Adam and Eve, they enjoyed this Garden and met with God in the cool of the day. God gave them every other tree to eat of, but He commanded them to not eat of the Tree of Knowledge of Good and Evil. God warned Adam that he would die on the day he ate of the Tree of Knowledge of Good and Evil.

Genesis 2:15-17 (KJV)

15 **And the Lord God took the man, and put him into the garden of Eden to dress it and to keep it.**

16 And the Lord God commanded the man, saying, Of every tree of the garden thou mayest freely eat:

17 **But of the tree of the knowledge of good and evil, thou shalt not eat of it: for in the day that thou eatest thereof thou shalt surely die.**

Adam and Eve ate the fruit of the Tree of Knowledge of Good and Evil when the devil tempted them. Obeying God's command to not eat of the Tree of the Knowledge of Good and Evil was Adam and Eve's requirement to access God's secret Garden of Eden and keep their *Supernatural Security Clearance.* They were being tested and did not know it. They lost their *Supernatural Security Clearance* and access to God's secret Garden when they failed the test. Let's read this story, where they lost their Heavenly access to the Garden of Eden and their *Supernatural Security Clearance.*

Genesis 3:1-13 (KJV)

1 Now the serpent was more subtil than any beast of the field which the Lord God had made. And he said unto the woman, Yea, hath God said, Ye shall not eat of every tree of the garden?

2 And the woman said unto the serpent, We may eat of the fruit of the trees of the garden:

3 But of the fruit of the tree which is in the midst of the garden, God hath said, Ye shall not eat of it, neither shall ye touch it, lest ye die.

4 And the serpent said unto the woman, Ye shall not surely die:

5 For God doth know that in the day ye eat thereof, then your eyes shall be opened, and ye shall be as gods, knowing good and evil.

6 **And when the woman saw that the tree was good for food, and that it was pleasant to the eyes, and a tree to be desired to make one wise, she took of the fruit thereof, and did eat, and gave also unto her husband with her; and he did eat.**

7 And the eyes of them both were opened, and they knew that they were naked; and they sewed fig leaves together, and made themselves aprons.

8 **And they heard the voice of the Lord God walking in the garden in the cool of the day: and Adam and his wife hid**

themselves from the presence of the Lord God amongst the trees of the garden.

9 And the Lord God called unto Adam, and said unto him, Where art thou?

10 And he said, I heard thy voice in the garden, and I was afraid, because I was naked; and I hid myself.

11 And he said, Who told thee that thou wast naked? Hast thou eaten of the tree, whereof I commanded thee that thou shouldest not eat?

12 **And the man said, The woman whom thou gavest to be with me, she gave me of the tree, and I did eat.**

13 And the Lord God said unto the woman, What is this that thou hast done? And the woman said, The serpent beguiled me, and I did eat.

After eating the fruit from the Tree of Knowledge of Good and Evil, the curse of death came upon them, as God said, and they were kicked out of the Garden of Eden. They were no longer allowed to partake of the Tree of Life and live forever. Furthermore, two Cherubims were placed at the entrance to the Garden of Eden with a flaming sword so they no longer had access to this secret location since they lost their *Supernatural Security Clearance.*

Genesis 3:22-24 (KJV)

22 And the Lord God said, Behold, the man is become as one of us, to know good and evil: **and now, lest he put forth his hand, and take also of the tree of life, and eat, and live for ever:**

23 Therefore the Lord God sent him forth from the garden of Eden, to till the ground from whence he was taken.

24 **So he drove out the man; and he placed at the east of the garden of Eden Cherubims, and a flaming sword which turned every way, to keep the way of the tree of life.**

Adam and Eve lost so much when they disobeyed God. God was coming to them every day and speaking with them. They also were granted a *Supernatural Security Clearance* from God to eat from the Tree of Life in the Garden of Eden to live forever. They did not appreciate this privilege as they should have, and it put a curse on the whole world when they disobeyed God.

Mount Sinai, the Mountain of God

God mightily used Moses to deliver the children of Israel from the bondage of Egypt. After God delivered the children of Israel from the hand of Pharaoh and the Egyptians, He led them into the desert to meet with them and give them the Law of Moses. These Laws were meant to be a guiding light to the children of Israel on how they should live and serve the living God.

As God was leading the children of Israel out of Egypt, He appeared to them as a pillar of cloud by day and a cloud of fire by night.

> **Exodus 13:21-22 (KJV)**
> 21 **And the Lord went before them by day in a pillar of a cloud, to lead them the way; and by night in a pillar of fire, to give them light; to go by day and night:**
> 22 He took not away the pillar of the cloud by day, nor the pillar of fire by night, from before the people.

God led Israel by His cloud to the backside of the desert to what is now known as Mount Sinai, which is also called the Mountain of God. God rested His cloud on this mountain and only allowed Moses and Aaron to come up and meet with Him. Moses was chosen by God to be given an extraordinary *Supernatural Security Clearance*. Moses was granted access to this privileged location to meet and talk with God. None of the other children of Israel were given this level of access. God also came down upon this mountain and spoke in an audible voice the Ten Commandments to the children of Israel.

> **Exodus 19:20-24 (KJV)**
> 20 **And the Lord came down upon mount Sinai, on the top of the mount: and the Lord called Moses up to the top of the mount; and Moses went up.**
> 21 And the Lord said unto Moses, Go down, charge the people, lest they break through unto the Lord to gaze, and many of them perish.
> 22 And let the priests also, which come near to the Lord, sanctify themselves, lest the Lord break forth upon them.
> 23 **And Moses said unto the Lord, The people cannot come up to mount Sinai: for thou chargedst us, saying, Set bounds about the mount, and sanctify it.**
> 24 **And the Lord said unto him, Away, get thee down, and thou shalt come up, thou, and Aaron with thee: but let not the priests and the people break through to come up unto the Lord, lest he break forth upon them.**

Mount Sinai became a top-secret location for God to come down on the earth and meet with Moses. This must have been a wonderful sight to behold. Moses was given such a high honor to meet with God face to face and hear His voice. Moses had a *Supernatural Security Clearance* that granted him far greater access to God than any man ever had before in the history of the world. Moses was even allowed to see the glory of God on this mountain when God made the two tables of stone that had the Ten Commandments written upon them.

> **Exodus 34:1-8 (KJV)**
> 1 And the Lord said unto Moses, Hew thee two tables of stone like unto the first: and I will write upon these tables the words that were in the first tables, which thou brakest.

2 **And be ready in the morning, and come up in the morning unto mount Sinai, and present thyself there to me in the top of the mount.**

3 **And no man shall come up with thee, neither let any man be seen throughout all the mount; neither let the flocks nor herds feed before that mount.**

4 And he hewed two tables of stone like unto the first; and Moses rose up early in the morning, and went up unto mount Sinai, as the Lord had commanded him, and took in his hand the two tables of stone.

5 And the Lord descended in the cloud, and stood with him there, and proclaimed the Name of the Lord.

6 And the Lord passed by before him, and proclaimed, The Lord, The Lord God, merciful and gracious, longsuffering, and abundant in goodness and truth,

7 Keeping mercy for thousands, forgiving iniquity and transgression and sin, and that will by no means clear the guilty; visiting the iniquity of the fathers upon the children, and upon the children's children, unto the third and to the fourth generation.

8 And Moses made haste, and bowed his head toward the earth, and worshipped.

Moses was highly honored and favored by God to have such access. Moses was chosen by God and faithfully carried out his mission from God and was granted one of the highest levels of *Supernatural Security Clearances* this world has ever witnessed.

The Tabernacle and Temple of God

When Moses met with God, he was given the ability to see into Heaven and the Throne of God, and this is how he was shown the pattern to construct the Tabernacle of God on the earth. The pattern of the

Tabernacle of Moses later became a blueprint for the Temple that King Solomon built. The Tabernacle of Moses was patterned after Heaven, where God dwells. The Tabernacle of Moses was to be a place where God would meet with the children of Israel on the earth. The Tabernacle of Moses was built to be a secret portal to the Throne of God, which is in Heaven.

> **Exodus 25:8-9 (KJV)**
> **8 And let them make me a sanctuary; that I may dwell among them.**
> **9 According to all that I shew thee, after the pattern of the tabernacle, and the pattern of all the instruments thereof, even so shall ye make it.**

Three main areas made up the Tabernacle of Moses:

1. **OUTER COURT** — This is where the children of Israel could come and make sacrifices to God on the Brazen Altar. The Outer Court of the Tabernacle contained the Brazen Altar and Brazen Laver. The Brazen Laver was filled with water where the priests could cleanse themselves before entering the inner court of the Tabernacle.

2. **INNER COURT** — The inner court contained the Table of Shewbread, Golden Candlestick, and Altar of Incense.

3. **HOLY OF HOLIES** — This was the most sacred place of the Tabernacle of Moses, where the Ark of the Covenant was placed. The High Priest was only allowed to enter this top-secret location once a year on the Day of Atonement to meet with God and make atonement for the sins of the children of Israel.

Not everyone was granted the same level of access to this top-secret Tabernacle. Also, no strangers or women were given access. Any stranger who attempted to go into the Tabernacle would be put to death. The Tabernacle of Moses was a highly guarded and secret location for God to meet with His people.

Numbers 3:38 (KJV)

38 But those that encamp before the tabernacle toward the east, even before the tabernacle of the congregation eastward, shall be Moses, and Aaron and his sons, keeping the charge of the sanctuary for the charge of the children of Israel; **and the stranger that cometh nigh shall be put to death.**

Below are the three levels of *Supernatural Security Clearances* granted to the children of Israel.

1. **OUTER COURT** – This level of access was granted to the men of Israel, Levites, and High Priest.

2. **INNER COURT** – This level of access was granted to the Levites and High Priest.

3. **HOLY OF HOLIES** – This level of access was granted only to the High Priest once a year on the Day of Atonement. A veil blocked the Holy of Holies from the Inner Court. The Levites could not see behind the veil into the Holy of Holies when they entered the Inner Court.

Numbers 18:1-7 (KJV)

1 And the Lord said unto Aaron, Thou and thy sons and thy father's house with thee shall bear the iniquity of the sanctuary: and thou and thy sons with thee shall bear the iniquity of your priesthood.

2 And thy brethren also of the tribe of Levi, the tribe of thy father, bring thou with thee, that they may be joined unto thee, and minister unto thee: **but thou and thy sons with thee shall minister before the tabernacle of witness.**

3 **And they shall keep thy charge, and the charge of all the tabernacle:** only they shall not come nigh the vessels of the sanctuary and the altar, that neither they, nor ye also, die.

4 **And they shall be joined unto thee, and keep the charge of the tabernacle of the congregation, for all the service of the tabernacle: and a stranger shall not come nigh unto you.**

5 And ye shall keep the charge of the sanctuary, and the charge of the altar: that there be no wrath any more upon the children of Israel.

6 And I, behold, I have taken your brethren the Levites from among the children of Israel: **to you they are given as a gift for the Lord, to do the service of the tabernacle of the congregation.**

7 Therefore thou and thy sons with thee shall keep your priest's office for everything of the altar, and within the vail; and ye shall serve: I have given your priest's office unto you as a service of gift: **and the stranger that cometh nigh shall be put to death.**

The Tabernacle of Moses and the Temple of King Solomon, which was later built, was a top-secret holy place for the children of Israel to meet with God for thousands of years. The children of Israel went to this highly sacred temple to meet with the unseen God, make sacrifices, offer gifts, and pray to God. *Supernatural Security Clearances* played a key role in who could and could not access God in His Tabernacle. The three access levels of security clearances were kept in place because God only allowed certain people to come before Him.

Once Jesus died on the cross, the Temple was no longer needed because the disciples of Christ became the Temple of God. Christians were now the Holy Place where the Spirit of God would reside. Therefore, to gain this new *Supernatural Security Clearance,* you had to believe that God raised Jesus from the dead and then confess with your mouth Jesus is Lord. Those willing to make Jesus their Lord would be saved and granted a *Supernatural Security Clearance.* When Jesus died on the cross, the veil that separated the Inner Court from the Holy of Holies was torn in two.

> **Matthew 27:50-51 (KJV)**
> 50 Jesus, when he had cried again with a loud voice, yielded up the ghost.
> 51 **And, behold, the veil of the temple was rent in twain from the top to the bottom**; and the earth did quake, and the rocks rent;

After the death, burial, and resurrection of Jesus, Christians became the Temple of God. The Temple in Jerusalem was no longer needed. The Temple was destroyed by the Romans 40 years after the crucifixion of Christ. It was destroyed in 70 AD and has never yet been rebuilt.

> **1 Corinthians 3:16-17 (KJV)**
> 16 **Know ye not that ye are the temple of God,** and that the Spirit of God dwelleth in you?
> 17 **If any man defile the temple of God, him shall God destroy; for the temple of God is holy, which temple ye are.**

> **2 Corinthians 6:16-18 (KJV)**
> 16 **And what agreement hath the temple of God with idols? for ye are the temple of the living God;** as God hath said, I will dwell in them, and walk in them; and I will be their God, and they shall be my people.

17 Wherefore come out from among them, and be ye separate, saith the Lord, and touch not the unclean thing; and I will receive you.

18 And will be a Father unto you, and ye shall be my sons and daughters, saith the Lord Almighty.

It is a privilege and honor to be the Temple of God, and there are requirements to keeping your *Supernatural Security Clearance.* If you sin against God and His Holy Spirit, you could lose access to you being the secret temple of God. Therefore, all *Supernatural Security Clearances* with God must be maintained and protected to remain active.

The Holy of Holies

The Holy of Holies was the most sacred place in the Tabernacle of Moses and the Temple of King Solomon. The Holy of Holies is where God instructed Moses to place the Ark of the Covenant. The Ark of the Covenant contained the Ten Commandments. The Ten Commandments were the Laws which God verbally spoke on Mount Sinai, which is the Mountain of God. Later, Aaron's rod that budded was placed with the Ark of the Covenant and a golden pot containing manna.

The Holy of Holies was undoubtedly the most sacred place on the earth. God said He would speak and meet with the children of Israel from the Mercy Seat located on top of the Ark of the Covenant. This place was so sacred that God placed a veil between the inner court and the Holy of Holies so no one could see inside where the Ark of the Covenant was located.

Exodus 26:31-34 (KJV)

31 And thou shalt make a vail of blue, and purple, and scarlet, and fine twined linen of cunning work: with cherubims shall it be made:

32 And thou shalt hang it upon four pillars of shittim wood overlaid with gold: their hooks shall be of gold, upon the four sockets of silver.

33 And thou shalt hang up the vail under the taches, **that thou mayest bring in thither within the vail the ark of the testimony: and the vail shall divide unto you between the holy place and the most holy.**

34 **And thou shalt put the mercy seat upon the ark of the testimony in the most holy place.**

Only the High Priest was granted a *Supernatural Security Clearance* to enter behind the veil once a year. If the High Priest had any sin in his life, he would instantly die upon entrance into this sacred place. So, the High Priest had to have a golden bell on the hem of his robe so he could be heard going in. There was an ancient Jewish tradition that the High Priest had a rope tied to either his foot or waist so the other priests of the Lord could pull him out of the Holy of Holies if he died to prevent them from entering and dying themselves.

Exodus 28:31-35 (KJV)

31 And thou shalt make the robe of the ephod all of blue.

32 And there shall be an hole in the top of it, in the midst thereof: it shall have a binding of woven work round about the hole of it, as it were the hole of an habergeon, that it be not rent.

33 And beneath upon the hem of it thou shalt make pomegranates of blue, and of purple, and of scarlet, round about the hem thereof; **and bells of gold between them round about:**

> 34 **A golden bell and a pomegranate, a golden bell and a**
> **pomegranate, upon the hem of the robe round about.**
> 35 And it shall be upon Aaron to minister: **and his sound shall**
> **be heard when he goeth in unto the holy place before the**
> **Lord, and when he cometh out, that he die not.**

The Holy of Holies was so special and sacred to God that the High Priest could only enter it once a year on the Day of Atonement to make a sacrifice to God for the people's sin. The High Priest also had to wear special garments to fulfill his duties.

Leviticus 16:2-4 (KJV)

> 2 And the Lord said unto Moses, Speak unto Aaron thy brother, **that he come not at all times into the holy place within the vail before the mercy seat, which is upon the ark; that he die not**: for I will appear in the cloud upon the mercy seat.
> 3 Thus shall Aaron come into the holy place: with a young bullock for a sin offering, and a ram for a burnt offering.
> 4 He shall put on the holy linen coat, and he shall have the linen breeches upon his flesh, and shall be girded with a linen girdle, and with the linen mitre shall he be attired: **these are holy garments;** therefore shall he wash his flesh in water, and so put them on.

The Holy of Holies is at the top of the list regarding secret locations and *Supernatural Security Clearances.* Getting this close to God was sacred, and secrecy was of the utmost importance. All the armies and priests of Israel guarded this top-secret location, and God also protected it.

The Throne of God

The Throne of God is the most important and highly sacred of all places in all creation. The Throne of God is where God rules, reigns, makes decrees, and is also a place where the worship of God takes place. The Throne of God is protected by the most powerful of God's creation, the Seraphims. The Seraphims are powerful, fierce, and dangerous Heavenly beings created to protect God and His Throne.

Very few people have ever been granted access to the Throne of God while living on the earth. The Throne of God takes the highest level of *Supernatural Security Clearance* to enter. Therefore, the Throne of God is the most guarded top-secret location in all creation.

The prophet Isaiah was granted access into the Throne of God and saw the Lord high and lifted up. Let us look at what he saw and experienced.

> **Isaiah 6:1-7 (KJV)**
> **1 In the year that king Uzziah died I saw also the Lord sitting upon a throne, high and lifted up, and his train filled the temple.**
> 2 Above it stood the seraphims: each one had six wings; with twain he covered his face, and with twain he covered his feet, and with twain he did fly.
> 3 And one cried unto another, and said, Holy, holy, holy, is the Lord of hosts: the whole earth is full of his glory.
> 4 And the posts of the door moved at the voice of him that cried, and the house was filled with smoke.
> **5 Then said I, Woe is me! for I am undone; because I am a man of unclean lips, and I dwell in the midst of a people of unclean lips: for mine eyes have seen the King, the Lord of hosts.**
> 6 Then flew one of the seraphims unto me, having a live coal in his hand, which he had taken with the tongs from off the altar:

7 And he laid it upon my mouth, and said, Lo, this hath touched thy lips; and thine iniquity is taken away, and thy sin purged.

The Throne of God is so holy that Isaiah knew he was undone when he saw it. The Seraphims had to take a coal from the altar to take his iniquity away and purge his sin. Isaiah saw Jesus in His glorified state as God before He came to the earth.

Now let us turn our attention to another prophet who came before the Throne of God. This prophet was Ezekiel, and what is interesting about Ezekiel's experience is that God's Throne was moveable. God's Throne is always seen with a rainbow over it to remind us of His covenant to not flood the earth as He did during the days of Noah.

Ezekiel 1:26-28 (KJV)

26 **And above the firmament that was over their heads was the likeness of a throne,** as the appearance of a sapphire stone: and upon the likeness of the throne was the likeness as the appearance of a man above upon it.

27 And I saw as the colour of amber, as the appearance of fire round about within it, from the appearance of his loins even upward, and from the appearance of his loins even downward, I saw as it were the appearance of fire, and it had brightness round about.

28 As the appearance of the bow that is in the cloud in the day of rain, so was the appearance of the brightness round about. This was the appearance of the likeness of the glory of the Lord. And when I saw it, I fell upon my face, and I heard a voice of one that spake.

You can read more about this experience by reading chapter 1 of Ezekiel. The last place I want to turn your attention to is the Throne of

God found in the Book of Revelation. John was taken up by the Spirit and granted a *Supernatural Security Clearance* to see what was happening before the Throne of God. John saw more of what was going on in the Throne of God than any other living person up to this point in history, and what he saw and experienced was astounding!

Revelation 4:1-11 (KJV)

1 After this I looked, and, behold, a door was opened in heaven: and the first voice which I heard was as it were of a trumpet talking with me; which said, Come up hither, and I will shew thee things which must be hereafter.

2 **And immediately I was in the spirit: and, behold, a throne was set in heaven, and one sat on the throne.**

3 And he that sat was to look upon like a jasper and a sardine stone: **and there was a rainbow round about the throne, in sight like unto an emerald.**

4 And round about the throne were four and twenty seats: and upon the seats I saw four and twenty elders sitting, clothed in white raiment; and they had on their heads crowns of gold.

5 And out of the throne proceeded lightnings and thunderings and voices: and there were seven lamps of fire burning before the throne, which are the seven Spirits of God.

6 And before the throne there was a sea of glass like unto crystal: and in the midst of the throne, and round about the throne, were four beasts full of eyes before and behind.

7 And the first beast was like a lion, and the second beast like a calf, and the third beast had a face as a man, and the fourth beast was like a flying eagle.

8 And the four beasts had each of them six wings about him; and they were full of eyes within: and they rest not day and

night, saying, Holy, holy, holy, Lord God Almighty, which was, and is, and is to come.

9 And when those beasts give glory and honour and thanks to him that sat on the throne, who liveth for ever and ever,

10 The four and twenty elders fall down before him that sat on the throne, and worship him that liveth for ever and ever, and cast their crowns before the throne, saying,

11 **Thou art worthy, O Lord, to receive glory and honour and power: for thou hast created all things, and for thy pleasure they are and were created.**

The Throne of God is not like any other place. This is where the most important top-secret things in God's kingdom occur. Decisions, decrees, and judgments are made from God's Throne, affecting all creation. For John to be granted a *Supernatural Security Clearance* and see the Throne of God is a high honor. All creation worships at the Throne of God for all the wonderful things He has done. It takes the highest of all *Supernatural Security Clearances* to access the Throne of God.

The Secret Place of the Most High

The *Secret Place* of the Most High is not a physical place you can find on the earth. The *Secret Place* of the Most High is a spiritual place located in the presence of God. We can abide and live in this place if given a *Supernatural Security Clearance*. The *Secret Place* is found in the Spirit of God and is a place of comfort and protection for the believer.

To better understand the Most High's *Secret Place*, we must read Psalm 91. This passage of Scripture gives one of the best descriptions of this secret and holy place only found in God.

Psalm 91:1 (KJV)

1 **He that dwelleth in the secret place of the most High shall abide under the shadow of the Almighty.**

The *Secret Place* of the Most High is a wonderful spiritual place of refuge for the believer to abide in. God has a *Secret Place* only found in His Spirit where a believer can seek fellowship and protection in God's presence. King David spent hours and years praying and seeking God while playing his harp before God in this *Secret Place*. King David was able to access a *Secret Place* in God's Spirit that helped him through all his trials while on earth.

Jesus talked about this *Secret Place* but used different terminology. Jesus referred to this place as the *Abiding*. Jesus taught His disciples that they could abide in Him if they obeyed Him. When you *Abide* in Christ, you bear fruit. When you *Abide* in Christ, you also have access to your prayers being answered.

Let's read what Jesus taught about this *Secret Place* of *Abiding* in Him.

John 15:4-11 (KJV)

4 **Abide in me, and I in you.** As the branch cannot bear fruit of itself, except it abide in the vine; no more can ye, except ye abide in me.

5 **I am the vine, ye are the branches: He that abideth in me, and I in him, the same bringeth forth much fruit: for without me ye can do nothing.**

6 If a man abide not in me, he is cast forth as a branch, and is withered; and men gather them, and cast them into the fire, and they are burned.

7 **If ye abide in me, and my words abide in you, ye shall ask what ye will, and it shall be done unto you.**

8 Herein is my Father glorified, that ye bear much fruit; so shall ye be my disciples.

9 As the Father hath loved me, so have I loved you: continue ye in my love.

10 If ye keep my Commandments, ye shall abide in my love; even as I have kept my Father's Commandments, **and abide in his love.**

11 These things have I spoken unto you, that my joy might remain in you, and that your joy might be full.

The *Abiding* in Christ and the *Secret Place* of the Most High are the same location. This wonderful and holy *Secret Place* can only be accessed by loving God and keeping His Commandments. God loves His people, and when you love Him back through your obedience, you can gain a *Supernatural Security Clearance* into this loving place of spiritual refuge.

The word *abide* means to remain, dwell, and live in. When you *Abide* in Christ by loving and obeying Him, you enter a living relationship that allows you to enter a secret relationship with Him. This intimate relationship of loving obedience to His Word gives you a *Supernatural Security Clearance* to access the *Secret Place* of the Most High. The main requirement to access this top-secret location is loving God and keeping His Commandments.

John 15:10 (KJV)

10 **If ye keep my Commandments, ye shall abide in my love; even as I have kept my Father's Commandments, and abide in his love.**

God grants you secret access to His presence when you love God with this type of obedient love. This is not an actual place in the natural, but more of a place where God surrounds you with Himself in the Spirit.

You can also call this being surrounded by His presence. Psalm 91 describes this as being covered with His feathers and wings.

Psalm 91:4 (KJV)
> 4 **He shall cover thee with his feathers, and under his wings shalt thou trust:** his truth shall be thy shield and buckler.

God uses feathers and wings as an example of how a bird covers and protects her children. Little birds can find protection from the elements, storms, and predators by coming under their mother's wings. Jesus used this same analogy when He came to Jerusalem and was rejected by the religious leaders.

Luke 13:34 (KJV)
> 34 O Jerusalem, Jerusalem, which killest the prophets, and stonest them that are sent unto thee; **how often would I have gathered thy children together, as a hen doth gather her brood under her wings,** and ye would not!

Jesus was offering them His protection, but they rejected Him and crucified Him on a cross, and because of this, they did not have the protection of God. Because God was not protecting them anymore, the Romans destroyed the Holy City of Jerusalem and the Temple of God 40 years later. God can protect and shelter His people from any storm if they love Him and obey His Commandments.

Psalm 91 goes into detail about God protecting those who *Abide* and dwell in the *Secret Place* of the Most High.

Psalm 91:2-13 (KJV)
> 2 **I will say of the Lord, He is my refuge and my fortress: my God; in him will I trust.**
> 3 Surely he shall deliver thee from the snare of the fowler, and from the noisome pestilence.

4 He shall cover thee with his feathers, and under his wings shalt thou trust: his truth shall be thy shield and buckler.

5 **Thou shalt not be afraid for the terror by night; nor for the arrow that flieth by day;**

6 **Nor for the pestilence that walketh in darkness; nor for the destruction that wasteth at noonday.**

7 **A thousand shall fall at thy side, and ten thousand at thy right hand; but it shall not come nigh thee.**

8 Only with thine eyes shalt thou behold and see the reward of the wicked.

9 **Because thou hast made the Lord, which is my refuge, even the most High, thy habitation;**

10 There shall no evil befall thee, neither shall any plague come nigh thy dwelling.

11 For he shall give his angels charge over thee, to keep thee in all thy ways.

12 They shall bear thee up in their hands, lest thou dash thy foot against a stone.

13 Thou shalt tread upon the lion and adder: the young lion and the dragon shalt thou trample under feet.

When you dwell in the *Secret Place* of the Most High, you are given protection from the terror by night, diseases, and any evil. God also surrounds you with His angels to protect you. God protects His children because He loves them, and when they bestow this love back in obedience to His Word, He grants them a *Supernatural Security Clearance*. This *Supernatural Security Clearance* gives them access to this *Secret Place* only found in Him.

Psalm 91:14-16 (KJV)

14 **Because he hath set his love upon me, therefore will I deliver him:** I will set him on high, because he hath known my name.

15 He shall call upon me, and I will answer him: **I will be with him in trouble; I will deliver him, and honour him.**

16 With long life will I satisfy him, and shew him my salvation.

Heavenly Jerusalem, the Eternal City of God

After the end of the world, God will create a new Heaven and a new earth. During this time, the New Jerusalem will descend out of Heaven. This city is described as a bride adorned for her husband. God uses the analogy of a bride and bridegroom because the only ones granted access to this city will be the Church and God. The Church is the Bride of Christ. God the Father and the Holy Spirit, along with Jesus and His Church, will be the only ones with access to this city. God will not grant a *Supernatural Security Clearance* to anyone other than the angels.

All evil people will be cast in the lake of fire with the devil, demons, fallen angels, and everyone else that rejected Christ. As harsh as this may seem to some, it is the Gospel truth revealed in the Book of Revelation. God has made every room for salvation for those who accept Him, but no room if you reject Him.

Let us look at the description of this city from the Book of Revelation.

> **Revelation 21:1-3 (KJV)**
> 1 **And I saw a new heaven and a new earth: for the first heaven and the first earth were passed away; and there was no more sea.**
> 2 **And I John saw the holy city, new Jerusalem, coming down from God out of heaven, prepared as a bride adorned for her husband.**
> 3 And I heard a great voice out of heaven saying, Behold, the tabernacle of God is with men, and he will dwell with them,

and they shall be his people, and God himself shall be with them, and be their God.

Revelation 21:10-14 (KJV)

10 And he carried me away in the spirit to a great and high mountain, **and shewed me that great city, the holy Jerusalem, descending out of heaven from God,**

11 Having the glory of God: and her light was like unto a stone most precious, even like a jasper stone, clear as crystal;

12 And had a wall great and high, and had twelve gates, and at the gates twelve angels, and names written thereon, which are the names of the twelve tribes of the children of Israel:

13 On the east three gates; on the north three gates; on the south three gates; and on the west three gates.

14 And the wall of the city had twelve foundations, and in them the names of the twelve apostles of the Lamb.

Revelation 21:18-26 (KJV)

18 And the building of the wall of it was of jasper: and the city was pure gold, like unto clear glass.

19 And the foundations of the wall of the city were garnished with all manner of precious stones. The first foundation was jasper; the second, sapphire; the third, a chalcedony; the fourth, an emerald;

20 The fifth, sardonyx; the sixth, sardius; the seventh, chrysolyte; the eighth, beryl; the ninth, a topaz; the tenth, a chrysoprasus; the eleventh, a jacinth; the twelfth, an amethyst.

21 And the twelve gates were twelve pearls: every several gate was of one pearl: and the street of the city was pure gold, as it were transparent glass.

22 And I saw no temple therein: for the Lord God Almighty and the Lamb are the temple of it.

23 And the city had no need of the sun, neither of the moon, to shine in it: for the glory of God did lighten it, and the Lamb is the light thereof.
24 And the nations of them which are saved shall walk in the light of it: and the kings of the earth do bring their glory and honour into it.
25 And the gates of it shall not be shut at all by day: for there shall be no night there.
26 And they shall bring the glory and honour of the nations into it.

After this beautiful description of how great this city is, let us see how God ends this chapter with a warning.

Revelation 21:27 (KJV)
27 And there shall in no wise enter into it any thing that defileth, neither whatsoever worketh abomination, or maketh a lie: but they which are written in the Lamb's Book of life.

God has requirements for anyone being granted access into this Heavenly city. Your name must be found written in the Lamb's Book of Life. Your name is written in this book when you repent of your evil ways and believe God raised Jesus from the dead in your heart. You must also confess that Jesus is Lord with your mouth. God will not allow anything to enter that will defile His Heavenly city.

God does have *Supernatural Security Clearances* and does not allow any evil person or wicked angel access into His New Jerusalem. Let us read what God has to say at the end of the Book of Revelation to confirm this truth.

Revelation 22:10-17 (KJV)

10 And he saith unto me, Seal not the sayings of the prophecy of this book: for the time is at hand.

11 He that is unjust, let him be unjust still: and he which is filthy, let him be filthy still: and he that is righteous, let him be righteous still: and he that is holy, let him be holy still.

12 And, behold, I come quickly; and my reward is with me, to give every man according as his work shall be.

13 I am Alpha and Omega, the beginning and the end, the first and the last.

14 **Blessed are they that do his Commandments, that they may have right to the tree of life, and may enter in through the gates into the city.**

15 For without are dogs, and sorcerers, and whoremongers, and murderers, and idolaters, and whosoever loveth and maketh a lie.

16 I Jesus have sent mine angel to testify unto you these things in the churches. I am the root and the offspring of David, and the bright and morning star.

17 And the Spirit and the bride say, Come. And let him that heareth say, Come. And let him that is athirst come. And whosoever will, let him take the water of life freely.

In conclusion, it is clear from all these examples that God has always had secret locations, and it takes a *Supernatural Security Clearance* to access them. God will not allow anything to defile His sacred locations. This chapter reveals these locations to understand how we can gain access to *Secret Places* found in God. It is an honor and privilege to be given a *Supernatural Security Clearance* into God's secret locations and must always be protected to avoid losing access.

CHAPTER 6
POWERFUL WEAPONS

Every nation needs powerful weapons to protect itself and defeat enemies. We live in a time where nations have developed some of the most powerful weapons this world has ever seen. Some countries have enough nuclear bombs to destroy the entire world many times over. They also have other secret weapons in their arsenal that could rain down terrible carnage on their enemies. Some nations even have secret weapons no one knows about that could do unheard of and unimaginable damage to their enemies. But, with all these powerful weapons, no nation has weapons as powerful as God's weapons. This chapter will reveal some of the supernatural weapons in the Bible that God used to destroy His enemies and who was given a *Supernatural Security Clearance* to have access to use these weapons.

God's weapons are not like human weapons. God's weapons are supernatural, voice-activated, and powerful at destroying the enemy. Some of God's most powerful weapons are the use of weather, elements of creation, plagues, cosmic power, and fire coming down from Heaven. God has a sword coming out of His mouth that can devastate any enemy with His spoken Word. God also has a fully equipped army with Divine weapons that can wipe out any opposing foe.

Revelation 19:11-21 (KJV)

11 And I saw heaven opened, and behold a white horse; **and he that sat upon him was called Faithful and True, and in righteousness he doth judge and make war.**

12 His eyes were as a flame of fire, and on his head were many crowns; and he had a name written, that no man knew, but he himself.

13 And he was clothed with a vesture dipped in blood: **and His Name is called The Word of God.**

14 **And the armies which were in heaven followed him upon white horses, clothed in fine linen, white and clean.**

15 **And out of his mouth goeth a sharp sword, that with it he should smite the nations: and he shall rule them with a rod of iron: and he treadeth the winepress of the fierceness and wrath of Almighty God.**

16 And he hath on his vesture and on his thigh a name written, King Of Kings, And Lord Of Lords.

17 And I saw an angel standing in the sun; and he cried with a loud voice, saying to all the fowls that fly in the midst of heaven, Come and gather yourselves together unto the supper of the great God;

18 That ye may eat the flesh of kings, and the flesh of captains, and the flesh of mighty men, and the flesh of horses, and of them that sit on them, and the flesh of all men, both free and bond, both small and great.

19 **And I saw the beast, and the kings of the earth, and their armies, gathered together to make war against him that sat on the horse, and against his army.**

20 And the beast was taken, and with him the false prophet that wrought miracles before him, with which he deceived them that had received the mark of the beast, and them that worshipped his image. These both were cast alive into a lake of fire burning with brimstone.

21 **And the remnant were slain with the sword of him that sat upon the horse, which sword proceeded out of his mouth:** and all the fowls were filled with their flesh.

When Jesus returns with His army to the earth, He will destroy His enemies with the sword coming out of His mouth; kings, captains, mighty men, them that sit on horses and all manner of men, both small and great. Jesus will also throw the beast, false prophet, and those who worship the beast into the lake of fire that burns with brimstone. No one can stand against God or defend themselves against God's weapons. God is unbeatable when it comes to war!

Throughout Biblical history, different individuals were granted supernatural access to use God's weapons to defeat their enemies. It took a *Supernatural Security Clearance* to access God's weapons, and they had to be very responsible in deploying them. Below is a list of some of the men of God used in the Bible to deploy some of God's most powerful weapons. We will study these men and see how God used them to defeat the enemies of their day with His weapons:

1. Noah and the Great Flood

2. Moses and the Judgments of Egypt

3. Joshua and the Promised Land

4. Samson and the Nazarite Vow

5. David the Giant Slayer

6. David's Mighty Men

7. Elijah and the Fire of God

8. The Two Witnesses

9. Christian Soldier

Noah and the Great Flood

During the days of Noah, after the fall of Adam and Eve, humanity had corrupted themselves and became very wicked before God. The imagination and thoughts of everyone's heart on the earth were continually evil, except Noah and his family. The wickedness of humankind was so evil that God's only solution was to wipe them all out. God's supernatural weapon of choice was to flood the whole earth, but He saved Noah by having him prepare an ark for himself, his family, and some of the animals of the world.

> **Genesis 6:5-7 (KJV)**
> 5 **And God saw that the wickedness of man was great in the earth, and that every imagination of the thoughts of his heart was only evil continually.**
> 6 And it repented the Lord that he had made man on the earth, and it grieved him at his heart.
> 7 **And the Lord said, I will destroy man whom I have created from the face of the earth;** both man, and beast, and the creeping thing, and the fowls of the air; for it repenteth me that I have made them.

> **Genesis 7:1-4 (KJV)**
> 1 And the Lord said unto Noah, Come thou and all thy house into the ark; for thee have I seen righteous before me in this generation.

2 Of every clean beast thou shalt take to thee by sevens, the male and his female: and of beasts that are not clean by two, the male and his female.

3 Of fowls also of the air by sevens, the male and the female; to keep seed alive upon the face of all the earth.

4 **For yet seven days, and I will cause it to rain upon the earth forty days and forty nights; and every living substance that I have made will I destroy from off the face of the earth.**

Genesis 7:10-12 (KJV)

10 **And it came to pass after seven days, that the waters of the flood were upon the earth.**

11 In the six hundredth year of Noah's life, in the second month, the seventeenth day of the month, **the same day were all the fountains of the great deep broken up, and the windows of heaven were opened.**

12 **And the rain was upon the earth forty days and forty nights.**

It is estimated that over four billion people were on the earth at the time of the flood. There were also mighty warring giants on the earth and wicked angels. God was able to defeat all the armies of the earth and defeat the wicked angels with just the flood. God does not fight like man fights. God fights with overwhelming power and supernatural elements that no man or angel can stand against.

Moses and the Judgments of Egypt

Moses was one of the most dangerous men of God who walked on this planet. God gave Moses a *Supernatural Security Clearance* to use weapons from God that defeated Egypt and their armies. God empowered Moses' staff, whereby he deployed the supernatural weaponry of God on the enemy. Pharaoh resisted the command of God through Moses to let His people go and suffered the wrath of God through an unparalleled series of plagues on Egypt. God's people were made to serve Egypt through hard bondage as enslaved people for over 400 years. God unleashed ten supernatural plagues upon Egypt and Pharaoh until he was forced to let God's people go and free them from slavery. Each of these plagues also judged the false gods Egypt was serving.

Here is a list of those plagues:

1. **The Water Turned to Blood** (Exodus 7:14-24)

2. **The Plague of Frogs** (Exodus 8:1-5)

3. **The Plague of Gnats** (Exodus 8:16-19

4. **The Plague of Flies** (Exodus 8:20-32)

5. **Diseased Livestock** (Exodus 9:1-7)

6. **The Plague of Boils** (Exodus 98-12)

7. **The Plague of Hail** (Exodus 9:13-35)

8. **The Plague of Locust** (Exodus 10:1-20)

9. **Thick Darkness for Three Days** (Exodus 10:21-29)

10. **Death of the Firstborn Son** (Exodus 11:1-10; 12:1-30)

After God unleashed these ten plagues, Pharaoh agreed to let God's people go. The death of Pharaoh's firstborn son was the straw that broke the camel's back that forced Pharoah to let God's people go. Pharaoh and Egypt were devastated and wiped out by these ten plagues. However, it is interesting to note that after God judged Pharaoh and all of Egypt with these ten plagues, Pharaoh still chased

Moses and the children of Israel with his army to the Red Sea and cornered them. Then, Moses used his staff with his *Supernatural Security Clearance* and parted the red sea so the children of Israel could pass. When Pharaoh's army chased them into the Red Sea, God closed the Red Sea upon them and wiped-out Pharaoh's army.

Exodus 14:21-30 (KJV)

21 **And Moses stretched out his hand over the sea; and the Lord caused the sea to go back by a strong east wind all that night, and made the sea dry land, and the waters were divided.**

22 And the children of Israel went into the midst of the sea upon the dry ground: and the waters were a wall unto them on their right hand, and on their left.

23 **And the Egyptians pursued, and went in after them to the midst of the sea, even all Pharaoh's horses, his chariots, and his horsemen.**

24 **And it came to pass, that in the morning watch the Lord looked unto the host of the Egyptians through the pillar of fire and of the cloud, and troubled the host of the Egyptians,**

25 **And took off their chariot wheels, that they drave them heavily: so that the Egyptians said, Let us flee from the face of Israel; for the Lord fighteth for them against the Egyptians.**

26 **And the Lord said unto Moses, Stretch out thine hand over the sea, that the waters may come again upon the Egyptians, upon their chariots, and upon their horsemen.**

27 **And Moses stretched forth his hand over the sea, and the sea returned to his strength when the morning appeared; and the Egyptians fled against it; and the Lord overthrew the Egyptians in the midst of the sea.**

28 **And the waters returned, and covered the chariots, and the horsemen, and all the host of Pharaoh that came into**

the sea after them; there remained not so much as one of them.

29 But the children of Israel walked upon dry land in the midst of the sea; and the waters were a wall unto them on their right hand, and on their left.

30 Thus the Lord saved Israel that day out of the hand of the Egyptians; **and Israel saw the Egyptians dead upon the sea shore.**

We can see through the story of Moses that God used the power of nature, supernatural phenomena, death, and the Red Sea to defeat the whole nation of Egypt, Pharaoh, and his armies. Never in the history of humankind had God brought such use of supernatural destruction upon His enemies. Moses was greatly used by God and was granted a *Supernatural Security Clearance* to access the incredible power of God.

Joshua and the Promised Land

Joshua was one of the most powerful military leaders of Israel. Joshua was the servant to Moses and witnessed the supernatural power of God wipe out the Egyptians. Now God was going to grant Joshua a *Supernatural Security Clearance* to take the children of Israel into the Promised Land and defeat the enemies of God.

Before Joshua started his crusade in taking the Promised Land, he had a supernatural encounter with the Captain of the host of the Lord. Many believe this is an appearance of Christ because this Captain tells Joshua to take off his shoes for the ground is holy. *Taking your shoes off* is only something you would only do in the presence of God.

Joshua 5:13-15 (KJV)

13 And it came to pass, when Joshua was by Jericho, **that he lifted up his eyes and looked, and, behold, there stood a**

man over against him with his sword drawn in his hand: and Joshua went unto him, and said unto him, Art thou for us, or for our adversaries?

14 **And he said, Nay; but as captain of the host of the Lord am I now come.** And Joshua fell on his face to the earth, and did worship, and said unto him, What saith my Lord unto his servant?

15 **And the captain of the Lord's host said unto Joshua, Loose thy shoe from off thy foot; for the place whereon thou standest is holy. And Joshua did so.**

After this experience with the Captain of the host of the Lord, Joshua successfully started taking the Promised Land and defeating God's enemies. No king could stand before Joshua because Joshua was granted access to a *Supernatural Security Clearance* to use Heavenly weapons to wipe out any army. In one of Joshua's battles in taking the Promised Land, God threw down great stones from Heaven upon His enemy. What army could stand against a supernatural attack such as this?

Joshua 10:10-14 (KJV)

10 And the Lord discomfited them before Israel, and slew them with a great slaughter at Gibeon, and chased them along the way that goeth up to Bethhoron, and smote them to Azekah, and unto Makkedah.

11 And it came to pass, as they fled from before Israel, and were in the going down to Bethhoron, **that the Lord cast down great stones from heaven upon them unto Azekah, and they died: they were more which died with hailstones than they whom the children of Israel slew with the sword.**

12 Then spake Joshua to the Lord in the day when the Lord delivered up the Amorites before the children of Israel, and

he said in the sight of Israel, Sun, stand thou still upon Gibeon; and thou, Moon, in the valley of Ajalon.

13 And the sun stood still, and the moon stayed, until the people had avenged themselves upon their enemies. Is not this written in the Book of Jasher? So the sun stood still in the midst of heaven, and hasted not to go down about a whole day.

14 And there was no day like that before it or after it, that the Lord hearkened unto the voice of a man: for the Lord fought for Israel.

Joshua asked God to stop the sun and moon to have more time to defeat their enemies. With God on his side, Joshua was more than a conqueror and became one of the great military leaders of all time. No one could stand and fight against Joshua. One of the secrets to his success and keeping his *Supernatural Security Clearance* is that he had to meditate on God's Law given to Moses and not let it depart from his mouth.

Joshua 1:7-9 (KJV)

7 **Only be thou strong and very courageous, that thou mayest observe to do according to all the law, which Moses my servant commanded thee: turn not from it to the right hand or to the left, that thou mayest prosper withersoever thou goest.**

8 **This Book of the law shall not depart out of thy mouth; but thou shalt meditate therein day and night, that thou mayest observe to do according to all that is written therein: for then thou shalt make thy way prosperous, and then thou shalt have good success.**

9 Have not I commanded thee? Be strong and of a good courage; be not afraid, neither be thou dismayed: for the Lord thy God is with thee whithersoever thou goest.

There are always requirements to accessing and maintaining a *Supernatural Security Clearance* from God. Joshua kept the commands of God and defeated the armies of Israel.

Samson and the Nazarite Vow

The story of Samson is one of the greatest stories in the Bible. It reveals the necessity of requirements to access and maintain a *Supernatural Security Clearance* from God. Before Samson was born, an angel came to Samson's mom and commanded that Samson take a Nazarite vow to become the deliverer and judge of Israel.

Israel, at that time, was under the dominion of the Philistines because they had done evil in the sight of the Lord. God, however, wanted to deliver them from the hand of the Philistines. God's way of delivering His people was always to raise up and send a deliverer that was granted a *Supernatural Security Clearance* to operate in the power of the anointing to defeat their enemy. During the time of Samson, God was using judges to be His deliverer.

A deliverer of Israel always had requirements from God to operate in this position and with the power of God's anointing. So, when the angel came to Samson's mom, he listed out these requirements for her son Samson to operate in a *Supernatural Security Clearance.* These requirements of a Nazarite vow were found in the Law of Moses.

Let's see what the angel said to Samson's mother.

> **Judges 13:3-5 (KJV)**
> 3 And the angel of the Lord appeared unto the woman, and said unto her, Behold now, thou art barren, and bearest not: but thou shalt conceive, and bear a son.

4 Now therefore beware, **I pray thee, and drink not wine nor strong drink, and eat not any unclean thing:**
5 **For, lo, thou shalt conceive, and bear a son; and no razor shall come on his head: for the child shall be a Nazarite unto God from the womb: and he shall begin to deliver Israel out of the hand of the Philistines.**

Samson's mother was told not to drink wine or strong drink, and she was also commanded not to eat anything unclean. Then she was told she would bear a son and no razor would come upon his head and that he would be a Nazarite to God from the womb. Here you can see God placed requirements for Samson to access his *Supernatural Security Clearance* to deliver Israel out of the hand of the Philistines.

Let's now go to the Law of Moses and see what the Laws of the Nazarite were.

Numbers 6:1-8 (KJV)

1 And the Lord spake unto Moses, saying,
2 **Speak unto the children of Israel, and say unto them, When either man or woman shall separate themselves to vow a vow of a Nazarite, to separate themselves unto the Lord:**
3 He shall separate himself from wine and strong drink, and shall drink no vinegar of wine, or vinegar of strong drink, neither shall he drink any liquor of grapes, nor eat moist grapes, or dried.
4 All the days of his separation shall he eat nothing that is made of the vine tree, from the kernels even to the husk.
5 **All the days of the vow of his separation there shall no razor come upon his head: until the days be fulfilled, in the which he separateth himself unto the Lord, he shall be holy, and shall let the locks of the hair of his head grow.**

6 All the days that he separateth himself unto the Lord he shall come at no dead body.

7 He shall not make himself unclean for his father, or for his mother, for his brother, or for his sister, when they die: **because the consecration of his God is upon his head.**

8 All the days of his separation he is holy unto the Lord.

These are the Nazarite Laws found in the Law of Moses (Numbers 6:1-8).

1. No wine or strong drink

2. No vinegar of wine or strong drink

3. No liquor from grapes

4. No eating of moist or dried grapes

5. No eating of anything made of the vine tree

6. No eating kernels or the husk

7. No razor is to come upon his head (He had to let the locks of his hair grow)

8. He cannot come near any dead body

9. He cannot make himself unclean by touching his father, mother, brother, or sister if they die

10. All the days of their separation, they are holy to the Lord

These were all the Laws of the Nazarites to follow to fulfill the Law of the Nazarite vow to God. God ordained Samson before he was born to keep the vow of the Nazarites. By keeping the Nazarite vow, he gained a *Supernatural Security Clearance* from God and was empowered to be a deliverer of Israel from the hand of the Philistines.

Later we read in the story of Samson that he was granted a supernatural weapon of Divine strength. The Spirit of God came upon Samson as he kept the vow of the Nazarite that gave him supernatural strength to defeat the enemies of Israel. Samson's strength was so incredible that he was able to kill a lion with his bare hands, pick up a city gate and carry it 20 miles, catch 300 foxes, tie their tails together and light them on fire. Samson also defeated 1,000 Philistines with the jawbone of a donkey. The Philistines were unable to fight this supernatural warrior of God.

However, Samson was seduced by a Philistine woman named Delilah, who wore him out asking about the secret to his unusual strength given to him by God. Samson gave in to her question, and he revealed the secret of his strength. He revealed to her that his hair had never been cut, which was a big part of the Nazarite vow that allowed him to be granted the ability to walk in the supernatural strength of God.

Delilah betrayed Samson and had his hair shaved off by a man while he slept. The Philistines captured Samson and cut his eyes out, and he could no longer defend himself because he lost his *Supernatural Security Clearance* of Divine strength. The Philistines also bound Samson with brass and made him grind at a mill as an enslaved prisoner.

> **Judges 16:16-21 (KJV)**
> 16 **And it came to pass, when she pressed him daily with her words, and urged him, so that his soul was vexed unto death;**

17 That he told her all his heart, and said unto her, **There hath not come a razor upon mine head; for I have been a Nazarite unto God from my mother's womb: if I be shaven, then my strength will go from me, and I shall become weak, and be like any other man.**

18 And when Delilah saw that he had told her all his heart, she sent and called for the lords of the Philistines, saying, Come up this once, for he hath shewed me all his heart. Then the lords of the Philistines came up unto her, and brought money in their hand.

19 **And she made him sleep upon her knees; and she called for a man, and she caused him to shave off the seven locks of his head; and she began to afflict him, and his strength went from him.**

20 And she said, The Philistines be upon thee, Samson. And he awoke out of his sleep, and said, I will go out as at other times before, and shake myself. **And he wist not that the Lord was departed from him.**

21 **But the Philistines took him, and put out his eyes, and brought him down to Gaza, and bound him with fetters of brass; and he did grind in the prison house.**

This is one of the best stories in revealing the requirements of walking in a *Supernatural Security Clearance* and how it can be lost if you disobey God's requirements. God does have *Supernatural Security Clearances,* and the conditions must be maintained to keep this level of clearance. Samson lost his supernatural weaponry of Divine strength because he allowed himself to be infiltrated by the enemy. Samson's weakness in women and sex was his downfall. This weakness to women and sex caused him to lose his most valuable possession, his *Supernatural Security Clearance*. After his hair was cut off, he didn't even know that the Lord had departed from him and taken his *Supernatural Security Clearance* away.

The story of Samson is a warning to everyone with a *Supernatural Security Clearance* and what can happen if you disobey God and fail to maintain His requirements. The enemy bound, blinded, and forced Samson to grind like a slave.

David the Giant Slayer

King David was a fearless warrior for God who took out a giant with a stone and a sling. This giant was no ordinary giant. This giant was a Philistine named Goliath who stood 9 feet and 6 inches tall. He was raised to be a warrior from his youth and was a scary sight to behold. Goliath's spear was 16 to 18 feet long and weighed about 15 pounds. His armor weighed over 91 pounds. Goliath was no one to fight with in the natural.

David was still a youth when he went out to fight Goliath. But a few things to note is that David loved the Lord with all his heart and was very brave. It is also important to note that before David went out and faced this giant, God had sent the prophet Samuel to anoint him to replace King Saul. King Saul had disobeyed God, and Samuel anointed David to replace him as king of Israel.

When Samuel anointed David to be king, the Spirit of God came upon him. So, when David went out to meet Goliath, the warring giant, he had a *Supernatural Security Clearance* of the anointing of God on his life.

1 Samuel 16:13 (KJV)

> 13 Then Samuel took the horn of oil, and anointed him in the midst of his brethren**: and the Spirit of the Lord came upon David from that day forward.** So Samuel rose up, and went to Ramah.

The anointing of God made all the difference going into this battle one-on-one with Goliath. It is also important to note that David was a prophet. He became a prophet and king when Samuel anointed him. To be a prophet in Israel, all your words had to come to pass. So, not only was he anointed to be the king of Israel, but he also had the prophetic Word of God in his mouth. When David faced Goliath, he prophesied his death. Goliath had no idea he would be fighting with God through this young shepherd boy.

Let's read how this battle goes down and how David used his *Supernatural Security Clearance* to defeat this wicked giant.

1 Samuel 17:40-51 (KJV)

> 40 And he took his staff in his hand, and chose him five smooth stones out of the brook, and put them in a shepherd's bag which he had, even in a scrip; and his sling was in his hand: and he drew near to the Philistine.
> 41 And the Philistine came on and drew near unto David; and the man that bare the shield went before him.
> 42 And when the Philistine looked about, and saw David, he disdained him: for he was but a youth, and ruddy, and of a fair countenance.
> 43 And the Philistine said unto David, Am I a dog, that thou comest to me with staves? And the Philistine cursed David by his gods.

44 And the Philistine said to David, Come to me, and I will give thy flesh unto the fowls of the air, and to the beasts of the field.

45 **Then said David to the Philistine, Thou comest to me with a sword, and with a spear, and with a shield: but I come to thee in the Name of the Lord of hosts, the God of the armies of Israel, whom thou hast defied.**

46 **This day will the Lord deliver thee into mine hand; and I will smite thee, and take thine head from thee; and I will give the carcases of the host of the Philistines this day unto the fowls of the air, and to the wild beasts of the earth; that all the earth may know that there is a God in Israel.**

47 **And all this assembly shall know that the Lord saveth not with sword and spear: for the battle is the Lord's, and he will give you into our hands.**

48 And it came to pass, when the Philistine arose, and came, and drew nigh to meet David, that David hastened, and ran toward the army to meet the Philistine.

49 **And David put his hand in his bag, and took thence a stone, and slang it, and smote the Philistine in his forehead, that the stone sunk into his forehead; and he fell upon his face to the earth.**

50 **So David prevailed over the Philistine with a sling and with a stone, and smote the Philistine, and slew him; but there was no sword in the hand of David.**

51 Therefore David ran, and stood upon the Philistine, and took his sword, and drew it out of the sheath thereof, and slew him, **and cut off his head therewith.** And when the Philistines saw their champion was dead, they fled.

David went on to become a great warring king of Israel, and during his reign as king, he defeated the remaining giants in the Promised Land.

David wisely used his *Supernatural Security Clearance* to serve God and defeat all the enemies of the Lord.

David's Mighty Men

When David became the king of Israel, he was given many men who had unusual supernatural abilities to fight. These mighty men were one of the main reasons King David had so much success on the battlefield. These men had *Supernatural Security Clearances* given to them by God to defeat His enemies.

Let's read the feats these mighty men supernaturally accomplished on the battlefield.

2 Samuel 23:8-12 (KJV)

8 These be the names of the mighty men whom David had: The Tachmonite that sat in the seat, chief among the captains; the same was Adino the Eznite: he lift up his spear against eight hundred, whom he slew at one time.

9 And after him was Eleazar the son of Dodo the Ahohite, one of the three mighty men with David, when they defied the Philistines that were there gathered together to battle, and the men of Israel were gone away:

10 He arose, and smote the Philistines until his hand was weary, and his hand clave unto the sword: and the Lord wrought a great victory that day; and the people returned after him only to spoil.

11 And after him was Shammah the son of Agee the Hararite. And the Philistines were gathered together into a troop, where was a piece of ground full of lentiles: and the people fled from the Philistines.

12 But he stood in the midst of the ground, and defended it, and slew the Philistines: and the Lord wrought a great victory.

2 Samuel 23:18-22 (KJV)

18 And Abishai, the brother of Joab, the son of Zeruiah, was chief among three. And he lifted up his spear against three hundred, and slew them, and had the name among three.

19 Was he not most honourable of three? therefore he was their captain: howbeit he attained not unto the first three.

20 And Benaiah the son of Jehoiada, the son of a valiant man, of Kabzeel, who had done many acts, he slew two lionlike men of Moab: he went down also and slew a lion in the midst of a pit in time of snow:

21 And he slew an Egyptian, a goodly man: and the Egyptian had a spear in his hand; but he went down to him with a staff, and plucked the spear out of the Egyptian's hand, and slew him with his own spear.

22 These things did Benaiah the son of Jehoiada, and had the name among three mighty men.

Elijah and the Fire of God

Elijah is undoubtedly one of the most powerful prophets of Israel. Elijah ministered as a prophet during some of the worst times in Israel. King Ahab was ruling with his wife Jezebel, and they went down as two of the wickedest rulers of Israel. God called Elijah to stand up to these corrupt rulers, and God gave him an unusual *Supernatural Security Clearance.*

During Elijah's ministry, at His Word, he started and stopped the rain, raised the dead, prophesied about future events, and many more unusual miracles. One of the supernatural abilities God gave to Elijah was to call down fire. He first called down fire on an altar when coming against the prophets of Baal. Later, Elijah called down this supernatural weapon of fire to destroy men sent to him by an evil king raised up after Ahab's death.

Let's read how Elijah killed military men with the secret weapon of God's fire.

2 Kings 1:1-15 (KJV)
1 Then Moab rebelled against Israel after the death of Ahab.
2 And Ahaziah fell down through a lattice in his upper chamber that was in Samaria, and was sick: and he sent messengers, and said unto them, Go, enquire of Baalzebub the God of Ekron whether I shall recover of this disease.
3 But the angel of the Lord said to Elijah the Tishbite, Arise, go up to meet the messengers of the king of Samaria, and say unto them, Is it not because there is not a God in Israel, that ye go to enquire of Baalzebub the God of Ekron?
4 Now therefore thus saith the Lord, Thou shalt not come down from that bed on which thou art gone up, but shalt surely die. And Elijah departed.
5 And when the messengers turned back unto him, he said unto them, Why are ye now turned back?
6 And they said unto him, There came a man up to meet us, and said unto us, Go, turn again unto the king that sent you, and say unto him, Thus saith the Lord, Is it not because there is not a God in Israel, that thou sendest to enquire of Baalzebub the God of Ekron? therefore thou shalt not come down from that bed on which thou art gone up, but shalt surely die.
7 And he said unto them, What manner of man was he which came up to meet you, and told you these words?
8 And they answered him, He was an hairy man, and girt with a girdle of leather about his loins. And he said, It is Elijah the Tishbite.
9 Then the king sent unto him a captain of fifty with his fifty. And he went up to him: and, behold, he sat on the top of an

hill. And he spake unto him, Thou man of God, the king hath said, Come down.

10 **And Elijah answered and said to the captain of fifty, If I be a man of God, then let fire come down from heaven, and consume thee and thy fifty. And there came down fire from heaven, and consumed him and his fifty.**

11 Again also he sent unto him another captain of fifty with his fifty. And he answered and said unto him, O man of God, thus hath the king said, Come down quickly.

12 **And Elijah answered and said unto them, If I be a man of God, let fire come down from heaven, and consume thee and thy fifty. And the fire of God came down from heaven, and consumed him and his fifty.**

13 And he sent again a captain of the third fifty with his fifty. And the third captain of fifty went up, and came and fell on his knees before Elijah, and besought him, and said unto him, O man of God, I pray thee, let my life, and the life of these fifty thy servants, be precious in thy sight.

14 **Behold, there came fire down from heaven, and burnt up the two captains of the former fifties with their fifties: therefore let my life now be precious in thy sight.**

15 And the angel of the Lord said unto Elijah, Go down with him: be not afraid of him. And he arose, and went down with him unto the king.

The Two Witnesses

In the last days, we know perilous times will come as the world is assaulted by the antichrist, the false prophet, and the devil. One of God's answers to these evil forces is to raise up two witnesses with powerful *Supernatural Security Clearances.* During their ministry in the last days, they will have many spiritual weapons at their disposal.

Let's read what these two witnesses accomplish with their *Supernatural Security Clearances* in the last days.

> **Revelation 11:3-6 (KJV)**
> 3 **And I will give power unto my two witnesses,** and they shall prophesy a thousand two hundred and threescore days, clothed in sackcloth.
> 4 These are the two olive trees, and the two candlesticks standing before the God of the earth.
> 5 **And if any man will hurt them, fire proceedeth out of their mouth, and devoureth their enemies: and if any man will hurt them, he must in this manner be killed.**
> 6 **These have power to shut heaven, that it rain not in the days of their prophecy: and have power over waters to turn them to blood, and to smite the earth with all plagues, as often as they will.**

During the ministry of the two witnesses, they will be granted incredible power to use the supernatural weaponry of God. The antichrist, false prophet, and the devil will be wreaking havoc on the earth. Also, many people will be blaspheming God for all the plagues hitting the world because of their sins. God sends the two witnesses to deal with the wicked people living on the planet during the last days. These two witnesses are given great power to judge the people of the earth with God's supernatural weapons.

Here is a list of their supernatural weapons from the Scriptures above:

1. Fire proceeds out of their mouth if anyone tries to hurt them and devours their enemies

2. They have the power to stop the rains during the days of their prophecy

3. They have power over the waters to turn them into blood

4. They have the power to strike the earth with all types of plagues as often as they want

As you can see, God's weapons are different than man's weapons. God uses unusual supernatural elements to defeat His enemies through men of God granted with *Supernatural Security Clearances.* In the last days, the battle between good and evil will escalate. The enemy will fight hard against God and His people but ultimately lose. These two witnesses are a sign the end is near when they come on the scene. When Jesus returns, He will defeat the antichrist, false prophet, and the devil with the sword coming out of His mouth, which is the Word of God.

Christian Soldier

God has called Christians to be spiritual warriors. The moment you become a Christian; you are enlisted in the army of God. As Christian warriors, we are called to endure hardness and not be entangled with the affairs of this life.

> **2 Timothy 2:3-4 (KJV)**
> 3 **Thou therefore endure hardness, as a good soldier of Jesus Christ.**
> 4 **No man that warreth entangleth himself with the affairs of this life; that he may please him who hath chosen him to be a soldier.**

As Christian warriors, we are called to fight the good fight of faith.

1 Timothy 6:12 (KJV)

> 12 **Fight the good fight of faith,** lay hold on eternal life, whereunto thou art also called, and hast professed a good profession before many witnesses.

To be effective as a soldier and fight the good fight of faith, you need high-power weaponry to defeat your enemy. Your weapons must also be more powerful than your enemy's weapons. Since it was God who called His people to be soldiers, it is God who equips them to battle the devil and his demons. God's answer to equipping His army is to give them His armor and weapon of choice, which is the sword of the Spirit. The sword of the Spirit is the Word of God that has the power to accomplish whatever it is sent to do.

Ephesians 6:13-17 (KJV)

> 13 **Wherefore take unto you the whole armour of God,** that ye may be able to withstand in the evil day, and having done all, to stand.
> 14 **Stand therefore, having your loins girt about with truth, and having on the breastplate of righteousness;**
> 15 **And your feet shod with the preparation of the Gospel of peace;**
> 16 **Above all, taking the shield of faith, wherewith ye shall be able to quench all the fiery darts of the wicked.**
> 17 **And take the helmet of salvation, and the sword of the Spirit, which is the word of God:**

We can read more about the armor of God in the Book of Isaiah. Christians are given the authority to wear the very armor God wears.

Isaiah 59:16-17 (KJV)

16 And he saw that there was no man, and wondered that there was no intercessor: therefore his arm brought salvation unto him; and his righteousness, it sustained him.

17 **For he put on righteousness as a breastplate, and an helmet of salvation upon his head; and he put on the garments of vengeance for clothing, and was clad with zeal as a cloak.**

Some people have taught that the armor of God is likened to Roman armor because that was the occupying force during the time of the early Church. I, however, disagree with this thought because the Bible says this is God's armor, and I would not want to face the devil with earthly Roman armor. The Bible says that this is an armor of light and is a special armor that no human can make.

Romans 13:12 (KJV)

12 The night is far spent, the day is at hand: let us therefore cast off the works of darkness, **and let us put on the armour of light.**

The sword we fight with is the sword of the Spirit. This is the same sword God fights with, and it is the Word of God. This sword is not of this world. The Bible says that God's sword glitters. The Hebrew definition for the word *glittering* is lightning, flashing, and bright. God's sword is bright and flashes with lightning, and besides having a sword God also has arrows.

Deuteronomy 32:41-42 (KJV)

41 **If I whet my glittering sword,** and mine hand take hold on judgment; I will render vengeance to mine enemies, and will reward them that hate me.

42 I **will make mine arrows drunk with blood,** and my sword shall devour flesh; and that with the blood of the slain and of the captives, from the beginning of revenges upon the enemy.

The sword of the Spirit is the Word of God, and this is the same sword that Jesus uses when He comes back to defeat the devil and the antichrist.

Revelation 19:11-16 (KJV)

11 And I saw heaven opened, and behold a white horse; and he that sat upon him was called Faithful and True, and in righteousness he doth judge and make war.

12 His eyes were as a flame of fire, and on his head were many crowns; and he had a name written, that no man knew, but he himself.

13 And he was clothed with a vesture dipped in blood: **and His Name is called The Word of God.**

14 And the armies which were in heaven followed him upon white horses, clothed in fine linen, white and clean.

15 **And out of his mouth goeth a sharp sword, that with it he should smite the nations: and he shall rule them with a rod of iron: and he treadeth the winepress of the fierceness and wrath of Almighty God.**

16 And he hath on his vesture and on his thigh a name written, King Of Kings, And Lord Of Lords.

We were born into an eternal conflict between God and the devil. The devil tries to deceive people, but the truth of God's Word sets people free. God's Word also affects all of creation when He speaks. God's weapons are more powerful than the devil's, and God has been working to raise up an army of believers who know who they are and how to speak His Word like a weapon.

2 Corinthians 10:4-6 (KJV)

> 4 **(For the weapons of our warfare are not carnal, but mighty through God to the pulling down of strong holds;)**
> 5 Casting down imaginations, and every high thing that exalteth itself against the knowledge of God, and bringing into captivity every thought to the obedience of Christ;
> 6 **And having in a readiness to revenge all disobedience, when your obedience is fulfilled.**

New Testament believers are equipped with the best armor and weapons in the universe. Christians are granted to wear God's armor and fight with God's sword. God is looking for those He can train and equip to fight His battles. The devil has tried to stop God, but that is impossible. Jesus defeated the devil at the cross and in every spiritual battle. As Christian soldiers, we are called to enforce the victory Jesus won for the entire world if they will believe. We are fighting from victory and not for victory. We are conquering liberators, sent to set the captives free from the devil's oppression.

Romans 8:37 (KJV)

> 37 **Nay, in all these things we are more than conquerors through him that loved us.**

1 Corinthians 15:57 (KJV)

> 57 **But thanks be to God, which giveth us the victory through our Lord Jesus Christ.**

2 Corinthians 2:14 (KJV)

> 14 **Now thanks be unto God, which always causeth us to triumph in Christ,** and maketh manifest the savour of his knowledge by us in every place.

In conclusion, we can see that God has equipped His people and chosen army with His weaponry and armor. The devil is no match for a man or woman of God who is armed as a soldier in God's army. God is looking for faithful warriors He can entrust with a *Supernatural Security Clearance* to access His powerful weapons and armor. Anyone wearing God's armor and carrying God's sword is not to be messed with. Today is the day for the people of God to rise up and defeat the enemies of God with their God-given *Supernatural Security Clearance.*

CHAPTER 7
CONFIDENTIAL SECRETS

E very nation has confidential information and top secrets to protect. These secrets are vital for the national security and safety of their country. Many nations also use different encrypted devices, so other nations cannot access their confidential information. But most importantly, every government needs trustworthy people who will not disclose any top-secret confidential information to their enemies. In this chapter, we will discover that God also has secrets to protect and needs trustworthy people for the success of the Gospel.

The word *secret* means something hidden, unexplained, or a mystery. It also means something containing confidential information that could endanger national security. Nations of this world have many top secrets and confidential information they do not want to be disclosed for their nation's protection. God also has many secrets He does not reveal to everyone. Even after we are granted entrance into His Heavenly Kingdom, it does not mean every secret God has will be revealed to us. God will only reveal on a *need-to-know basis* to those who have the level of *Supernatural Security Clearance* needed to access His deeper Heavenly secrets.

> **Deuteronomy 29:29 (KJV)**
>
> 29 **The secret things belong unto the Lord our God:** but those things which are revealed belong unto us and to our children for ever, that we may do all the words of this law.

God's Kingdom is no different than any other kingdom in that it has secrets to protect, and only those that can be trusted can gain access to these top secrets. God only reveals His secrets to the righteous.

> **Proverbs 3:32 (KJV)**
>
> 32 For the froward is abomination to the Lord: **but his secret is with the righteous.**

He also reveals His secrets to those who fear Him, and He will also show them His covenant.

> **Psalm 25:14 (KJV)**
>
> 14 **The secret of the Lord is with them that fear him; and he will shew them his covenant.**

Untrustworthy people, flatterers, and talebearers give up secrets and cannot be trusted.

> **Proverbs 11:13 (KJV)**
>
> 13 **A talebearer revealeth secrets:** but he that is of a faithful spirit concealeth the matter.

> **Proverbs 20:19 (KJV)**
>
> 19 **He that goeth about as a talebearer revealeth secrets: therefore meddle not with him that flattereth with his lips.**

Not everyone can be trusted with highly classified secrets from God. God is looking for trustworthy servants that can be trusted with His most sacred secrets. There are many people found in the Bible that God could trust with His secrets, and He used them during crucial times in Biblical history. God also revealed that He would reveal His secrets to His prophets before He did anything. These prophets would then prophesy the secrets of what God was about to do.

> **Amos 3:7-8 (KJV)**
> 7 **Surely the Lord God will do nothing, but he revealeth his secret unto his servants the prophets.**
> 8 The lion hath roared, who will not fear? **the Lord God hath spoken, who can but prophesy?**

In this chapter, we will study people that God entrusted in the Bible with His secrets. Here is a list of the people we will study in this book, along with the subjects of prophecy and the mysteries of God:

1. Abraham, Sodom, and Gomorrah

2. Joseph and the Interpretation of Dreams

3. Daniel, the Beloved Prophet of God

4. The Apostle Paul

5. John, the Revelator

6. Prophecy

7. The Mysteries of God

Abraham, Sodom, and Gomorrah

The patriarch and father of our faith, Abraham, witnessed a powerful display of God's supernatural power when God destroyed Sodom and

Gomorrah. Sodom and Gomorrah had corrupted themselves with all manner of evil. God gave Abraham a *Supernatural Security Clearance* to know what He was about to do. God also allowed Abraham to negotiate with Him over the minimum number of righteous people being in the cities whereby God would spare the cities. One of the reasons God granted Abraham a *Supernatural Security Clearance* is because He knew that Abraham would command his children to keep the way of the Lord to do justice and judgment.

> **Genesis 18:17-19 (KJV)**
> 17 **And the Lord said, Shall I hide from Abraham that thing which I do;**
> 18 Seeing that Abraham shall surely become a great and mighty nation, and all the nations of the earth shall be blessed in him?
> 19 **For I know him, that he will command his children and his household after him, and they shall keep the way of the Lord, to do justice and judgment;** that the Lord may bring upon Abraham that which he hath spoken of him.

Abraham negotiated with God to there only being ten righteous in the city; to stop the destruction of Sodom and Gomorrah. After this Divine negotiation, God sent in two Heavenly beings, and the people of Sodom and Gomorrah attempted to rape them. These Heavenly beings could not find ten righteous, so God supernaturally destroyed Sodom and Gomorrah. God did, however, spare Abrahams' nephew Lot and his family.

Let's read how God supernaturally destroyed Sodom and Gomorrah.

> **Genesis 18:20-21 (KJV)**
> 20 And the Lord said, Because the cry of Sodom and Gomorrah is great, **and because their sin is very grievous;**

21 **I will go down now, and see whether they have done altogether according to the cry of it, which is come unto me; and if not, I will know.**

Genesis 19:23-25 (KJV)

23 The sun was risen upon the earth when Lot entered into Zoar.

24 **Then the Lord rained upon Sodom and upon Gomorrah brimstone and fire from the Lord out of heaven;**

25 And he overthrew those cities, and all the plain, and all the inhabitants of the cities, and that which grew upon the ground.

God wiped Sodom and Gomorrah off the map with fire and brimstone raining down from Heaven. God secretly revealed to Abraham what He was about to do because He trusted him. Many natural disasters that occur on the earth are displays of God's judgments. Most people have no idea what is happening behind the scenes in the unseen world, which causes these events to occur.

God trusted Abraham to know what would happen to Sodom and Gomorrah. Abraham was also authorized to negotiate with God on what numbers of righteous people would be the limit for God not to destroy these cities. When God trusts you, He can give you a *Supernatural Security Clearance* to see what judgments will take place on the earth. You can also be given a *Supernatural Security Clearance* to pray about the event before it takes place, and you might be able to persuade God to hold off His judgment. This is called standing in the gap, and God is looking for people who will stand in the gap.

Ezekiel 22:30 (KJV)
> 30 **And I sought for a man among them, that should make up the hedge, and stand in the gap before me for the land, that I should not destroy it: but I found none.**

God is fair and merciful with His judgments. God is looking for people on this earth He can entrust to negotiate the judgments He must enforce. If you are found faithful like Abraham, you too could be used to stop a judgment and negotiate with God by standing in the gap for people, lands, and nations. The great mystery of God is that He has invited a select few to be granted a *Supernatural Security Clearance* and assist Him with the judgments of the world.

Joseph and the Interpretation of Dreams

The story of Joseph is one of the most beautiful stories in the Bible of how God can turn a terrible situation into an amazing testimony to the glory of God. Joseph was betrayed by his brothers and sold into Egyptian slavery. While in Egypt, Joseph was falsely accused of raping his master's wife. Joseph was then thrown into Pharaoh's prison by his Egyptian master. At every turn, we see Joseph going from one tragedy to the next, but Joseph kept his integrity and faith in God. God had a bigger plan in all that was happening to Joseph.

While Joseph was in prison, Pharaoh had two dreams that no one could interpret.

Genesis 41:1-8 (KJV)
> 1 And it came to pass at the end of two full years, that Pharaoh dreamed: and, behold, he stood by the river.
> 2 And, behold, there came up out of the river seven well favoured kine and fatfleshed; and they fed in a meadow.

3 And, behold, seven other kine came up after them out of the river, ill favoured and leanfleshed; and stood by the other kine upon the brink of the river.

4 And the ill favoured and leanfleshed kine did eat up the seven well favoured and fat kine. So Pharaoh awoke.

5 And he slept and dreamed the second time: and, behold, seven ears of corn came up upon one stalk, rank and good.

6 And, behold, seven thin ears and blasted with the east wind sprung up after them.

7 And the seven thin ears devoured the seven rank and full ears. And Pharaoh awoke, and, behold, it was a dream.

8 **And it came to pass in the morning that his spirit was troubled; and he sent and called for all the magicians of Egypt, and all the wise men thereof: and Pharaoh told them his dream; but there was none that could interpret them unto Pharaoh.**

No one could give Pharaoh the secret interpretation of his two dreams. However, Joseph was known for having dreams and interpreting dreams. He accurately interpreted the dreams of two of Pharaoh's servants thrown into jail by Pharoah. One of them was killed and the other spared. Both servants had dreams while in prison, and Joseph accurately interpreted their dreams on who would not live and who would be restored. The restored servant informed Pharaoh that Joseph had accurately interpreted his dream and could interpret Pharaoh's dream.

Joseph was quickly pulled out of prison, cleaned up, and brought before Pharaoh to interpret his dream. Joseph knew the top-secret confidential information about Pharaoh's dream because he had a *Supernatural Security Clearance* granted to him by God for his faithfulness. Joseph revealed to Pharaoh that God would send seven years of plenty followed by seven years of famine. Joseph also gave Pharaoh wisdom on what to do with the top-secret information revealed in his dreams from God.

Because Joseph had access to the secret interpretation of this dream, Pharaoh promoted him to second in command to Pharoah to collect and store harvested corn in preparation for the famine. Joseph was used mightily to save the Egyptians and all of Israel during this famine because of his access to Heavenly confidential information. Joseph was also used to save his whole family during the famine.

Jacob, the father of Joseph, came down to Egypt during the famine. Jacob thought he was dead because his other sons lied to him about Joseph when they sold him into slavery. Joseph was restored to his family and forgave his brothers. Joseph is a beautiful story in that it reveals if you will stay faithful to God, even if injustice is done to you, you can receive a *Supernatural Security Clearance* and be promoted to a place of great authority.

Daniel, the Beloved Prophet of God

Daniel was a mighty prophet of God during the Babylonian captivity of Judah. The children of Israel had sinned, and God had them defeated and carried off to Babylon for their transgressions. Daniel was among those exiled with all the children of Israel to Babylon. Daniel, however, was faithful to God and was promoted in Babylon as one of the king's wise men to bring counsel to the king of Babylon. Daniel was also made a eunuch during his captivity, which was a common practice when foreigners were brought into the king's palace.

While Daniel was serving in Babylon, the king of Babylon, Nebuchadnezzar, had a dream that troubled him. What is interesting about this dream is that Nebuchadnezzar could not remember the dream, but it still troubled him. Then king Nebuchadnezzar required something that no other king in the history of humanity demanded, and that was for his counselors to not only interpret the dream but tell him what the dream was. King Nebuchadnezzar also ordered that they would all be killed if they could not tell him his dream, but on the other hand, they would receive gifts, rewards, and great honor if they could tell him his dream.

Daniel, at this time, informs king Nebuchadnezzar that he can tell him his dream and the interpretation, but he needs time to seek God.

Daniel 2:16-23 (KJV)

16 **Then Daniel went in, and desired of the king that he would give him time, and that he would shew the king the interpretation.**

17 Then Daniel went to his house, and made the thing known to Hananiah, Mishael, and Azariah, his companions:

18 **That they would desire mercies of the God of heaven concerning this secret;** that Daniel and his fellows should not perish with the rest of the wise men of Babylon.

19 **Then was the secret revealed unto Daniel in a night vision.** Then Daniel blessed the God of heaven.

20 Daniel answered and said, Blessed be the name of God for ever and ever: for wisdom and might are his:

21 And he changeth the times and the seasons: he removeth kings, and setteth up kings: he giveth wisdom unto the wise, and knowledge to them that know understanding:

22 **He revealeth the deep and secret things:** he knoweth what is in the darkness, and the light dwelleth with him.

23 I thank thee, and praise thee, O thou God of my fathers, who hast given me wisdom and might, and hast made known

unto me now what we desired of thee: **for thou hast now made known unto us the king's matter.**

Daniel not only received the interpretation of the king of Babylon's dream, but God, in His mercy, revealed the secret dream to him. Daniel had a *Supernatural Security Clearance* never before seen on the earth up to this point in time. Daniel revealed the dream to King Nebuchadnezzar and revealed the future events of kingdoms to come. The dream was a secret revealing by God of future events. God knows the future, and for anyone to access the secret knowledge of future events, they need a *Supernatural Security Clearance.*

The prophet Daniel went on to have many more experiences and visions about the secret prophetic future events of the world. When you read the Book of Daniel, you can see he was a man greatly beloved of the Lord to know the secrets of the future. Some of the secret events of the future that Daniel saw thousands of years ago are soon to take place on the earth. God wants to reveal His top secrets and confidential information, but He needs people He can trust, as He trusted Daniel. Daniel was a faithful servant of God who could be trusted with *a Supernatural Security Clearance.*

The Apostle Paul

The Apostle Paul is an interesting man to study in the Bible. Paul started out persecuting the early Church to become a prominent New Testament apostle. Paul had an amazing experience when he met Jesus in a Heavenly vision on his way to Damascus, where he was going to persecute the early Church. We can read about this experience in the Book of Acts.

Acts 9:1-6 (KJV)

> 1 And Saul, yet breathing out threatenings and slaughter against the disciples of the Lord, went unto the high priest,
>
> 2 And desired of him letters to Damascus to the synagogues, that if he found any of this way, whether they were men or women, he might bring them bound unto Jerusalem.
>
> 3 And as he journeyed, he came near Damascus: and suddenly there shined round about him a light from heaven:
>
> 4 And he fell to the earth, and heard a voice saying unto him, Saul, Saul, why persecutest thou me?
>
> 5 And he said, Who art thou, Lord? And the Lord said, I am Jesus whom thou persecutest: it is hard for thee to kick against the pricks.
>
> 6 And he trembling and astonished said, Lord, what wilt thou have me to do? And the Lord said unto him, Arise, and go into the city, and it shall be told thee what thou must do.

After this experience in meeting Jesus, Paul spent years receiving Divine secret revelations about God, the Gospel, and the destiny of the Church.

Galatians 1:11-20 (KJV)

> 11 But I certify you, brethren, that the Gospel which was preached of me is not after man.
>
> 12 For I neither received it of man, neither was I taught it, but by the revelation of Jesus Christ.
>
> 13 For ye have heard of my conversation in time past in the Jews' religion, how that beyond measure I persecuted the church of God, and wasted it:
>
> 14 And profited in the Jews' religion above many my equals in mine own nation, being more exceedingly zealous of the traditions of my fathers.

15 But when it pleased God, who separated me from my mother's womb, and called me by his grace,

16 To reveal his Son in me, that I might preach him among the heathen; immediately I conferred not with flesh and blood:

17 Neither went I up to Jerusalem to them which were apostles before me; but I went into Arabia, and returned again unto Damascus.

18 Then after three years I went up to Jerusalem to see Peter, and abode with him fifteen days.

19 But other of the apostles saw I none, save James the Lord's brother.

20 Now the things which I write unto you, behold, before God, I lie not.

Paul received many revelations and wisdom from God that Peter said was hard to understand.

2 Peter 3:13-18 (KJV)

13 Nevertheless we, according to his promise, look for new heavens and a new earth, wherein dwelleth righteousness.

14 Wherefore, beloved, seeing that ye look for such things, be diligent that ye may be found of him in peace, without spot, and blameless.

15 And account that the longsuffering of our Lord is salvation; **even as our beloved brother Paul also according to the wisdom given unto him hath written unto you;**

16 **As also in all his epistles, speaking in them of these things; in which are some things hard to be understood,** which they that are unlearned and unstable wrest, as they do also the other scriptures, unto their own destruction.

17 Ye therefore, beloved, seeing ye know these things before, beware lest ye also, being led away with the error of the wicked, fall from your own stedfastness.

18 But grow in grace, and in the knowledge of our Lord and Saviour Jesus Christ. To him be glory both now and for ever. Amen.

The Apostle Paul taught the remarkable secret mysteries given to him from God about the Church. Paul is also responsible for writing most of the New Testament. He wrote many letters to the early Churches spread across the world, and these letters became a big part of the Bible we read today. Paul went from a persecutor of the Church to a leader of the Church and was granted a powerful *Supernatural Security Clearance* from God.

John, the Revelator

The Apostle John was given some of the most accurate secret details concerning the end of the world and the coming kingdom of God that staggers the natural mind. John was given access to the Throne of God and granted the ability to see what was about to take place on the earth. John's *Supernatural Security Clearance* is astounding. The Book of Revelation reveals many hidden secrets about the end of the world.

This prophetic book reveals what is going on in the unseen world, and what is about to take place before Christ returns.

Revelation 1:19 (KJV)
19 **Write the things which thou hast seen, and the things which are, and the things which shall be hereafter;**

John also wrote that whoever read, heard and kept what was written in the Book of Revelation would be blessed.

Revelation 1:1-3 (KJV)
1 The Revelation of Jesus Christ, which God gave unto him, to shew unto his servants things which must shortly come to

pass; and he sent and signified it by his angel unto his servant John:

2 Who bare record of the Word of God, and of the testimony of Jesus Christ, and of all things that he saw.

3 Blessed is he that readeth, and they that hear the words of this prophecy, and keep those things which are written therein: for the time is at hand.

I will not go into detail about what he saw and prophesied. But I will say it is important that every Christian read and pray to understand what John wrote in this Book. The Book of Revelation reveals important secrets about what will happen on the earth during the seven-year Tribulation and the coming of God's restored kingdom. John was also given access to see the Heavenly Jerusalem descending out of Heaven.

John was the beloved apostle of Jesus and God granted him unprecedented access to His secrets and a powerful *Supernatural Security Clearance.* John saw into the unseen world of God's kingdom as no one living on earth had ever seen before. As hard as it is for some to understand, the Book of Revelation is a blessing for us to read. It still takes *Supernatural Security Clearances* to understand what John wrote about. May you be blessed as you discover the future of the world, the fate of all humanity, and the eternal blessing of God's Heavenly Kingdom found in the Book of Revelation.

Prophecy

Prophecy plays a significant role in the Bible and our personal lives. Prophecy is the foretelling of future events. The Bible is filled with prophetic words spoken by prophets that came to pass or are about to come to pass. Daniel prophesied many events that came to pass throughout history and some events that will soon take place.

There are over 500 verses in the Old Testament alluding to the coming Messiah, and Jesus fulfilled over 300 of them. Some of the prophecies are yet to be fulfilled when He returns. The odds of Jesus fulfilling that many prophecies during His life is like dropping a feather out of a plane 20,000 feet in the air and landing on a specific target. The probability and impossibility of one man fulfilling all the Old Testament prophecy in His life is an impossible feat that only God could perform.

God also gives personal prophetic words to people so they can meditate on them about a spiritual gift given to them by God and mature them in Christ to where others can see their growth.

> **1 Timothy 4:14-16 (KJV)**
> 14 **Neglect not the gift that is in thee, which was given thee by prophecy,** with the laying on of the hands of the presbytery.
> 15 **Meditate upon these things; give thyself wholly to them; that thy profiting may appear to all.**
> 16 Take heed unto thyself, and unto the doctrine; continue in them: for in doing this thou shalt both save thyself, and them that hear thee.

Prophecy also helps us in our spiritual battles. God will give some people a prophetic word about their future. This secret insight into someone's future can help them in the battles they face. For instance, someone may be given a promise about living a long life and prospering. So, when they are faced with a deadly symptom, they can know that God will heal them because the prophetic word hasn't come to pass yet. We can use personal prophetic words in the battles we face.

Prophecy is also used to reveal the secrets of people's hearts and assist in them getting saved.

> **1 Corinthians 14:23-25 (KJV)**
> 23 If therefore the whole church be come together into one place, and all speak with tongues, and there come in those that are unlearned, or unbelievers, will they not say that ye are mad?
> 24 **But if all prophesy,** and there come in one that believeth not, or one unlearned, he is convinced of all, he is judged of all:
> 25 **And thus are the secrets of his heart made manifest; and so falling down on his face he will worship God, and report that God is in you of a truth.**

Prophecy is one of the most powerful of all nine gifts of the Spirit. We are to desire to have this gift because God can use this gift to reveal secrets. God can reveal the secrets of people's hearts and future destinies by the gift of prophecy. The secret insight revealed in each prophetic word can have a profound effect on people's lives.

The Mysteries of God

God has many mysteries, and they are not always revealed or understood by humanity. The word *mystery* means sacred secrets that are hidden and can only be revealed by Divine Revelation. The word *mystery* also means something hidden, not fully manifest, and challenging to understand. The Divine secret mysteries of God were revealed by Christ, apostles, prophets, and many of the anointed men of God in the Bible. These secrets are hidden behind commitment levels to Christ and the message of the Gospel. Distractions of this life can keep someone from focusing long enough for God to reveal His secrets to them. God is looking for those who are faithful and committed to His kingdom whereby He can reveal the mysteries of His kingdom to them.

Mark 4:11 (KJV)
> **11 And he said unto them, Unto you it is given to know the mystery of the kingdom of God: but unto them that are without, all these things are done in parables:**

I wrote in an earlier chapter on this subject, but I want to reveal some more aspects of God's kingdom secrets. In my early chapter on Kingdom of God Top Secrets, I revealed secrets to the parable of the sower sows the Word, and I also revealed the personal requirements to gaining access to the mysteries of God's kingdom. You have to understand, be committed to, and not lose focus on what was preached to gain a harvest of the kingdom of God. The parable of the sower sows the Word reveals God's requirements to gain a *Supernatural Security Clearance.*

I will not write about all the secrets revealed to me in this book about God's secret kingdom mysteries. This book is more about meeting the requirements to gain a *Supernatural Security Clearance* so you, too, can have access to the mysteries of the kingdom of God. God has revealed many secrets to me through dreams, visions, prophetic words, and Divine revelation into His Word about His kingdom, which I cannot fully disclose. I can only reveal that which God leads me to reveal.

The beauty of what I am revealing in the book is that you, too, can enter a relationship with God, where He will start to reveal Divine secrets to you about the mysteries of His kingdom. I believe that we will have the opportunity to access the many hidden secrets of God's kingdom throughout all of eternity, but we must be counted faithful to God.

God has many mysteries He desires to reveal to humankind. Below is a list of all the mysteries mentioned in the New Testament. I highly advise that you look up each of the Scriptures attached to the mysteries listed below to gain greater knowledge and understanding into the secret mysteries of God:

1. Mysteries of the Kingdom of God (Matthew 13:11; Mark 4:11 and Luke 8:10)

2. Mystery of the blindness of the Jews and Grafting in of the Fullness of the Gentiles (Romans 11:25)

3. Mystery of the Revelation of Jesus Christ (Romans 16:25)

4. Mysteries of God (1 Corinthians 2:7; 4:1)

5. Mysteries When you Speak in Unknown Tongues (1 Corinthians 14:2)

6. Mystery of the Christians being Changed When the Trumpet Sounds (1 Corinthians 15:51,52)

7. Mystery of His Will which is the Gathering Together in One All Things in Christ, Both Which are in Heaven and on Earth (Ephesians 1:9,10)

8. Mystery of Christ (Ephesians 3:4; Colossians 4:3)

9. Mystery of the Fellowship (Ephesians 3:9)

10. Mystery of Christ and the Church (Ephesians 5:32)

11. Mystery of the Gospel (Ephesians 6:19)

12. Mystery of the Riches of the Glory Among the Gentiles, Which is Christ in You, the Hope of Glory (Colossians 1:26,27)

13. Mystery of God, and the Father, and of Christ (Colossians 2:2)

14. Mystery of Iniquity (2 Thessalonians 2:7)

15. Mystery of Faith (1Timothy 3:9)

16. Mystery of Godliness (I Timothy 3:16)

17. Mystery of the Seven Stars in the Right Hand of Christ (Revelation 1:20)

18. Mystery of God Being Finished (Revelation 10:7)

The Bible even says that Jesus going to the cross was a secret mystery. If it were revealed that Jesus going to the cross, dying, and being risen again would defeat the devil, the devil never would have had Jesus crucified. Jesus secretly defeated the devil by going to the cross to die and rise again on the third day.

1 Corinthians 2:6-8 (KJV)
6 **Howbeit we speak wisdom among them that are perfect: yet not the wisdom of this world,** nor of the princes of this world, that come to nought:
7 **But we speak the wisdom of God in a mystery, even the hidden wisdom, which God ordained before the world unto our glory:**
8 **Which none of the princes of this world knew: for had they known it, they would not have crucified the Lord of glory.**

The death of Jesus enabled Him to take back what was lost in the Garden of Eden by the first Adam. There are many Divine secret mysteries of God's kingdom to be discovered in the Holy Scriptures. God has hidden these mysteries, and they are waiting to be revealed by those who will meet the requirements to obtain a *Supernatural Security Clearance.* When you are granted a *Supernatural Security*

Clearance, you will gain access to the mysteries of God's kingdom. You cannot function and operate by faith if you do not understand the mysteries of God's kingdom. You also cannot operate in the anointing and power of God without your eyes being opened to see into God's kingdom mysteries.

Jesus taught a parable about the kingdom of God and used the example of a householder who brought out of their treasure things new and old.

> **Matthew 13:52 (KJV)**
> 52 Then said he unto them, **Therefore every scribe which is instructed unto the kingdom of heaven is like unto a man that is an householder, which bringeth forth out of his treasure things new and old.**

In this man's treasure, things new and old are a hidden meaning of new revelations and ancient revelations of things concerning God's kingdom. When someone is taught secrets of the kingdom of God, Divine secret mysteries of the past, the present mysteries of life on earth, and events that are going to happen in the future are revealed to them.

The Bible is filled with the secret history and destiny of all humanity. Not everyone agrees with what God has revealed in the Bible. Many people have come up with different teachings about the past creation of humankind, how things work in the world, and the future of humanity. It is imperative as a Christian you seek God for the truth about the kingdom of God, so the enemy does not deceive you. These lies can keep you from the blessings and inheritance found in Christ and His kingdom.

You are open to deception when you don't have access to and understanding of God's kingdom. Jesus warned people not to let any man deceive them.

Matthew 24:4 (KJV)
4 And Jesus answered and said unto them, **Take heed that no man deceive you.**

Jesus also warned that many would come in His Name before the end, saying they were the Christ.

Mark 13:6 (KJV)
6 **For many shall come in my name, saying, I am Christ; and shall deceive many.**

The Apostle Paul taught that the five-fold leadership of the Church was to edify the body of Christ and bring them into maturity so they would not be deceived.

Ephesians 4:11-15 (KJV)
11 **And he gave some, apostles; and some, prophets; and some, evangelists; and some, pastors and teachers;**
12 For the perfecting of the saints, for the work of the ministry, for the edifying of the body of Christ:
13 Till we all come in the unity of the faith, and of the knowledge of the Son of God, unto a perfect man, unto the measure of the stature of the fulness of Christ:
14 **That we henceforth be no more children, tossed to and fro, and carried about with every wind of doctrine, by the sleight of men, and cunning craftiness, whereby they lie in wait to deceive;**
15 But speaking the truth in love, may grow up into him in all things, which is the head, even Christ:

In conclusion, God has many incredible Divine mysteries of His kingdom and the future events of the world that He wants to reveal to humankind. Humankind, however, must receive a *Supernatural Security Clearance* to access these secrets. To access the mysteries of God, you will have to understand, stay committed, and focused on God and His Word. Those who make this commitment will gain a *Supernatural Security Clearance,* access God's Heavenly Kingdom, and live forever with God. Those granted the secret mysteries of God's kingdom will not be deceived.

CHAPTER 8
THE MANTLE OF ELIJAH

E lijah was one of the most powerful prophets to walk this earth. As a prophet of God, Elijah was granted the authority to start and stop the rains at His Word, raise the dead, perform miracles, prophesy future events, decree the judgments of God, part the waters of the Jordan River, and call down fire from Heaven. Elijah's mantle represented the God-given spiritual authority he was walking in as a prophet. Before Elijah left this earth, he gave his mantle to his servant Elisha. However, Elisha had to pass specific requirements before being granted the authority to wear Elijah's prophetic mantle. In this chapter, we will discover what was required of Elisha to wear this prophetic anointed mantle and obtain a *Supernatural Security Clearance* from God.

First, we need to define what a mantle is and what it represents. A mantle during the time of the Old Testament was a loose sleeveless cloak or cape that was worn as an outer garment. The word *mantle* means something that covers or wraps. When referring to the mantle of Elijah, we are talking about the outer garment he wore that represented the authority of God he was clothed in as a prophet of God. Elijah's mantle was an outward symbol of his *Supernatural*

Security Clearance given to him by God to function as a prophet of Israel.

Elijah's mantle was also transferable where he could grant his servant Elisha a *Supernatural Security Clearance* to walk in his God-given authority as a prophet. When Elijah left this earth and went up in a whirlwind, Elisha was able to pick up Elijah's mantle, wear it, and walk in the miraculous authority and power Elijah walked in. The moment Elisha took up and wore Elijah's mantle, he was granted a *Supernatural Security Clearance* from God to walk in the same authority and power as a prophet like Elijah.

However, although it seemed as easy as just picking up a garment to walk in the authority of God as a prophet, it was not that easy. Before Elijah left this earth in a whirlwind, he passed through specific locations with Elisha. All these locations represented something spiritually significant that Elisha would have to walk through before being granted the opportunity to wear Elijah's mantle. Elisha had to pass these locations, tests, and requirements before being given the *Supernatural Security Clearance* to wear Elijah's mantle.

Elisha followed Elijah through each of these symbolic locations as a sign. He was willing to do whatever was required of him to be granted the honor to wear the mantle of Elijah and become a mighty prophet of God. Before we get into these locations and their spiritual significance, I want to reveal a few noteworthy events leading to Elisha being given Elijah's mantle.

God gave Elijah a word to anoint Elisha to be a prophet in place of him while he was on Horeb, the mountain of God. During this experience, God told Elijah to anoint three people, and Elisha was one of those three.

1 Kings 19:15-17 (KJV)

> 15 And the Lord said unto him, Go, return on thy way to the wilderness of Damascus: and when thou comest, anoint Hazael to be king over Syria:
>
> 16 And Jehu the son of Nimshi shalt thou anoint to be king over Israel: **and Elisha the son of Shaphat of Abelmeholah shalt thou anoint to be prophet in thy room.**
>
> 17 And it shall come to pass, that him that escapeth the sword of Hazael shall Jehu slay: **and him that escapeth from the sword of Jehu shall Elisha slay.**

Elijah left the mountain of God, found Elisha, and threw his mantle on Elisha while he was plowing with his twelve yokes of oxen. Elisha responded by killing his yoke of oxen and giving those with him to eat and went after Elijah and ministered to him.

1 Kings 19:19-21 (KJV)

> 19 So he departed thence, and found Elisha the son of Shaphat, who was plowing with twelve yoke of oxen before him, and he with the twelfth: and Elijah passed by him, **and cast his mantle upon him.**
>
> 20 And he left the oxen, and ran after Elijah, and said, Let me, I pray thee, kiss my father and my mother, and then I will follow thee. And he said unto him, Go back again: for what have I done to thee?
>
> 21 **And he returned back from him, and took a yoke of oxen, and slew them, and boiled their flesh with the instruments of the oxen, and gave unto the people, and they did eat. Then he arose, and went after Elijah, and ministered unto him.**

It is believed that Elisha ministered and served Elijah for six years before Elijah was taken up into Heaven by a whirlwind. Later, when two kings needed a prophet's help, Elisha was mentioned as one who could help them because he poured water on the hands of Elijah. This meant Elisha was worthy and capable of assisting them prophetically because he served as Elijah's minister.

2 Kings 3:11 (KJV)

11 But Jehoshaphat said, Is there not here a prophet of the Lord, that we may enquire of the Lord by him? And one of the king of Israel's servants answered and said, **Here is Elisha the son of Shaphat, which poured water on the hands of Elijah.**

This statement of pouring water on Elijah's hands and Elisha ministering to Elijah's needs for years reveals a vital aspect of obtaining a *Supernatural Security Clearance* from God. Both facts show it takes a servant's heart to be granted the authority of high positions in God's kingdom. Jesus revealed in His teachings that the greatest of all was the servant of all. When Jesus was on the earth, He served the spiritual needs of all humanity, washed the apostle's feet, and died on the cross. Jesus, the King of the universe, is the greatest servant of all. To be granted a *Supernatural Security Clearance* to access a powerful mantle, we must also follow the examples of Elisha and Jesus, who had servant's hearts.

Mark 10:42-45 (KJV)

42 But Jesus called them to him, and saith unto them, Ye know that they which are accounted to rule over the Gentiles exercise lordship over them; and their great ones exercise authority upon them.
43 **But so shall it not be among you: but whosoever will be great among you, shall be your minister:**
44 **And whosoever of you will be the chiefest, shall be servant of all.**

45 For even the Son of man came not to be ministered unto, but to minister, and to give his life a ransom for many.

Now, getting back to Elijah and Elisha's story, I want to reveal what was required of Elisha by the four locations the Lord sent Elijah to with Elisha. Each of these four locations played a vital role in the history of the children of Israel. These locations reveal essential requirements placed upon Elisha before he could be granted a *Supernatural Security Clearance* to walk in God's authority and wear the prophetic mantle of Elijah. The four locations and what Elijah said to Elisha right before a whirlwind took him into Heaven are essential to understand and know the secrets required by God to be granted a *Supernatural Security Clearance.*

Here is a list of the four locations Elijah went to with Elisha before being taken by God in a whirlwind:

1. Gilgal

2. Bethel

3. Jericho

4. Jordan River

We will study the significance of these locations in Biblical history and how they apply to Elisha receiving Elijah's mantle. We will also see Elisha's response to Elijah in each of these significant locations before receiving Elijah's mantle and being granted a *Supernatural Security Clearance* from God. Let us read this story, and then I will get into the significance of each of these locations and how Elisha responded.

2 Kings 2:1-15 (KJV)

1 And it came to pass when the Lord would take up Elijah into heaven by a whirlwind, **that Elijah went with Elisha from Gilgal.**

2 **And Elijah said unto Elisha, Tarry here, I pray thee; for the Lord hath sent me to Bethel.** And Elisha said unto him, As the Lord liveth, and as thy soul liveth, I will not leave thee. **So they went down to Bethel.**

3 And the sons of the prophets that were at Bethel came forth to Elisha, and said unto him, Knowest thou that the Lord will take away thy master from thy head to day? And he said, Yea, I know it; hold ye your peace.

4 **And Elijah said unto him, Elisha, tarry here, I pray thee; for the Lord hath sent me to Jericho. And he said, As the Lord liveth, and as thy soul liveth, I will not leave thee. So they came to Jericho.**

5 And the sons of the prophets that were at Jericho came to Elisha, and said unto him, Knowest thou that the Lord will take away thy master from thy head to day? And he answered, Yea, I know it; hold ye your peace.

6 **And Elijah said unto him, Tarry, I pray thee, here; for the Lord hath sent me to Jordan. And he said, As the Lord liveth, and as thy soul liveth, I will not leave thee. And they two went on.**

7 And fifty men of the sons of the prophets went, and stood to view afar off: and they two stood by Jordan.

8 And Elijah took his mantle, and wrapped it together, and smote the waters, and they were divided hither and thither, so that they two went over on dry ground.

9 And it came to pass, when they were gone over, that Elijah said unto Elisha, **Ask what I shall do for thee, before I be taken away from thee. And Elisha said, I pray thee, let a double portion of thy spirit be upon me.**

10 **And he said, Thou hast asked a hard thing: nevertheless, if thou see me when I am taken from thee, it shall be so unto thee; but if not, it shall not be so.**

11 **And it came to pass, as they still went on, and talked, that, behold, there appeared a chariot of fire, and horses of fire, and parted them both asunder; and Elijah went up by a whirlwind into heaven.**

12 And Elisha saw it, and he cried, My father, my father, the chariot of Israel, and the horsemen thereof. **And he saw him no more: and he took hold of his own clothes, and rent them in two pieces.**

13 **He took up also the mantle of Elijah that fell from him, and went back, and stood by the bank of Jordan;**

14 **And he took the mantle of Elijah that fell from him, and smote the waters, and said, Where is the Lord God of Elijah? and when he also had smitten the waters, they parted hither and thither: and Elisha went over.**

15 And when the sons of the prophets which were to view at Jericho saw him, they said, **The spirit of Elijah doth rest on Elisha.** And they came to meet him, and bowed themselves to the ground before him.

Gilgal

Gilgal is located eight miles north of Jericho in the Promised Land, where the Israelites first encamped after crossing the Jordan River. Gilgal was the headquarters war camp from which Joshua led the armies of Israel to conquer enemy cities in the Promised Land. This camp was a vital secret location for the armies of Israel to prepare for war.

A few key events took place at this location before Joshua led the armies of Israel into the Promised Land to defeat the enemies of God.

These key events apply to why Elijah took Elisha to Gilgal before he could walk in his mantle as a prophet. First, God commanded Joshua to circumcise all the children of Israel. This circumcision represented a rolling away of the reproach of Egypt. Being circumcised also tied them in with the covenant God made with Abraham and their Divine right to possess the Promised Land. God gave the Promised Land to Abraham and his seed. The Promised Land is known as the nation of Israel today. Circumcision also represented the children of Israel being freed as enslaved people to serving as God's children. They went from a slave mentality to a conquering son of God mentality.

Joshua 5:2-9 (KJV)
> 2 At that time the Lord said unto Joshua, **Make thee sharp knives, and circumcise again the children of Israel the second time.**
> 3 **And Joshua made him sharp knives, and circumcised the children of Israel at the hill of the foreskins.**
> 4 And this is the cause why Joshua did circumcise: All the people that came out of Egypt, that were males, even all the men of war, died in the wilderness by the way, after they came out of Egypt.
> 5 Now all the people that came out were circumcised: but all the people that were born in the wilderness by the way as they came forth out of Egypt, them they had not circumcised.
> 6 For the children of Israel walked forty years in the wilderness, till all the people that were men of war, which came out of Egypt, were consumed, because they obeyed not the voice of the Lord: unto whom the Lord sware that he would not shew them the land, which the Lord sware unto their fathers that he would give us, a land that floweth with milk and honey.

7 And their children, whom he raised up in their stead, them Joshua circumcised: for they were uncircumcised, because they had not circumcised them by the way.
8 And it came to pass, when they had done circumcising all the people, that they abode in their places in the camp, till they were whole.
9 And the Lord said unto Joshua, **This day have I rolled away the reproach of Egypt from off you. Wherefore the name of the place is called Gilgal unto this day.**

The name Gilgal means *rolling*. God named this camp Gilgal because this is where the reproach of Egypt was *rolled away* from the children of Israel. The children of Israel were to be circumcised eight days after they were born according to the Law of Moses, but the parents of this generation were disobedient to God. Circumcision started with Abraham, the father of faith, but these disobedient parents did not keep God's command. That rebellious generation was not allowed into the Promised Land because of their disobedience and lack of faith. They rebelled against God's Commandments and repeatedly refused to believe God.

Another important event during this time was the first celebration of Passover. Passover was instituted during the time of Moses as one of the last ten plagues to judge the Egyptians. Passover is a Feast of the Lord where the blood of a lamb was placed on the children of Israel's doorposts. The death angel killed any firstborn males in a home where he did not see the blood of the lamb on the doorposts. The Egyptians did not keep the laws of this feast, and the death angel killed all the firstborn males of the Egyptians. The death angel also killed the firstborn male of Pharaoh, the king of Egypt. This was the final straw that broke the will of Pharaoh, who kept refusing to let the children of

Israel go. After this plague, Pharoah released the children of Israel from bondage as enslaved people to serve God in their own land.

Later in history, we know that Passover was also a representation of Jesus dying as the Lamb of God. Jesus died on the cross and was offered as a sacrifice for our sins on the Day of Passover. We are saved and delivered by His precious blood. The blood of Jesus was spilled for our redemption so we could be forgiven, no longer be enslaved to sin, go to Heaven, and live as one of God's children forever.

> **Romans 6:14-18 (KJV)**
> 14 **For sin shall not have dominion over you:** for ye are not under the law, but under grace.
> 15 What then? shall we sin, because we are not under the law, but under grace? God forbid.
> 16 **Know ye not, that to whom ye yield yourselves servants to obey, his servants ye are to whom ye obey; whether of sin unto death, or of obedience unto righteousness?**
> 17 **But God be thanked, that ye were the servants of sin,** but ye have obeyed from the heart that form of doctrine which was delivered you.
> 18 **Being then made free from sin, ye became the servants of righteousness.**

> **Colossians 1:14 (KJV)**
> 14 **In whom we have redemption through his blood, even the forgiveness of sins:**

> **1 Corinthians 5:7 (KJV)**
> 7 Purge out therefore the old leaven, that ye may be a new lump, as ye are unleavened. **For even Christ our passover is sacrificed for us:**

Jesus established the New Covenant when He died on the cross. His blood was the payment for us to be able to enter this New Covenant if we would believe that God raised Jesus from the dead. We also must confess that Jesus is Lord with our mouths to be saved. When you become a Christian, you are no longer a slave to sin, and you can now walk in the newness of life.

> **Matthew 26:27-29 (KJV)**
> 27 And he took the cup, and gave thanks, and gave it to them, saying, Drink ye all of it;
> 28 **For this is my blood of the new testament, which is shed for many for the remission of sins.**
> 29 But I say unto you, I will not drink henceforth of this fruit of the vine, until that day when I drink it new with you in my Father's kingdom.

Another important event during this time was the children of Israel eating fruit in the Promised Land for the first time. Up to that point, they were still eating manna which was God's Heavenly angel food falling upon the ground every morning. The children of Israel were now entering into all that God promised Abraham.

From studying these noteworthy events at Gilgal and their prophetic symbolism, we can see why Elijah brought Elisha to this place. For Elisha to take on the mantle of Elijah, he had to be circumcised and partake of the Passover. This meant that Elisha had to go from a slave mentality to a son of God warrior mentality. Elijah taught Elisha the historical and prophetic value of what God did at Gilgal and how it applied to becoming God's prophet and being granted a *Supernatural Security Clearance*.

God revealed many spiritual truths at historical Biblical locations. Spiritual locations serve as a reminder of what God wants us to implement in our lives. Elisha was being reminded of God's spiritual truths by coming to Gilgal. He had to be a committed warrior for God with a circumcised heart. He also had to understand the significance of Passover and the application of the blood of the lamb. Elisha had to be proven to be entrusted with God's spiritual truths before being able to wear Elijah's Mantle.

Bethel

Bethel is the historical location where Abraham first pitched his tent when he came into the Promised Land. Bethel is also the famous location where Jacob had a dream where he saw a ladder from Heaven, and the angels of God were ascending and descending upon the ladder. Bethel is located twelve miles north of Jerusalem and is one of the most mentioned cities in the Old Testament. Bethel is mentioned in over sixty verses in the Bible.

The word Bethel means the *House of God* and the *Gate of Heaven*. The city was formerly named Luz, and it was changed to Bethel when Jacob had a dream of the angels of God ascending and descending from the ladder going from earth to Heaven. In this dream, the Lord stood at the top of the ladder.

> **Genesis 28:10-19 (KJV)**
> 10 And Jacob went out from Beersheba, and went toward Haran.
> 11 And he lighted upon a certain place, and tarried there all night, because the sun was set; and he took of the stones of that place, and put them for his pillows, and lay down in that place to sleep.

12 **And he dreamed, and behold a ladder set up on the earth, and the top of it reached to heaven: and behold the angels of God ascending and descending on it.**

13 **And, behold, the Lord stood above it, and said, I am the Lord God of Abraham thy father, and the God of Isaac: the land whereon thou liest, to thee will I give it, and to thy seed;**

14 **And thy seed shall be as the dust of the earth, and thou shalt spread abroad to the west, and to the east, and to the north, and to the south: and in thee and in thy seed shall all the families of the earth be blessed.**

15 **And, behold, I am with thee, and will keep thee in all places whither thou goest, and will bring thee again into this land; for I will not leave thee, until I have done that which I have spoken to thee of.**

16 And Jacob awaked out of his sleep, **and he said, Surely the Lord is in this place; and I knew it not.**

17 **And he was afraid, and said, How dreadful is this place! this is none other but the house of God, and this is the gate of heaven.**

18 **And Jacob rose up early in the morning, and took the stone that he had put for his pillows, and set it up for a pillar, and poured oil upon the top of it.**

19 **And he called the name of that place Bethel: but the name of that city was called Luz at the first.**

Bethel became known as a place or house where people met with God. Bethel served as a point where people could communicate with God. People were able to encounter and experience God at Bethel. This location reminds us to be more Heavenly-minded than earthly-minded. People would also go to Bethel during times of trouble to ask the counsel of God for help.

Bethel is also the first place in the Bible where a vow was made to God. Jacob vowed to God that if God brought him back to his father's house in peace, the Lord would be his God. Jacob also vowed to God that he would give a tenth back to God of all that God gave him. The stone Jacob slept on would be set as a pillar to God's house.

Genesis 28:20-22 (KJV)

20 And Jacob vowed a vow, saying, If God will be with me, and will keep me in this way that I go, and will give me bread to eat, and raiment to put on,

21 **So that I come again to my father's house in peace; then shall the Lord be my God:**

22 **And this stone, which I have set for a pillar, shall be God's house: and of all that thou shalt give me I will surely give the tenth unto thee.**

Vows play a very important role in the life of believers. Samson had the vow of the Nazarite upon him from his birth. In this vow, he was not supposed to cut his hair. When his hair was cut by the trickery of Delilah, he lost his supernatural strength. Vows are meant to bind your soul to an oath that you will be faithful to God and to the vow you make.

In the New Testament, there is a passage frequently quoted about the sick being healed by the prayer of faith. This verse is found in James 5:13-20.

James 5:13-20 (KJV)

13 Is any among you afflicted? let him **pray**. Is any merry? let him sing psalms.

14 Is any sick among you? let him call for the elders of the church; and let them **pray** over him, anointing him with oil in the Name of the Lord:

146

15 And the **prayer of faith** shall save the sick, and the Lord shall raise him up; and if he have committed sins, they shall be forgiven him.

16 Confess your faults one to another, and **pray** one for another, that ye may be healed. The effectual fervent **prayer** of a righteous man availeth much.

17 Elias was a man subject to like passions as we are, and he **prayed** earnestly that it might not rain: and it rained not on the earth by the space of three years and six months.

18 And he **prayed** again, and the heaven gave rain, and the earth brought forth her fruit.

19 Brethren, if any of you do err from the truth, and one convert him;

20 Let him know, that he which converteth the sinner from the error of his way shall save a soul from death, and shall hide a multitude of sins.

The word *prayer* is mentioned seven times in this passage of Scripture. The first few times, it is mentioned in verses 13 and 14. The Greek word for prayer means to worship and pray to God to obtain something good or to avert evil from their life. When the word prayer is mentioned in verse 15, where it says *the prayer of faith*, a different Greek word is used, which has to do with making a vow or votive obligation prayer. Votive obligation prayer is a prayer that is offered in the fulfillment of a vow of gratitude and devotion to God.

The prayer of faith has everything to do with making a vow. If you read the passage James 5:13-20, you can see it is clearly talking about getting healed if you confess your sins. This passage is dealing with sin and why someone is sick. Not everyone is sick because of sin, but this passage refers to those who are sick because they sinned.

Tying these Scriptures together, the person who needs healing needs to make a vow to quit sinning. Repentance has to do with past sins, but a vow to quit sinning has to do with future sins. This is why Jesus told the man He healed in John Chapter 5 to sin no more. Jesus also told the woman caught in adultery to go and sin no more. They needed to make a vow to quit sinning in the future.

John 5:14 (KJV)
14 Afterward Jesus findeth him in the temple, and said unto him, Behold, thou art made whole: **sin no more**, lest a worse thing come unto thee.

John 8:11 (KJV)
11 She said, No man, Lord. And Jesus said unto her, Neither do I condemn thee: go, and **sin no more**.

We also see that the effectual fervent prayer of a righteous man avails much and it refers to Elijah starting and stopping the rains.

James 5:16-18 (KJV)
16 Confess your faults one to another, and pray one for another, that ye may be healed. **The effectual fervent prayer of a righteous man availeth much.**
17 **Elias was a man subject to like passions as we are, and he prayed earnestly that it might not rain: and it rained not on the earth by the space of three years and six months.**
18 **And he prayed again, and the heaven gave rain, and the earth brought forth her fruit.**

A righteous man refers to a man who made a vow to God to walk in holiness and not sin. Therefore, Elijah was teaching Elisha that he had to make vows to God to not sin and walk as a righteous man for his prayers to be answered. God does not hear the prayers of those who regard iniquity in their heart.

Psalm 66:18 (KJV)
> 18 **If I regard iniquity in my heart, the Lord will not hear me:**

Elijah was able to offer the prayer of faith because he had made vows to God to remain faithful by not sinning and Elijah kept his vows.

Numbers 30:2 (KJV)
> 2 If a man vow a vow unto the Lord, or swear an oath to bind his soul with a bond; he shall not break His Word, he shall do according to all that proceedeth out of his mouth.

What I am revealing here is a powerful mystery. God wants believers to make vows that they will not sin and keep this vow if they are to be granted a *Supernatural Security Clearance.* God is looking for people He can trust to make vows of commitments to Him and keep them. This type of vow is no different than a husband and wife vowing to remain faithful to each other and treat each other with love and respect.

Elijah brought Elisha to Bethel to remind him to always be Heavenly-minded and faithful to God. For a prophet of Israel to be successful, they had to stay in constant communication with God and keep their vows. God would communicate with the prophet through dreams, visions, prophecy, and the Word of the Lord. For Elisha to carry the mantle of Elijah and be given a *Supernatural Security Clearance,* he had to hear from God regularly and remain faithful to his vows to God. Elisha had to be willing to vow to God like Jacob made a vow to God and fulfilled the vow.

Jericho

Jericho was the first city destroyed by Joshua when the children of Israel entered the Promised Land. God commanded the children of

Israel not to take any of the spoils of this city. All the spoils from the destruction of Jericho were to be dedicated to God. The children of Israel marched around Jericho for seven days with the Ark of the Covenant without saying a word. On the seventh day, after they marched around the city seven times, they shouted at the command of God, and the walls of Jericho fell flat before the armies of Israel. Joshua and his army destroyed everything in this city. They killed all the men, women, young, old, ox, sheep, and donkeys with the edge of the sword. Only Rahab, the harlot, was saved because she hid the spies of Israel when they came to spy out the city.

After this city was destroyed, Joshua cursed anyone who would try to rebuild Jericho.

Joshua 6:26 (KJV)

26 And Joshua adjured them at that time, saying, **Cursed be the man before the Lord, that riseth up and buildeth this city Jericho: he shall lay the foundation thereof in his firstborn, and in his youngest son shall he set up the gates of it.**

However, during the time of the wicked reign of Ahab, Jericho was rebuilt, and the prophecy of Joshua came to pass.

1 Kings 16:33-34 (KJV)

33 And Ahab made a grove; and Ahab did more to provoke the Lord God of Israel to anger than all the kings of Israel that were before him.
34 **In his days did Hiel the Bethelite build Jericho: he laid the foundation thereof in Abiram his firstborn, and set up the gates thereof in his youngest son Segub, according to the word of the Lord, which he spake by Joshua the son of Nun.**

Jericho was a cursed city that never should have been rebuilt. Jericho is believed to be one of the oldest cities in the world. Jericho is close to where the children of Israel crossed the Jordan River and about ten miles northwest of the Dead Sea. Jericho was also called the *City of Palms* because of its abundance of palm trees.

Jericho is spiritually symbolic of a place where we die to all that the world offers and give everything to God. Elijah brought Elisha to this city to know he had to give everything to God and forsake the world. This city was never to be rebuilt as a symbol for believers to never return to the world once they were saved. For Elisha to take up the mantle of Elijah and be given a *Spiritual Security Clearance,* he had to be committed to giving everything to God and forsake all that the world had to offer and never go back.

Jordan River

The Jordan River has always played an essential role in the history of Israel. The Jordan River runs for 156 miles dividing Israel from eastern Arab countries. The Jordan River starts in Syria and runs south through the Sea of Galilee into the Dead Sea. The Jordan River is where Joshua miraculously crossed over into the Promised Land when it parted as the priests stepped into the water with the Ark of the Covenant.

The miraculous parting of the Jordan River was a sign that God was with the children of Israel and would perform miracles in the taking of the Promised Land. The miracle of the Jordan River parting also magnified Joshua in the sight of the Israelites. The Jordan River is a place of God magnifying His leadership by performing miracles. Signs and wonders serve as a sign to reveal who God is with.

Joshua 3:1-17 (KJV)

1 And Joshua rose early in the morning; and they removed from Shittim, and came to Jordan, he and all the children of Israel, and lodged there before they passed over.

2 And it came to pass after three days, that the officers went through the host;

3 And they commanded the people, saying, When ye see the ark of the covenant of the Lord your God, and the priests the Levites bearing it, then ye shall remove from your place, and go after it.

4 Yet there shall be a space between you and it, about two thousand cubits by measure: come not near unto it, that ye may know the way by which ye must go: for ye have not passed this way heretofore.

5 And Joshua said unto the people, **Sanctify yourselves: for to morrow the Lord will do wonders among you.**

6 And Joshua spake unto the priests, saying, Take up the ark of the covenant, and pass over before the people. And they took up the ark of the covenant, and went before the people.

7 **And the Lord said unto Joshua, This day will I begin to magnify thee in the sight of all Israel, that they may know that, as I was with Moses, so I will be with thee.**

8 And thou shalt command the priests that bear the ark of the covenant, saying, When ye are come to the brink of the water of Jordan, ye shall stand still in Jordan.

9 And Joshua said unto the children of Israel, Come hither, and hear the words of the Lord your God.

10 And Joshua said, **Hereby ye shall know that the living God is among you,** and that he will without fail drive out from before you the Canaanites, and the Hittites, and the Hivites, and the Perizzites, and the Girgashites, and the Amorites, and the Jebusites.

11 Behold, the ark of the covenant of the Lord of all the earth passeth over before you into Jordan.

12 Now therefore take you twelve men out of the tribes of Israel, out of every tribe a man.

13 **And it shall come to pass, as soon as the soles of the feet of the priests that bear the ark of the Lord, the Lord of all the earth, shall rest in the waters of Jordan, that the waters of Jordan shall be cut off from the waters that come down from above; and they shall stand upon an heap.**

14 And it came to pass, when the people removed from their tents, to pass over Jordan, and the priests bearing the ark of the covenant before the people;

15 **And as they that bare the ark were come unto Jordan, and the feet of the priests that bare the ark were dipped in the brim of the water, (for Jordan overfloweth all his banks all the time of harvest,)**

16 That the waters which came down from above stood and rose up upon an heap very far from the city Adam, that is beside Zaretan: and those that came down toward the sea of the plain, even the salt sea, failed, and were cut off: and the people passed over right against Jericho.

17 **And the priests that bare the ark of the covenant of the Lord stood firm on dry ground in the midst of Jordan, and all the Israelites passed over on dry ground, until all the people were passed clean over Jordan.**

God wants His people to know He is with them and will do wonders among them. He also uses signs and wonders to show who He appoints as spiritual leaders over His people. God revealed He was with Joshua when He miraculously parted the Jordan River.

Elijah also miraculously parted the Jordan River with his mantle. He revealed to Elisha that if he were granted a *Supernatural Security*

Clearance to wear his mantle, God would also be with him and do miracles. On top of that, people would know that he was God's appointed spiritual leader as a prophet of God. God is looking for people who will pass His tests so He can anoint them into a God-given spiritual leadership position ordained by Him and not man.

It is also important to note that the Jordan River was where John the Baptist anointed Jesus before His ministry began on the earth. When Jesus was being baptized, the Holy Spirit descended upon Him while the Father spoke from Heaven. Water baptism represents dying to oneself and putting on Christ for a believer. Just like Elisha would take off his clothing and wear Elijah's mantle, we must also put off the work of the flesh and put on Christ to be anointed by God.

> **Galatians 3:27 (KJV)**
> 27 **For as many of you as have been baptized into Christ have put on Christ.**

Baptism represents us dying to ourselves in recognition of Christ's death and walking in the newness of life. When you go under the water, it means you are dying to yourself, and when you come up out of the water, it represents you walking in the newness of life.

> **Romans 6:3-6 (KJV)**
> 3 **Know ye not, that so many of us as were baptized into Jesus Christ were baptized into his death?**
> 4 **Therefore we are buried with him by baptism into death: that like as Christ was raised up from the dead by the glory of the Father, even so we also should walk in newness of life.**
> 5 **For if we have been planted together in the likeness of his death, we shall be also in the likeness of his resurrection:**

6 Knowing this, that our old man is crucified with him, that the body of sin might be destroyed, that henceforth we should not serve sin.

Elisha would have to die to himself and take on a new life to be granted a *Supernatural Security Clearance.* In this newness of life, Elisha would walk in the anointing of Elijah and wear his prophetic mantle.

The Passing of Elijah's Mantle to Elisha

Now came the time for Elijah to be taken up into Heaven by a whirlwind, and Elijah asked Elisha what he wanted. Elisha responded by saying he wanted a double portion of his spirit. Elijah said that Elisha asked a hard thing, but he would be granted his request if he saw him taken up into Heaven.

I want to look back at the response Elisha gave Elijah at Gilgal, Bethel, and Jericho when Elijah asked Elisha to stay behind at each one of these locations. Elisha responded to Elijah the same way every time Elijah challenged him to stay at a location. Elisha responded to Elijah by saying, *"As the Lord liveth, and as thy soul liveth, I will not leave thee."* Interestingly, Elijah had another servant before Elisha; however, this servant stayed behind at a location when Elijah told him to stay. This servant did not have that key characteristic of never giving up or quitting as Elisha had.

When Elijah was on the run from a death threat from Jezebel after killing the prophets of Baal in Carmel, Elijah's servant did not say to Elijah what Elisha said. Elijah's first servant did not show a loyal commitment to stay with Elijah no matter what. This servant could have refused to stay behind, and he could have made a strong commitment like Elisha did to stay with Elijah despite any challenging circumstances.

1 Kings 19:1-3 (KJV)

> 1 And Ahab told Jezebel all that Elijah had done, and withal how he had slain all the prophets with the sword.
> 2 Then Jezebel sent a messenger unto Elijah, saying, **So let the gods do to me, and more also, if I make not thy life as the life of one of them by to morrow about this time.**
> 3 **And when he saw that, he arose, and went for his life**, and came to Beersheba, which belongeth to Judah, **and left his servant there.**

If you want to receive a mantle from an anointed man or woman of God on this earth, you will have to commit to staying with them, and you must make every sacrifice to be with them to the end. You have to say what Ruth said to Naomi when Naomi persisted in telling Ruth and her sister-in-law to go back to their own country after the death of their husbands. Let us read what Ruth said to Naomi to gain insight into the commitment level it takes to receive a mantle from a prophetic leader and gain a *Supernatural Security Clearance* from God.

Ruth 1:16-18 (KJV)

> 16 **And Ruth said, Intreat me not to leave thee, or to return from following after thee: for whither thou goest, I will go; and where thou lodgest, I will lodge: thy people shall be my people, and thy God my God:**
> 17 **Where thou diest, will I die, and there will I be buried: the Lord do so to me, and more also, if ought but death part thee and me.**
> 18 When she saw that she was stedfastly minded to go with her, she left speaking unto her.

Ruth was not about to leave Naomi and committed unto death to follow her and her God. Elisha made a similar commitment to stay with Elijah to the end, and he was not about to let him out of his sight until

156

he was taken away by God. Let us read the story of Elisha with Elijah and what they said to each other before Elijah was taken away after they miraculously crossed over the Jordan River.

2 Kings 2:8-15 (KJV)

8 And Elijah took his mantle, and wrapped it together, and smote the waters, and they were divided hither and thither, so that they two went over on dry ground.

9 And it came to pass, when they were gone over, that Elijah said unto Elisha, **Ask what I shall do for thee, before I be taken away from thee. And Elisha said, I pray thee, let a double portion of thy spirit be upon me.**

10 **And he said, Thou hast asked a hard thing: nevertheless, if thou see me when I am taken from thee, it shall be so unto thee; but if not, it shall not be so.**

11 And it came to pass, as they still went on, and talked, that, behold, there appeared a chariot of fire, and horses of fire, and parted them both asunder; **and Elijah went up by a whirlwind into heaven.**

12 And Elisha saw it, and he cried, My father, my father, the chariot of Israel, and the horsemen thereof. **And he saw him no more: and he took hold of his own clothes, and rent them in two pieces.**

13 **He took up also the mantle of Elijah that fell from him, and went back, and stood by the bank of Jordan;**

14 **And he took the mantle of Elijah that fell from him, and smote the waters, and said, Where is the Lord God of Elijah? and when he also had smitten the waters, they parted hither and thither: and Elisha went over.**

15 And when the sons of the prophets which were to view at Jericho saw him, they said, **The spirit of Elijah doth rest on Elisha.** And they came to meet him, and bowed themselves to the ground before him.

Elijah asked Elisha what he wanted, and Elisha asked for a double portion of his spirit to be upon him. Elijah said he asked a hard thing, but if Elisha saw Elijah taken from him, he would receive his mantle, and if he did not see Elijah taken from him, he would not receive it. So, we know from the whole story that it was a lot more than just seeing him being taken from him to receive his mantle. Seeing Elijah taken to Heaven was just the last requirement of all the other requirements Elisha had already met to receive Elijah's mantle and a *Supernatural Security Clearance* from God to operate as an anointed prophet of Israel.

Elisha was so committed to staying with Elijah that it took a chariot of fire to separate him from Elijah. Elisha was faithful to God and Elijah to the end and received the highly coveted mantle of Elijah. This symbolic mantle granted him access to the High Calling of God and a *Supernatural Security Clearance.* Elisha went on to perform twice as many miracles as Elijah performed. Elisha walked boldly in this prophetic mantle from Elijah and ministered to kings and mighty men while on the earth.

With this understanding of the four locations and their significance, we can see there are requirements for obtaining a *Supernatural Security Clearance* from God. God left us these clues and what it takes to receive a mantle from the story of Elijah and Elisha. These clues are so the people of God can access a powerful anointing and mantle during their generation.

Many people of God throughout history have answered the call and committed to wearing a mantle as Elisha did. Today is the day for men and women of God to rise up and be committed and have an all-in, no-quit mentality to the kingdom of God. These will be the ones granted a *Supernatural Security Clearance* from God and help establish His kingdom on earth.

In conclusion, if you are to be granted a high honor of receiving a mantle from God, you must be willing to pass all the tests of God. You must also meet all the requirements of God without giving up if you are going to receive a *Supernatural Security Clearance.* If you pass the tests and meet all the requirements, you will be granted a powerful mantle like Elisha. Mantles and anointings from God are very valuable, and He only gives them to mature people who are committed to doing what it takes to walk in them. God is looking for the next generation of faithful believers committed to answering His High Calling, no matter what it costs.

CHAPTER 9
REVOKED SECURITY CLEARANCES

Just as one can meet the requirements to be trusted with a *Supernatural Security Clearance,* someone can do untrustworthy acts and have their *Supernatural Security Clearance* revoked by God. God is both angered and disappointed when He is put into a position where He must revoke a *Supernatural Security Clearance* from one of His children. *Supernatural Security Clearances* are hard to obtain, so it is a big disappointment when someone loses one through sin and disobedience to God and His Word. This chapter will reveal people in the Bible who were granted the privilege of being entrusted with a *Supernatural Security Clearance* and why God revoked His *Supernatural Security Clearance* from them.

What does it mean when a *Supernatural Security Clearance* is revoked? When a *Supernatural Security Clearance* is revoked, the person can no longer access secret locations, powerful weapons, or confidential information in God's kingdom. When God revokes a *Supernatural Security Clearance*, He cuts that person off from operating in their High Call and anointing. They may stay in the natural position for a time, but they are no longer given access to God and His kingdom privileges as they were before.

Supernatural Security Clearances are only given out and maintained by trustworthy people who love God and keep His Commandments. It is a high honor to be granted the privilege of obtaining a *Supernatural Security Clearance* from God. Anyone who has a *Supernatural Security Clearance* must walk worthy of it, and it is a shame to lose such a coveted privilege. It does not bring honor to God when the action of an untrustworthy servant causes them to lose their *Supernatural Security Clearance.*

This study will begin with the stories of people in the Bible who were granted a *Supernatural Security Clearance* and how they lost it. This study will teach people not to make the same mistakes as these rebellious individuals who lost their *Supernatural Security Clearance* from God. If we learn from their bad example, we will be able to please God and can keep our *Supernatural Security Clearance.*

Here is a list of who we will be studying in this chapter:

1. Adam and Eve

2. Esau

3. Samson

4. King Saul

5. Judas Iscariot, the Betrayer of Jesus

6. Disobedient Christians

Adam and Eve

Adam and Eve were the first to be granted a *Supernatural Security Clearance* in the Bible. Their *Supernatural Security Clearance* gave them access to the Garden of Eden and God. The Garden of Eden was a place where God was accessible to Adam and Eve as He came to them each day in the cool of the day. The Tree of Life and the Tree of Knowledge of Good and Evil were planted in the Garden of Eden.

God gave Adam and Eve only one Commandment of something they should not do, and that was not to eat of the Tree of Knowledge of Good and Evil. God warned them that they would die on the day they ate of the Tree of Knowledge of Good and Evil.

> **Genesis 2:15-17 (KJV)**
> 15 And the Lord God took the man, and put him into the garden of Eden to dress it and to keep it.
> 16 **And the Lord God commanded the man, saying, Of every tree of the garden thou mayest freely eat:**
> 17 **But of the tree of the knowledge of good and evil, thou shalt not eat of it: for in the day that thou eatest thereof thou shalt surely die.**

Eve is tempted by the devil, eats of the Tree of Knowledge of Good and Evil, and betrays God's command. She then takes the fruit from the Tree of Knowledge of Good and Evil and gives it to her husband to eat. The Bible reveals in the New Testament that Eve was deceived, but Adam knew what he was doing.

> **1 Timothy 2:14 (KJV)**
> 14 **And Adam was not deceived, but the woman being deceived was in the transgression.**

When Adam and Eve sinned, many terrible things occurred, and they were the first humans on earth to have their *Supernatural Security Clearance* revoked. They lost their access to the Garden of Eden and the Tree of Life. Death entered the world, and they could no longer live forever by eating from the Tree of Life. Many other curses also occurred by them losing their *Supernatural Security Clearance.* We can see by what they lost in the curse placed upon them that their *Supernatural Security Clearance* gave them greater access and abilities than humankind has today. To understand Adam and Eve's *Supernatural Security Clearance,* we must study what they lost and the curse that was brought upon them.

To do this, we will have to reverse engineer by looking at what they lost, and then we will have a deeper understanding of what they had. We can do this by reading what happened to them after eating from the Tree of Knowledge of Good and Evil. Let us read Genesis Chapter 3 and then dissect everything that happened to them to reveal what they had before their fall. This will show what their *Supernatural Security Clearance* gave them access to.

Genesis 3:1-24 (KJV)

1 Now the serpent was more subtil than any beast of the field which the Lord God had made. And he said unto the woman, Yea, hath God said, Ye shall not eat of every tree of the garden?

2 And the woman said unto the serpent, We may eat of the fruit of the trees of the garden:

3 But of the fruit of the tree which is in the midst of the garden, God hath said, Ye shall not eat of it, neither shall ye touch it, lest ye die.

4 And the serpent said unto the woman, Ye shall not surely die:

5 For God doth know that in the day ye eat thereof, then your eyes shall be opened, and ye shall be as gods, knowing good and evil.

6 And when the woman saw that the tree was good for food, and that it was pleasant to the eyes, and a tree to be desired to make one wise, she took of the fruit thereof, and did eat, and gave also unto her husband with her; and he did eat.

7 And the eyes of them both were opened, and they knew that they were naked; and they sewed fig leaves together, and made themselves aprons.

8 And they heard the voice of the Lord God walking in the garden in the cool of the day: and Adam and his wife hid themselves from the presence of the Lord God amongst the trees of the garden.

9 And the Lord God called unto Adam, and said unto him, Where art thou?

10 And he said, I heard thy voice in the garden, and I was afraid, because I was naked; and I hid myself.

11 And he said, Who told thee that thou wast naked? **Hast thou eaten of the tree, whereof I commanded thee that thou shouldest not eat?**

12 And the man said, The woman whom thou gavest to be with me, she gave me of the tree, and I did eat.

13 And the Lord God said unto the woman, What is this that thou hast done? And the woman said, The serpent beguiled me, and I did eat.

14 And the Lord God said unto the serpent, Because thou hast done this, thou art cursed above all cattle, and above every beast of the field; upon thy belly shalt thou go, and dust shalt thou eat all the days of thy life:

15 And I will put enmity between thee and the woman, and between thy seed and her seed; it shall bruise thy head, and thou shalt bruise his heel.

16 **Unto the woman he said, I will greatly multiply thy sorrow and thy conception; in sorrow thou shalt bring forth children; and thy desire shall be to thy husband, and he shall rule over thee.**

17 **And unto Adam he said, Because thou hast hearkened unto the voice of thy wife, and hast eaten of the tree, of which I commanded thee, saying, Thou shalt not eat of it: cursed is the ground for thy sake; in sorrow shalt thou eat of it all the days of thy life;**

18 **Thorns also and thistles shall it bring forth to thee; and thou shalt eat the herb of the field;**

19 **In the sweat of thy face shalt thou eat bread, till thou return unto the ground; for out of it wast thou taken: for dust thou art, and unto dust shalt thou return.**

20 And Adam called his wife's name Eve; because she was the mother of all living.

21 Unto Adam also and to his wife did the Lord God make coats of skins, and clothed them.

22 **And the Lord God said, Behold, the man is become as one of us, to know good and evil: and now, lest he put forth his hand, and take also of the tree of life, and eat, and live for ever:**

23 **Therefore the Lord God sent him forth from the garden of Eden, to till the ground from whence he was taken.**

24 **So he drove out the man; and he placed at the east of the garden of Eden Cherubims, and a flaming sword which turned every way, to keep the way of the tree of life.**

Here is a list of everything they lost when their *Supernatural Security Clearance* was revoked. We can use this list to see what their *Supernatural Security Clearance* gave them access to by reverse engineering it:

1. Their eyes were opened, and they knew they were naked.

2. They feared God's voice.

3. Eve had to conceive in sorrow.

4. Eve would try to rule over her husband, but he would rule over her.

5. The ground was cursed due to Adam's sin.

6. Adam would eat of the ground in sorrow all his days.

7. The ground would bring forth thorns and thistles.

8. Adam would have to eat bread by the sweat of his face.

9. They would return to the ground.

10. They became like God to know good and evil and were kicked out of the Garden of Eden so they could not partake of the Tree of Life and live forever.

11. God sent them out of the Garden of Eden to till the ground where they were taken from.

Now let us reverse engineer these curses, and it will reveal what their *Supernatural Security Clearance* granted them before their fall. Here is a list of what they had before they fell:

1. They had direct access to God and could talk with Him daily.

2. They must have been clothed with something, so they did not know they were naked. They had Heavenly clothing, or they were clothed in the glory of God.

3. They must have only had faith and no fear. They were walking by faith.

4. Eve could have children without pain. So, there was no pain.

5. Eve knew her proper place, and there was no rebellion.

6. The ground of the earth had no curse and fully yielded its fruit.

7. Adam had joy and no sorrow or depression.

8. There were no thorns or thistles whereby man could be hurt.

9. Adam did not work by the sweat of his brow. Adam worked as God worked, and that was with his voice. Adam could command things to happen with His Word, and all of creation would obey him.

10. The body God gave Adam and Eve could live forever.

11. Adam and Eve were pure from the thoughts of evil. Their minds were free from sinful thinking.

12. They had access to God's secret Garden of Eden.

The above list is everything Adam and Eve's *Supernatural Security Clearance* gave them access to. So, when Adam and Eve sinned, they lost a lot, and so did all of humanity. When we go to Heaven, all these things will be restored and then some.

When we go to Heaven, we will be given a *Supernatural Security Clearance* to all these things and supernatural abilities:

1. Access to God (Revelation 21:3)

2. Access to God's Throne (Revelation 22:3)

3. Access to God's Heavenly Jerusalem (Revelation 22:14)

4. Ability to see God's face (Revelation 22:4)

5. Access to the Tree of Life (Revelation 22:2;14)

6. Access to the Water of Life (Revelation 22:1,2)

7. Access to the new Heaven (Revelation 21:1)

8. Access to the new earth (Revelation 21:1)

9. Given a glorified body that is just like Jesus' glorified body (1 John 3:1-3)

10. Granted to be a son of God (Revelation 21:7)

11. Granted to live eternally (John 3:16)

12. Given a mansion to live in (John 14:2)

13. Granted the ability to live under God's blessing and no more curse (Revelation 22:3)

14. Given a Heavenly position and job from God (Luke 19:11-26)

15. Stress-free living (Revelation 21:4)

From looking at it from this perspective, we can see that although Adam and Eve lost a lot when they gave up their *Supernatural Security Clearance,* God had a plan to restore everything lost in the Garden of Eden and more. Those who obey God and keep His Commandments by accepting Jesus as their Lord will be given an incredible *Supernatural Security Clearance* throughout all of eternity.

In conclusion, Adam and Eve lost a lot more than they realized. We can see what they lost by reverse-engineering the curse placed upon them.

However, God always had a plan to restore humankind and bring them into a glorious destiny. They could be allowed to come into this destiny if they believed in their heart that God raised Jesus from the dead, confessed Him as Lord, repented of their sins, and obeyed His commands. Those who make Jesus their Lord will be granted a *Supernatural Security Clearance* far greater than has ever before been given while living on this earth. Adam and Eve had their *Supernatural Security Clearance's* revoked, and it affected the entire world, but God has made a way through Jesus for humanity to be restored and granted a powerful *Supernatural Security Clearance* that will last for all eternity.

Esau

Esau sold his God-given *Supernatural Security Clearance* for one meal. Esau returned to his home from hunting in the field and was faint for lack of eating. Jacob, his brother, had made a boiled pot of stew, and Esau asked Jacob to feed him. Jacob responds by asking Esau to sell him his birthright. The Bible says that Esau despised his birthright by doing this.

> **Genesis 25:29-34 (KJV)**
> 29 And Jacob sod pottage: and Esau came from the field, and he was faint:
> 30 And Esau said to Jacob, Feed me, I pray thee, with that same red pottage; for I am faint: therefore was His Name called Edom.
> 31 **And Jacob said, Sell me this day thy birthright.**
> 32 **And Esau said, Behold, I am at the point to die: and what profit shall this birthright do to me?**
> 33 And Jacob said, Swear to me this day; and he sware unto him: **and he sold his birthright unto Jacob.**

34 Then Jacob gave Esau bread and pottage of lentiles; and he did eat and drink, and rose up, and went his way: **thus Esau despised his birthright.**

When Esau sold his firstborn right to the birthright, he disrespected God and gave up the most powerful and special inheritance he had rights to. Esau's birthright was God's covenant with his grandfather Abraham to bless him and his seed after him. The Blessing of Abraham is the foundation of all blessings from God and the granting of all *Supernatural Security Clearances* for both the Jews and Christians. The Blessing of Abraham extended to the Jews and was the Covenant that Jesus walked in and performed miracles. Let's read about this birthright found in the Book of Genesis.

Genesis 12:1-3 (KJV)

1 Now the Lord had said unto Abram, Get thee out of thy country, and from thy kindred, and from thy father's house, unto a land that I will shew thee:

2 **And I will make of thee a great nation, and I will bless thee, and make thy name great; and thou shalt be a blessing:**

3 **And I will bless them that bless thee, and curse him that curseth thee: and in thee shall all families of the earth be blessed.**

Genesis 17:1-8 (KJV)

1 And when Abram was ninety years old and nine, the Lord appeared to Abram, and said unto him, I am the Almighty God; walk before me, and be thou perfect.

2 **And I will make my covenant between me and thee, and will multiply thee exceedingly.**

3 And Abram fell on his face: and God talked with him, saying,

4 **As for me, behold, my covenant is with thee, and thou shalt be a father of many nations.**

5 Neither shall thy name any more be called Abram, but thy name shall be Abraham; for a father of many nations have I made thee.

6 **And I will make thee exceeding fruitful, and I will make nations of thee, and kings shall come out of thee.**

7 And I will establish my covenant between me and thee and thy seed after thee in their generations for an everlasting covenant, to be a God unto thee, and to thy seed after thee.

8 **And I will give unto thee, and to thy seed after thee, the land wherein thou art a stranger, all the land of Canaan, for an everlasting possession; and I will be their God.**

God spoke many powerful covenant blessings to Abraham. Abraham believed God and became a friend of God. The New Testament reveals how miracles are performed through faith by the Spirit based upon the Blessing of Abraham.

Galatians 3:5-9 (KJV)

5 **He therefore that ministereth to you the Spirit, and worketh miracles among you,** doeth he it by the works of the law, or by the hearing of faith?

6 Even as Abraham believed God, and it was accounted to him for righteousness.

7 **Know ye therefore that they which are of faith, the same are the children of Abraham.**

8 **And the scripture, foreseeing that God would justify the heathen through faith, preached before the Gospel unto Abraham, saying, In thee shall all nations be blessed.**

9 So then they which be of faith are blessed with faithful Abraham.

When God promised that all nations would be blessed through the Blessing of Abraham, it was a prophetic declaration of the Gospel that

Jesus preached. The preaching of the good news of the Gospel was a promise that God would bless people. Jesus proclaimed this message during His ministry while on the earth, and this is how He performed miracles.

Matthew 4:23 (KJV)

23 And Jesus went about all Galilee, teaching in their synagogues, and preaching the **Gospel of the kingdom,** and healing all manner of sickness and all manner of disease among the people.

Matthew 9:35 (KJV)

35 And Jesus went about all the cities and villages, teaching in their synagogues, **and preaching the Gospel of the kingdom,** and healing every sickness and every disease among the people.

The Blessing of Abraham is the foundation of the Law of Moses and the preaching of the Gospel through Jesus. The Church of today is still operating from the foundation of the Blessing of Abraham. Anyone in Christ, by faith, is entitled to the inherited blessings found in the covenant that God made with Abraham.

Galatians 3:26-29 (KJV)

26 For ye are all the children of God by faith in Christ Jesus.
27 **For as many of you as have been baptized into Christ have put on Christ.**
28 There is neither Jew nor Greek, there is neither bond nor free, there is neither male nor female: for ye are all one in Christ Jesus.
29 **And if ye be Christ's, then are ye Abraham's seed, and heirs according to the promise.**

This is the birthright that Esau despised and sold for one meal. Esau did not have any faith in what God promised Abraham. Esau disrespected God and His promises. When it came time to announce the firstborn blessing over Esau from his father Isaac, God allowed Jacob to steal the blessing from Esau. God had no respect for Esau because Esau had no respect for God, and Esau's *Supernatural Security Clearance* was revoked.

We never read of Esau having any Divine encounters with God, while the rest of his family enjoyed multiple encounters with God. Esau rejected God, and therefore God rejected Esau. The New Testament uses the story of Esau as a warning for Christians that they can also sell their birthright by being a fornicator or profane person. The word *profane* means: unholy, wicked, irreverent, disrespectful, and hateful to God.

> **Hebrews 12:14-17 (KJV)**
> 14 Follow peace with all men, and holiness, without which no man shall see the Lord:
> 15 Looking diligently lest any man fail of the grace of God; lest any root of bitterness springing up trouble you, and thereby many be defiled;
> 16 **Lest there be any fornicator, or profane person, as Esau, who for one morsel of meat sold his birthright.**
> 17 **For ye know how that afterward, when he would have inherited the blessing, he was rejected: for he found no place of repentance, though he sought it carefully with tears.**

Esau is a grave example of who and what not to be and how not to treat God. Esau was irreverent and disrespectful to God. Esau also had a murderous spirit because he wanted to kill Jacob over the blessing that his father Isaac spoke over Jacob. It is interesting to note that Esau wanted his father Isaac to bless him with the Blessing of Abraham but disrespected God at the same time. This is like anyone who wants God's blessings but does not want to have a pure relationship with God by obeying His Commands. A *Supernatural Security Clearance* has everything to do with how you respect your God-given inheritance through Christ and the Blessing of Abraham. Anyone granted a *Supernatural Security Clearance* must value God's promises in the covenant of Abraham and the New Covenant of Christ. Esau disrespected God at the highest level and God revoked his *Supernatural Security Clearance* because of it.

Our birthright found in Christ through the Abrahamic Covenant is the most valuable inheritance anyone could ever possess. Some Christians do not realize or value their God-given birthright and sell it for the most foolish of things. When Christians sin through fornication or being profane, they are selling their birthright. When you sell your birthright through sinning against God, you are no better than Esau, who sold his birthright for one meal. Never give away your birthright to anyone or for anything. Your God-given birthright through Christ gives you access to God, Heaven, and your *Supernatural Security Clearance.*

Samson

Samson was granted one of the most unusual *Supernatural Security Clearances* from God in the Bible. Before Samson was born, an angel appeared to Samson's mother and gave her instructions and commands to follow. The angel told Samson's mom that she was not to drink wine or strong drink or eat any unclean thing. The angel also said to her that she would conceive a son and that no razor was to come upon his head and that he was supposed to be a Nazarite from the womb. If she and her son Samson obeyed what he said, Samson would deliver Israel out of the hand of the Philistines who were oppressing them at that time.

Judges 13:3-5 (KJV)
> 3 And the angel of the Lord appeared unto the woman, and said unto her, Behold now, thou art barren, and bearest not: but thou shalt conceive, and bear a son.
> 4 **Now therefore beware, I pray thee, and drink not wine nor strong drink, and eat not any unclean thing:**
> 5 **For, lo, thou shalt conceive, and bear a son; and no razor shall come on his head: for the child shall be a Nazarite unto God from the womb: and he shall begin to deliver Israel out of the hand of the Philistines.**

The laws of the Nazarite can be found in the Law of Moses.

Numbers 6:1-8 (KJV)
> 1 And the Lord spake unto Moses, saying,
> 2 Speak unto the children of Israel, and say unto them, When either man or woman shall separate themselves to vow a vow of a Nazarite, to separate themselves unto the Lord:
> 3 **He shall separate himself from wine and strong drink, and shall drink no vinegar of wine, or vinegar of strong drink, neither shall he drink any liquor of grapes, nor eat moist grapes, or dried.**
> 4 **All the days of his separation shall he eat nothing that is made of the vine tree, from the kernels even to the husk.**
> 5 **All the days of the vow of his separation there shall no razor come upon his head: until the days be fulfilled, in the which he separateth himself unto the Lord, he shall be holy, and shall let the locks of the hair of his head grow.**
> 6 **All the days that he separateth himself unto the Lord he shall come at no dead body.**

7 He shall not make himself unclean for his father, or for his mother, for his brother, or for his sister, when they die: because the consecration of his God is upon his head.
8 All the days of his separation he is holy unto the Lord.

Samson obeyed and followed all the Commandments of the vow of a Nazarite as he was growing up. When it came time for him to deliver Israel, the Spirit of God came upon him with unusual strength. When the Spirit of God came upon Samson, he became stronger than any other man. His vow as a Nazarite by not cutting his hair granted him access to a powerful *Supernatural Security Clearance* of Divine strength never witnessed before or since on the earth.

The physical strength that came upon Samson by the Spirit was no earthly match for God's enemies. Samson was able to do supernatural acts of strength that astounded the natural mind. *Supernatural Security Clearances* can allow someone to do things not capable of by mere humans. The Philistines were stopped dead in their tracks by this powerful anointing of strength given to Samson by God.

Here are supernatural acts Samson performed with his God-given strength:

1. Killed a lion with his bare hands

2. Massacred thirty Philistines and took their garments

3. Caught three hundred foxes, tied their tails together, and set them on fire to burn the Philistine's cornfield

4. Singlehandedly Killed 1,000 Philistines with a donkey's jawbone

5. Carried the doors of the gate of a city and the two posts upon his shoulders thirty-seven miles

6. Broke free from all of Delilah's traps to find his strength before she had his hair cut off

7. Pulled down the pillars of the house of the Philistines, killing 3,000 Philistines

Samson's supernatural strength astounded his enemies. Samson revealed the secret of his strength to Delilah, and she had Samson's hair cut off while he slept. When Samson awoke after his hair was cut off, he did not realize that his *Supernatural Security Clearance* was revoked, and the Spirit of God had left him. Samson lost his supernatural strength because he broke God's command not to cut his hair. The Philistines ended up poking out his eyes and forced him to grind like a slave. The Philistines then brought Samson into their house, where a great sacrifice was being made to their god Dagon. Samson's hair, at this time, had grown back some, and he called upon God one last time to give him the strength to pull down the pillars of the Philistine's house. God granted him this request, and Samson died as he killed 3,000 Philistines by pulling down the house's pillars.

The story of Samson is amazing and tragic at the same time. The story of Samson reveals the mighty anointing that comes upon someone who meets God's requirement to be granted a *Supernatural Security Clearance.* Samson maintained his *Supernatural Security Clearance* for most of his life. However, this story reveals that we must keep our requirements secret from the enemy. The enemy will always tempt people to violate their requirements to maintain a *Supernatural Security Clearance* and have it revoked by disobedience to God.

Supernatural Security Clearances are very sacred and must be kept secret from the enemy. The enemy is looking for who he can deceive and cause a *Supernatural Security Clearance* to be revoked by God through disobedience. This book is designed to help people access a *Supernatural Security Clearance* and keep one from being revoked. The story of Samson is a powerful example of what not to do when granted such a great and powerful anointing to walk in a *Supernatural Security Clearance.*

King Saul

Saul was granted the privilege to be the first king of Israel and granted a *Supernatural Security Clearance.* As the king of Israel, he was called to lead the armies of Israel into battle. The armies of Israel were given a supernatural ability from God to defeat large armies from the time of Abraham, Moses, and Joshua because God was with them. God wrote in the Law of Moses for them not to be afraid when they went into battle because He would be with them to fight against their enemies.

> **Deuteronomy 20:1-4 (KJV)**
> 1 When thou goest out to battle against thine enemies, and seest horses, and chariots, and a people more than thou, **be not afraid of them: for the Lord thy God is with thee, which brought thee up out of the land of Egypt.**
> 2 And it shall be, when ye are come nigh unto the battle, that the priest shall approach and speak unto the people,
> 3 And shall say unto them, Hear, O Israel, ye approach this day unto battle against your enemies: **let not your hearts faint, fear not, and do not tremble, neither be ye terrified because of them;**
> 4 **For the Lord your God is he that goeth with you, to fight for you against your enemies, to save you.**

Saul was anointed to be king by the prophet Samuel during the time when judges were leading the children of Israel. Samuel was the last of the judges to rule over the nation of Israel. God directed Samuel to anoint Saul as the king of Israel because the children of Israel wanted to be like all the nations and have a king over them to lead their armies. God chose Saul and granted him a *Supernatural Security Clearance* to lead the armies of Israel.

I want to add that although Saul was chosen to be king, and the children of Israel had to repent for wanting to be like all the other nations, it was still God's will for a king to be raised up in Israel. God first prophesied to Abraham that kings and nations would be born in his lineage hundreds of years before Saul became the first king of Israel.

Genesis 17:3-8 (KJV)

3 And Abram fell on his face: and God talked with him, saying,

4 As for me, behold, my covenant is with thee, and thou shalt be a father of many nations.

5 Neither shall thy name any more be called Abram, but thy name shall be Abraham; for a father of many nations have I made thee.

6 And I will make thee exceeding fruitful, **and I will make nations of thee, and kings shall come out of thee.**

7 And I will establish my covenant between me and thee and thy seed after thee in their generations for an everlasting covenant, to be a God unto thee, and to thy seed after thee.

8 And I will give unto thee, and to thy seed after thee, the land wherein thou art a stranger, all the land of Canaan, for an everlasting possession; and I will be their God.

God also wrote laws in the Laws of Moses hundreds of years before Saul became the first king of Israel. The future king was commanded in the Law of Moses to obey a number of items, but most importantly, they were to make a copy of the Law of Moses for them to read all the days of their life. The king was to learn to fear the Lord by reading the Law of Moses and keeping all the Words of the Law. If the future king kept God's Commandments, God would prolong his days and kingdom.

Deuteronomy 17:14-20 (KJV)

14 When thou art come unto the land which the Lord thy God giveth thee, and shalt possess it, and shalt dwell therein, **and shalt say, I will set a king over me, like as all the nations that are about me;**

15 **Thou shalt in any wise set him king over thee, whom the Lord thy God shall choose:** one from among thy brethren shalt thou set a king over thee: thou mayest not set a stranger over thee, which is not thy brother.

16 But he shall not multiply horses to himself, nor cause the people to return to Egypt, to the end that he should multiply horses: forasmuch as the Lord hath said unto you, Ye shall henceforth return no more that way.

17 Neither shall he multiply wives to himself, that his heart turn not away: neither shall he greatly multiply to himself silver and gold.

18 **And it shall be, when he sitteth upon the throne of his kingdom, that he shall write him a copy of this law in a book out of that which is before the priests the Levites:**

19 **And it shall be with him, and he shall read therein all the days of his life: that he may learn to fear the Lord his God, to keep all the words of this law and these statutes, to do them:**

20 **That his heart be not lifted up above his brethren, and that he turn not aside from the commandment, to the right hand, or to the left: to the end that he may prolong his days in his kingdom, he, and his children, in the midst of Israel.**

After King Saul came into the authority of being king over Israel, he faced his first test. The Philistines had positioned themselves to fight against the Israelites. The Philistines had a vast army, and the people of Israel were distressed and began to hide. Saul was supposed to wait for Samuel to come and pray to God and make a sacrifice to be blessed as they went into battle with the Philistines.

King Saul, however, gets impatient while waiting for the prophet Samuel to show up and makes the sacrifice. King Saul took it upon himself to make a sacrifice and broke the Commandment of God because only the priests were to make this sacrifice. Samuel was not only a prophet, but he was also a priest. When he arrived on the scene, Samuel revoked King Saul's *Supernatural Security Clearance* to be the king of Israel. He disobeyed God's Commandment by making a sacrifice that only priests were allowed to make. Samuel said to Saul that his kingdom would not continue, and God was going to seek another man to be captain over His people.

1 Samuel 13:8-15 (KJV)
8 And he tarried seven days, according to the set time that Samuel had appointed: **but Samuel came not to Gilgal; and the people were scattered from him.**
9 And Saul said, Bring hither a burnt offering to me, and peace offerings. And he offered the burnt offering.
10 **And it came to pass, that as soon as he had made an end of offering the burnt offering, behold, Samuel came; and Saul went out to meet him, that he might salute him.**
11 And Samuel said, What hast thou done? And Saul said, Because I saw that the people were scattered from me, and that thou camest not within the days appointed, and that the Philistines gathered themselves together at Michmash;

12 **Therefore said I, The Philistines will come down now upon me to Gilgal, and I have not made supplication unto the Lord: I forced myself therefore, and offered a burnt offering.**

13 **And Samuel said to Saul, Thou hast done foolishly: thou hast not kept the commandment of the Lord thy God, which he commanded thee: for now would the Lord have established thy kingdom upon Israel for ever.**

14 **But now thy kingdom shall not continue: the Lord hath sought him a man after his own heart, and the Lord hath commanded him to be captain over his people, because thou hast not kept that which the Lord commanded thee.**

15 And Samuel arose, and gat him up from Gilgal unto Gibeah of Benjamin. And Saul numbered the people that were present with him, about six hundred men.

After this event, God secretly gives King Saul another chance to redeem himself. God tells Samuel to command King Saul to utterly destroy the Amalekites. The Amalekites came behind the children of Israel when they were in the wilderness during the time of Moses and killed the weak and feeble. Therefore, God commanded them to be destroyed when the children of Israel were given rest from their enemies. It had been years since this occurred, but now was the time for God to judge the Amalekites.

Deuteronomy 25:17-19 (KJV)

17 Remember what Amalek did unto thee by the way, when ye were come forth out of Egypt;

18 **How he met thee by the way, and smote the hindmost of thee, even all that were feeble behind thee, when thou wast faint and weary; and he feared not God.**

19 **Therefore it shall be, when the Lord thy God hath given thee rest from all thine enemies round about, in the land**

which the Lord thy God giveth thee for an inheritance to possess it, that thou shalt blot out the remembrance of Amalek from under heaven; thou shalt not forget it.

After many years, King Saul was given the responsibility to wipe the Amalekites clean off the earth. King Saul, however, fails to obey God fully and keeps back the king of the Amalekites and spared the best of the sheep, oxen, fatlings, lambs, and anything good. At this point, the prophet Samuel arrives with a Word from God that is a full revoking of Saul being king over Israel. This is the final straw, and God entirely revokes all of Saul's *Supernatural Security Clearance* because of his rebellion against the command of God.

1 Samuel 15:22-29 (KJV)

22 **And Samuel said, Hath the Lord as great delight in burnt offerings and sacrifices, as in obeying the voice of the Lord? Behold, to obey is better than sacrifice, and to hearken than the fat of rams.**

23 **For rebellion is as the sin of witchcraft, and stubbornness is as iniquity and idolatry. Because thou hast rejected the word of the Lord, he hath also rejected thee from being king.**

24 And Saul said unto Samuel, I have sinned: for I have transgressed the commandment of the Lord, and thy words: because I feared the people, and obeyed their voice.

25 Now therefore, I pray thee, pardon my sin, and turn again with me, that I may worship the Lord.

26 **And Samuel said unto Saul, I will not return with thee: for thou hast rejected the word of the Lord, and the Lord hath rejected thee from being king over Israel.**

27 And as Samuel turned about to go away, he laid hold upon the skirt of his mantle, and it rent.

28 And Samuel said unto him, The Lord hath rent the kingdom of Israel from thee this day, and hath given it to a neighbour of thine, that is better than thou.
29 And also the Strength of Israel will not lie nor repent: for he is not a man, that he should repent.

A demonic spirit came upon Saul from this point on, and he started to do terrible acts. Saul repeatedly chased and tried to kill David, who was anointed by the prophet Samuel to be the next king of Israel. Saul killed the priests of the Lord who he thought were helping David. Saul also went to the witch of Endor to call up Samuel from the dead. Finally, Saul ends up committing suicide after a terrible defeat at the hands of the Philistines.

Another crucial fact to note in the story of Saul is that God stopped communicating with Saul through dreams, Urim, or the prophets. When you lose a *Supernatural Security Clearance,* you no longer have access to communicate with God. God stopped listening to Saul because Saul stopped listening to God. Therefore, Saul sought out the witch of Endor to talk to Samuel, who was already dead.

1 Samuel 28:5-20 (KJV)

5 And when Saul saw the host of the Philistines, he was afraid, and his heart greatly trembled.
6 **And when Saul enquired of the Lord, the Lord answered him not, neither by dreams, nor by Urim, nor by prophets.**
7 Then said Saul unto his servants, Seek me a woman that hath a familiar spirit, that I may go to her, and enquire of her. And his servants said to him, Behold, there is a woman that hath a familiar spirit at Endor.
8 And Saul disguised himself, and put on other raiment, and he went, and two men with him, and they came to the woman by night: and he said, I pray thee, Divine unto me by

185

the familiar spirit, and bring me him up, whom I shall name unto thee.

9 And the woman said unto him, Behold, thou knowest what Saul hath done, how he hath cut off those that have familiar spirits, and the wizards, out of the land: wherefore then layest thou a snare for my life, to cause me to die?

10 And Saul sware to her by the Lord, saying, As the Lord liveth, there shall no punishment happen to thee for this thing.

11 Then said the woman, Whom shall I bring up unto thee? **And he said, Bring me up Samuel.**

12 And when the woman saw Samuel, she cried with a loud voice: and the woman spake to Saul, saying, Why hast thou deceived me? for thou art Saul.

13 And the king said unto her, Be not afraid: for what sawest thou? And the woman said unto Saul, I saw gods ascending out of the earth.

14 And he said unto her, What form is he of? And she said, An old man cometh up; and he is covered with a mantle. And Saul perceived that it was Samuel, and he stooped with his face to the ground, and bowed himself.

15 And Samuel said to Saul, Why hast thou disquieted me, to bring me up? **And Saul answered, I am sore distressed; for the Philistines make war against me, and God is departed from me, and answereth me no more, neither by prophets, nor by dreams:** therefore I have called thee, that thou mayest make known unto me what I shall do.

16 **Then said Samuel, Wherefore then dost thou ask of me, seeing the Lord is departed from thee, and is become thine enemy?**

17 And the Lord hath done to him, as he spake by me: for the Lord hath rent the kingdom out of thine hand, and given it to thy neighbour, even to David:

18 **Because thou obeyedst not the voice of the Lord, nor executedst his fierce wrath upon Amalek, therefore hath the Lord done this thing unto thee this day.**

19 Moreover the Lord will also deliver Israel with thee into the hand of the Philistines: and to morrow shalt thou and thy sons be with me: the Lord also shall deliver the host of Israel into the hand of the Philistines.

20 Then Saul fell straightway all along on the earth, and was sore afraid, because of the words of Samuel: and there was no strength in him; for he had eaten no bread all the day, nor all the night.

King Saul was granted one of the most important *Supernatural Security Clearances* to be the king of Israel at a crucial time in history for the children of Israel. His disobedience and rebellion to God caused his *Supernatural Security Clearance* to be revoked, and many people died because of it. King Saul's life and disobedience serve as a grave reminder to everyone that just as God can promote you to a significant position in His kingdom, your *Supernatural Security Clearance* will be revoked through rebellion and disobedience to God.

Judas Iscariot, the Betrayer of Jesus

The story of Judas Iscariot is the most disgusting story of betrayal in the Bible. Judas Iscariot was granted the most incredible privilege and honor of walking next to the Son of God and being one of Jesus' twelve chosen apostles. Judas Iscariot was given one of the highest levels of *Supernatural Security Clearances* possible. It is utterly revolting how Judas Iscariot took this highly privileged position by stealing from God and betraying Jesus. We will investigate this betrayer's life and see how his *Supernatural Security Clearance* was revoked.

Judas Iscariot walked with Jesus from the beginning of His ministry and was also sent out to perform miracles with the other apostles of Jesus. Judas was also given the position to hold the money bag for the poor that Jesus was using to help them. Judas, however, was stealing from this money bag for the poor and ended up betraying Jesus on the night before His crucifixion for thirty pieces of silver.

Judas Iscariot was complaining that a woman who poured expensive oil on the feet of Jesus before His crucifixion should have sold it to give to the poor. The Bible reveals that Judas was stealing from the money bag of Jesus.

> **John 12:4-8 (KJV)**
> 4 **Then saith one of his disciples, Judas Iscariot, Simon's son, which should betray him,**
> 5 Why was not this ointment sold for three hundred pence, and given to the poor?
> 6 **This he said, not that he cared for the poor; but because he was a thief, and had the bag, and bare what was put therein.**
> 7 Then said Jesus, Let her alone: against the day of my burying hath she kept this.
> 8 For the poor always ye have with you; but me ye have not always.

Judas Iscariot was a part of the ministry of Jesus from the beginning until the end. Judas, however, was not good-natured; he had evil plans the whole time. He started by stealing from Jesus' ministry, resulting in total betrayal.

On the night that Judas betrayed Jesus, he had sat down with all the other apostles, and Jesus even washed his feet. Judas had plotted, in advance with the chief priest, to betray Jesus for money.

Mark 14:10-11 (KJV)

> 10 **And Judas Iscariot, one of the twelve, went unto the chief priests, to betray him unto them.**
> 11 **And when they heard it, they were glad, and promised to give him money. And he sought how he might conveniently betray him.**

From these Scriptures, we can see that Judas Iscariot was greedy for money, which was his prime motive in betraying Jesus. Therefore, it is crucial for someone to receive a *Supernatural Security Clearance* to be free from stealing and covetousness. If not, they could end up betraying God.

Judas was granted a special security clearance to walk and live with the Son of God. On the night that Jesus was betrayed, they did not know where Jesus was located. Judas Iscariot, however, knew the secret location where Jesus could be found, and Judas gave up His location for thirty pieces of silver.

John 18:1-3 (KJV)

> 1 **When Jesus had spoken these words, he went forth with his disciples over the brook Cedron, where was a garden, into the which he entered, and his disciples.**
> 2 **And Judas also, which betrayed him, knew the place: for Jesus ofttimes resorted thither with his disciples.**
> 3 Judas then, having received a band of men and officers from the chief priests and Pharisees, cometh thither with lanterns and torches and weapons.

Judas also betrayed Jesus with a kiss. It was dark at night in the Garden of Gethsemane, and Judas could only reveal who Jesus was by kissing Him.

Mark 14:43-46 (KJV)

> 43 And immediately, while he yet spake, cometh Judas, one of the twelve, and with him a great multitude with swords and staves, from the chief priests and the scribes and the elders.
>
> 44 **And he that betrayed him had given them a token, saying, Whomsoever I shall kiss, that same is he; take him, and lead him away safely.**
>
> 45 **And as soon as he was come, he goeth straightway to him, and saith, Master, master; and kissed him.**
>
> 46 And they laid their hands on him and took him.

The story of Judas Iscariot has gone down in history as the worst of all betrayals. Jesus even said that it would have been better if Judas Iscariot had never been born. Judas Iscariot is an example of the dangers of greed, stealing, and betrayal. Thieves always end up as betrayers. Judas Iscariot lost the most valuable *Supernatural Security Clearance* offered to man. Judas walked with the Son of God and could have been privileged to rule and reign with Him in His coming Kingdom. Judas chose this world and lost everything. Judas ended up hanging himself on a tree after he betrayed Jesus. The lesson of Judas and his betrayal is a scary example of someone's *Supernatural Security Clearance* being revoked.

Disobedient Christians

There are heavy warnings in the Bible for anyone who becomes a Christian and falls away by sinning against the Lord. Being allowed the privilege of becoming a Christian is the highest honor one can attain in this life. Being granted a *Supernatural Security Clearance* through the blood of Jesus is very valuable in this life and in the life to come. God's grace freely saves us, but God takes it very seriously when we count the blood of the Covenant as a light thing by committing sin.

Hebrews 10:26-31 (KJV)

> 26 **For if we sin wilfully after that we have received the knowledge of the truth, there remaineth no more sacrifice for sins,**
>
> 27 **But a certain fearful looking for of judgment and fiery indignation, which shall devour the adversaries.**
>
> 28 He that despised Moses' law died without mercy under two or three witnesses:
>
> 29 **Of how much sorer punishment, suppose ye, shall he be thought worthy, who hath trodden under foot the Son of God, and hath counted the blood of the covenant, wherewith he was sanctified, an unholy thing, and hath done despite unto the Spirit of grace?**
>
> 30 For we know him that hath said, Vengeance belongeth unto me, I will recompense, saith the Lord. And again, The Lord shall judge his people.
>
> 31 **It is a fearful thing to fall into the hands of the living God.**

When Christians willfully sin against the Lord, they despise the Spirit of grace that saved them. The Apostle Peter wrote in his letter it would be better not to have known the way of righteousness and turn away from the holy Commandment delivered to them. He also said that their latter end would be worse than their beginning. These people are like dogs returning to their vomit.

2 Peter 2:20-22 (KJV)

> 20 For if after they have escaped the pollutions of the world through the knowledge of the Lord and Saviour Jesus Christ, they are again entangled therein, and overcome, **the latter end is worse with them than the beginning.**
>
> 21 **For it had been better for them not to have known the way of righteousness, than, after they have known it, to turn from the holy commandment delivered unto them.**

22 But it is happened unto them according to the true proverb, **The dog is turned to his own vomit again; and the sow that was washed to her wallowing in the mire.**

The Book of Hebrews says that if a Christian falls away, they crucify the Son of God all over again and put Him to an open shame. They are putting Jesus to an open shame because they publicly disrespect Him in front of everyone by sinning and doing the very sin(s) He died for.

Hebrews 6:4-6 (KJV)

4 For it is impossible for those who were once enlightened, and have tasted of the heavenly gift, and were made partakers of the Holy Ghost,
5 And have tasted the good word of God, and the powers of the world to come,
6 **If they shall fall away, to renew them again unto repentance; seeing they crucify to themselves the Son of God afresh, and put him to an open shame.**

Jesus bled and died on a cross so humankind could be saved from their sins. Jesus died and rose again for people to be given a second chance. When we accept Jesus and repent of our sins, we are given a second chance and a fresh start to serve God. This second chance is God forgiving someone of their sins and granting them a *Supernatural Security Clearance.* Therefore, if someone goes back to the sins they repented of, they publicly crucify the Lord again.

Everything about God and His kingdom is of great value and must be honored. God will hold anyone accountable who accepts Jesus and turns away. The Bible is full of examples of people who fell away and were judged by God. Nobody wants to go to hell, but there is a real chance for someone to go to hell when they fall away from the Lord. Jesus said narrow is the way that leads to life, and few find it.

Matthew 7:13-14 (KJV)

> 13 **Enter ye in at the strait gate: for wide is the gate, and broad is the way, that leadeth to destruction, and many there be which go in thereat:**
>
> 14 **Because strait is the gate, and narrow is the way, which leadeth unto life, and few there be that find it.**

As wonderful as the good news of the Gospel is, it comes with heavy warnings. God expects His children that He saves through the blood of Jesus to walk a narrow line. The free grace of God demands that we walk holy and obey His Commands once given a second chance. Why would anyone go back to their sinful vomit once saved? When you sin against the Lord, your heart becomes hardened, and we are commanded not to harden our hearts.

Hebrews 3:7-12 (KJV)

> 7 Wherefore (as the Holy Ghost saith, To day if ye will hear his voice,
>
> 8 **Harden not your hearts,** as in the provocation, in the day of temptation in the wilderness:
>
> 9 When your fathers tempted me, proved me, and saw my works forty years.
>
> 10 Wherefore I was grieved with that generation, and said, They do alway err in their heart; and they have not known my ways.
>
> 11 So I sware in my wrath, They shall not enter into my rest.)
>
> 12 **Take heed, brethren, lest there be in any of you an evil heart of unbelief, in departing from the living God.**

The fastest way to have a *Supernatural Security Clearance* revoked is to sin against the Lord. A real Christian is responsible for obeying God and keeping their conscience pure. Jesus paid too heavy a price with His blood for someone to turn their back on Him through disobedience to the Word of God and sin. It's a beautiful thing to accept Jesus in our hearts with a promise to go to Heaven and live forever, but we must understand the responsibility of this *precious gift.* God will hold you accountable for how you live your life after you experience the grace of God through Jesus Christ.

In conclusion, we can see that God expects His children to walk worthy of the calling when given a *Supernatural Security Clearance.* It is a fearful thing to fall into the hands of the living God, who has done everything to save us from our sins. This chapter reveals the dangers of falling away from God. The Book of Proverbs says we are to keep our hearts with all diligence (Proverbs 4:23). Just the smallest of sins can harden your heart against the Lord. Therefore, to keep and protect your *Supernatural Security Clearance* from God, always be careful to flee from sin.

CHAPTER 10
THE TEMPTATIONS
OF CHRIST

One of the fascinating mysteries in the Bible is that Jesus, who is God, became a man to live in the natural world. Jesus is the God we read about in the Book of Genesis who created everything with His spoken Word. Jesus, who is God Almighty, became a man to die on a cross to regain what was lost by the first Adam and redeem all of humanity back to God. However, Jesus becoming a man is an extraordinary mystery that not everyone understands. In this chapter, we will reveal how Jesus became *a man* and was tested *as a man* before accessing a *Supernatural Security Clearance* as a man.

To understand this mysterious truth of Jesus emptying Himself and relinquishing His rights to operate as God while being formed in the fashion of a man, we must go to the Book of Philippians in the New Testament. The Book of Philippians powerfully reveals this truth.

> **Philippians 2:5-8 (KJV)**
> 5 Let this mind be in you, which was also in Christ Jesus:
> 6 **Who, being in the form of God, thought it not robbery to be equal with God:**

7 But made himself of no reputation, and took upon him the form of a servant, and was made in the likeness of men:
8 And being found in fashion as a man, he humbled himself, and became obedient unto death, even the death of the cross.

If you are going to understand the temptations of Christ, it must be established that Jesus became a man when He was born from the virgin Mary. This is important to understand because God cannot be tempted with evil in His glorified state.

> **James 1:13 (KJV)**
> 13 Let no man say when he is tempted, I am tempted of God: **for God cannot be tempted with evil,** neither tempteth he any man:

God cannot be tempted with evil; therefore, for Christ to be tempted with evil, He could not be in His form of God while living as a man on the earth. This is a fundamental truth to understand when you are studying the life and ministry of Jesus Christ. There are some facts you must consider to better understand the impact of this revelation.

Here are some facts to consider about Jesus:

1. Jesus did not do any miracles until the age of thirty when the Holy Spirit Anointed Him.

2. Jesus' stepfather Joseph died before the Holy Spirit anointed Jesus, and we do not have any record of Joseph being healed or raised from the dead by Jesus.

3. Jesus was crucified and died just like any other mortal man.

4. Jesus could be tempted to sin like any other mortal man.

These facts reveal that Jesus was not operating in His God capacity while on the earth. Jesus was operating as a man to win back what the first Adam lost when he sinned. He was also operating as a man to be our example of how to live and obey God as a man. Jesus was the living example of obeying God and how to obtain a *Supernatural Security Clearance* from God.

Jesus had to go through three temptations of the devil as a man before He could be granted a *Supernatural Security Clearance* and walk in a powerful anointing of the Holy Spirit. Jesus did not gain access to the supernatural power of the Holy Spirit until He passed these tests in the wilderness while He was fasting for 40 days.

Jesus was baptized by John the Baptist in the Jordan River, and the Holy Spirit descended upon Him, the Heavens were opened, and God the Father said in an audible voice, "This is My Beloved Son, in whom I am well pleased." After this experience, Jesus was led by the Holy Spirit into the wilderness to be tempted by the devil. Let's look at the temptations Jesus went through and how it applies to us.

> **Luke 4:1-14 (KJV)**
> 1 And Jesus being full of the Holy Ghost returned from Jordan, **and was led by the Spirit into the wilderness,**
> 2 **Being forty days tempted of the devil.** And in those days he did eat nothing: and when they were ended, he afterward hungered.
> 3 And the devil said unto him, If thou be the Son of God, command this stone that it be made bread.
> 4 And Jesus answered him, saying, It is written, That man shall not live by bread alone, but by every Word of God.
> 5 And the devil, taking him up into an high mountain, shewed unto him all the kingdoms of the world in a moment of time.

6 And the devil said unto him, All this power will I give thee, and the glory of them: for that is delivered unto me; and to whomsoever I will I give it.

7 If thou therefore wilt worship me, all shall be thine.

8 And Jesus answered and said unto him, Get thee behind me, Satan: for it is written, Thou shalt worship the Lord thy God, and him only shalt thou serve.

9 And he brought him to Jerusalem, and set him on a pinnacle of the temple, and said unto him, If thou be the Son of God, cast thyself down from hence:

10 For it is written, He shall give his angels charge over thee, to keep thee:

11 And in their hands they shall bear thee up, lest at any time thou dash thy foot against a stone.

12 And Jesus answering said unto him, It is said, Thou shalt not tempt the Lord thy God.

13 And when the devil had ended all the temptation, he departed from him for a season.

14 **And Jesus returned in the power of the Spirit into Galilee:** and there went out a fame of him through all the region round about.

The devil tempted Jesus three times. So, I want to reemphasize the point that if Jesus could not sin as a man because He was God, then these three temptations were not a real test. These temptations were a real test, and Jesus had the possibility of sinning, but He chose not to.

Let's look at another Scripture to understand this truth.

Hebrews 2:14-18 (KJV)

14 Forasmuch then as the children are partakers of flesh and blood, he also himself likewise took part of the same; that

through death he might destroy him that had the power of death, that is, the devil;

15 And deliver them who through fear of death were all their lifetime subject to bondage.

16 For verily he took not on him the nature of angels; but he took on him the seed of Abraham.

17 **Wherefore in all things it behoved him to be made like unto his brethren, that he might be a merciful and faithful high priest in things pertaining to God, to make reconciliation for the sins of the people.**

18 **For in that he himself hath suffered being tempted, he is able to succour them that are tempted.**

Jesus became a man and was made like those He was going to save by His sacrificial death on the cross. Jesus can also help those being tempted because He was tempted in all ways like us, but He was without sin. Jesus could have sinned, but He never did. He was like any other mortal man in that He could sin as they could.

Hebrews 4:14-15 (KJV)

14 Seeing then that we have a great high priest, that is passed into the heavens, **Jesus the Son of God,** let us hold fast our profession.

15 For we have not an high priest which cannot be touched with the feeling of our infirmities; **but was in all points tempted like as we are, yet without sin.**

My purpose in going into detail about Jesus being a man is that He had to pass tests and overcome temptations before He was granted a *Supernatural Security Clearance* from God. Jesus is our example of how to obtain a *Supernatural Security Clearance*. Too many believers have misunderstood the humanity and deity of Christ and lost the truth that He is our example. We should look to and follow Christ as an example of how to obtain a *Supernatural Security Clearance* from God. If He could do it, then we can do it too.

Hebrews 12:2-4 (KJV)

2 **Looking unto Jesus the author and finisher of our faith;** who for the joy that was set before him endured the cross, despising the shame, and is set down at the right hand of the Throne of God.

3 For consider him that endured such contradiction of sinners against himself, **lest ye be wearied and faint in your minds.**

4 **Ye have not yet resisted unto blood, striving against sin.**

Jesus even told His apostles that they could do the works He was doing and even greater if they believed. Jesus said if we asked anything in His Name, He would do it.

John 14:12-14 (KJV)

12 **Verily, verily, I say unto you, He that believeth on me, the works that I do shall he do also; and greater works than these shall he do; because I go unto my Father.**

13 **And whatsoever ye shall ask in my name, that will I do,** that the Father may be glorified in the Son.

14 **If ye shall ask any thing in my name, I will do it.**

For an apostle or anyone else to perform greater miracles than Christ, they need a *Supernatural Security Clearance*. We also know from the history of the Bible, in the Book of Acts, the apostles did perform many miracles like Jesus and even greater! The Apostle Peter's shadow healed people. We do not see anywhere in the Bible where the shadow of Jesus healed anyone.

Acts 5:14-16 (KJV)

14 And believers were the more added to the Lord, multitudes both of men and women.)

15 **Insomuch that they brought forth the sick into the streets, and laid them on beds and couches, that at the least the shadow of Peter passing by might overshadow some of them.**

16 There came also a multitude out of the cities round about unto Jerusalem, bringing sick folks, and them which were vexed with unclean spirits: and they were healed every one.

All the apostles were granted a *Supernatural Security Clearance* from God and were doing miracles, signs, and wonders.

Acts 5:12 (KJV)

12 **And by the hands of the apostles were many signs and wonders wrought among the people;** (and they were all with one accord in Solomon's porch.

Acts 4:33 (KJV)

33 **And with great power gave the apostles witness of the resurrection of the Lord Jesus:** and great grace was upon them all.

With all these examples of Scripture, it is clear to see that Jesus had to pass tests and temptations before He could be granted an earthly *Supernatural Security Clearance* to operate in the power of the Holy Spirit. The early apostles also had to pass these same tests and temptations to be granted a *Supernatural Security Clearance.* We also have many examples of people in the Old Testament who passed tests to be given a *Supernatural Security Clearance* to walk in the power of God.

The three basic temptations that need to be overcome are the lusts of the flesh, the lust of the eyes, and the pride of life before you can be granted a *Supernatural Security Clearance.*

1 John 2:15-17 (KJV)

> 15 Love not the world, neither the things that are in the world. If any man love the world, the love of the Father is not in him.
> 16 **For all that is in the world, the lust of the flesh, and the lust of the eyes, and the pride of life, is not of the Father, but is of the world.**
> 17 And the world passeth away, and the lust thereof: but he that doeth the will of God abideth for ever.

In conclusion, Jesus is our example of how to overcome temptations, please God, defeat the devil, and be granted a *Supernatural Security Clearance* from God as He did. Jesus showed us what it took to obtain a *Supernatural Security Clearance.* Some believers today and throughout history do not even know there is a *Supernatural Security Clearance* to be obtained from God. The thought of God looking for trusted people who have overcome temptation is foreign to them. God has *Supernatural Security Clearances*, and the Bible is full of examples of people gaining and losing them. God is revealing this truth to people in this generation so they will seek Him, be found faithful, and be granted their *Supernatural Security Clearance* to fulfill the High Call of God on their lives.

CHAPTER 11
PETER, JAMES, AND JOHN

Jesus chose Peter, James, and John to be His closest friends and associates during His earthly ministry. Jesus' ministry reached thousands of people, but He only granted a few people to get close to Him. Out of everyone He could have chosen to be near to Him, for some reason, He chose Peter, James, and John to be granted a remarkable *Supernatural Security Clearance.* Peter, James, and John shared some of the most secret experiences with Jesus while He was on this earth. This chapter will discover some of the reasons Jesus chose these men to be close to Him, what they experienced together, and why they were granted the most sacred of all *Supernatural Security Clearances* that God has ever handed out.

When Jesus ministered on the earth, He needed to find people He could be friends with, trust, learn His sacred teachings, and help Him fulfill His God-given mission. Jesus, although He was the Son of God, needed men He could trust with His most sacred secrets. The earthly ministry of Jesus was not just a job to Him; He wanted to share His mission with men He could call friends. Jesus chose twelve men whom He called apostles to be the closest to Him.

Mark 3:13-19 (KJV)

13 And he goeth up into a mountain, and calleth unto him whom he would: and they came unto him.

14 And he ordained twelve, **that they should be with him**, and that he might send them forth to preach,

15 And to have power to heal sicknesses, and to cast out devils:

16 And Simon he surnamed Peter;

17 And James the son of Zebedee, and John the brother of James; and he surnamed them Boanerges, which is, The sons of thunder:

18 And Andrew, and Philip, and Bartholomew, and Matthew, and Thomas, and James the son of Alphaeus, and Thaddaeus, and Simon the Canaanite,

19 **And Judas Iscariot, which also betrayed him:** and they went into an house.

Before Jesus sent these twelve men out to preach, He wanted them to be with Him. Jesus wanted to get close to these men. However, one of these men, Judas Iscariot, betrayed Him. Jesus knew He needed to find men He could trust at the deepest level to continue His mission of preaching the Gospel to the lost. Also, the mission of Jesus was about restoring humanity from their fallen position back into the family of God.

God has a kingdom and a government, but He runs it with His trusted family members. These trusted family members are called sons of God.

John 1:12 (KJV)

12 **But as many as received him, to them gave he power to become the sons of God,** even to them that believe on His Name:

On the first day of creation, the Father, Son, and Holy Spirit had family on their minds while creating. Just because everyone created is an offspring of God does not mean they are His genuine family members. Many people and angels have disobeyed, rebelled, and become enemies of God. God is very relational and wants to share His deepest secrets, secret locations, powerful weapons, and His kingdom only with those He can trust like a family member.

The statement that blood is thicker than water is true in God's kingdom. Those who have been redeemed by the blood of the Lamb have been grafted into the family of God and are closer to God than any of His creation. The blood of Jesus was the ultimate price to bring us back to God.

> **Ephesians 2:13 (KJV)**
> 13 **But now in Christ Jesus ye who sometimes were far off are made nigh by the blood of Christ.**

> **Colossians 1:19-21 (KJV)**
> 19 For it pleased the Father that in him should all fulness dwell;
> 20 **And, having made peace through the blood of his cross,** by him to reconcile all things unto himself; by him, I say, whether they be things in earth, or things in heaven.
> 21 And you, that were sometime alienated and enemies in your mind by wicked works, yet now hath he reconciled

> **Revelation 12:11 (KJV)**
> 11 **And they overcame him by the blood of the Lamb, and by the word of their testimony;** and they loved not their lives unto the death.

Jesus spilled His blood on the cross so we believers could be restored to the family of God by becoming sons of God. God did not send Jesus to redeem us so we could be His servants, but He redeemed us to be a part of His family.

Galatians 4:4-7 (KJV)
4 But when the fulness of the time was come, God sent forth his Son, made of a woman, made under the law,
5 To redeem them that were under the law, **that we might receive the adoption of sons.**
6 **And because ye are sons, God hath sent forth the Spirit of his Son into your hearts, crying, Abba, Father.**
7 **Wherefore thou art no more a servant, but a son; and if a son, then an heir of God through Christ.**

Romans 8:14-17 (KJV)
14 **For as many as are led by the Spirit of God, they are the sons of God.**
15 **For ye have not received the spirit of bondage again to fear; but ye have received the Spirit of adoption, whereby we cry, Abba, Father.**
16 **The Spirit itself beareth witness with our spirit, that we are the children of God:**
17 **And if children, then heirs; heirs of God, and joint-heirs with Christ;** if so be that we suffer with him, that we may be also glorified together.

Jesus loves the entire world and died for everyone, but that does not mean all the world loves Him. Jesus died that all people might be saved, but many people refuse His free gift of salvation. These people cannot be trusted with anything sacred from God because they hate the light of God, which is His glory and goodness.

John 3:16-21 (KJV)

> 16 **For God so loved the world, that he gave his only begotten Son, that whosoever believeth in him should not perish, but have everlasting life.**
>
> 17 **For God sent not his Son into the world to condemn the world; but that the world through him might be saved.**
>
> 18 He that believeth on him is not condemned: but he that believeth not is condemned already, because he hath not believed in the name of the only begotten Son of God.
>
> 19 **And this is the condemnation, that light is come into the world, and men loved darkness rather than light, because their deeds were evil.**
>
> 20 **For every one that doeth evil hateth the light, neither cometh to the light, lest his deeds should be reproved.**
>
> 21 **But he that doeth truth cometh to the light, that his deeds may be made manifest, that they are wrought in God.**

Jesus was looking for friendship and family when He was born on this earth, and He found this in Peter, James, and John. Jesus trusted these men above all the men He could have been with. These men must have opened themselves up to Jesus as much as He opened Himself to them. Jesus needed these men and His other disciples to help Him on His mission of love to restore humanity back to the Father as loving sons of God.

Now let us look at who Peter, James, and John were and the special top-secret encounters they were granted by God when Jesus was on the earth. Peter, James, and John were fishermen by trade, and Jesus used their trade as an example of them becoming fishers of men.

Mark 1:16-20 (KJV)

> 16 **Now as he walked by the sea of Galilee, he saw Simon** and Andrew his brother **casting a net into the sea: for they were fishers.**
>
> 17 **And Jesus said unto them, Come ye after me, and I will make you to become fishers of men.**
>
> 18 **And straightway they forsook their nets, and followed him.**
>
> 19 And when he had gone a little farther thence, **he saw James the son of Zebedee, and John his brother, who also were in the ship mending their nets.**
>
> 20 **And straightway he called them: and they left their father Zebedee in the ship with the hired servants, and went after him.**

All three of these men were willing to leave their profession and follow Jesus immediately. This quickness of action to quit what they were doing was the first stage of them getting close to Jesus. This must have impressed Jesus deeply and moved Him to make them a part of the first twelve chosen apostles.

Later, we find that Peter is the first of the apostles to acknowledge that Jesus was the Christ. Peter confessed that Jesus was the Christ when it was not popular or safe because of the religious leaders of that day.

Matthew 16:13-19 (KJV)

> 13 When Jesus came into the coasts of Caesarea Philippi, he asked his disciples, saying, **Whom do men say that I the Son of man am?**
>
> 14 And they said, Some say that thou art John the Baptist: some, Elias; and others, Jeremias, or one of the prophets.
>
> 15 He saith unto them, But whom say ye that I am?

16 And Simon Peter answered and said, Thou art the Christ, the Son of the living God.

17 And Jesus answered and said unto him, Blessed art thou, Simon Barjona: for flesh and blood hath not revealed it unto thee, but my Father which is in heaven.

18 And I say also unto thee, That thou art Peter, and upon this rock I will build my church; and the gates of hell shall not prevail against it.

19 And I will give unto thee the keys of the kingdom of heaven: and whatsoever thou shalt bind on earth shall be bound in heaven: and whatsoever thou shalt loose on earth shall be loosed in heaven.

Jesus referred to James and John as the sons of thunder, and they were two of the apostles who said they were willing to suffer for Jesus' sake.

Matthew 20:20-23 (KJV)

20 Then came to him the mother of Zebedees children with her sons, worshipping him, and desiring a certain thing of him.

21 And he said unto her, What wilt thou? She saith unto him, Grant that these my two sons may sit, the one on thy right hand, and the other on the left, in thy kingdom.

22 But Jesus answered and said, Ye know not what ye ask. Are ye able to drink of the cup that I shall drink of, and to be baptized with the baptism that I am baptized with? They say unto him, We are able.

23 And he saith unto them, Ye shall drink indeed of my cup, and be baptized with the baptism that I am baptized with: but to sit on my right hand, and on my left, is not mine to give, but it shall be given to them for whom it is prepared of my Father.

Zebedee was the father of James and John. Their mother requested from Jesus that her sons sit with Him in His kingdom, one on His left and the other on the right. Jesus replied by asking if they could drink the cup He would drink of. This cup was referring to the cup of His death. He also asked if they could be baptized with His baptism, referring to His baptism of persecution. James and John both replied that they were able, which meant they were willing to die and suffer persecution for Christ.

History tells us that Peter was hung upside down on a cross when he died for his confession of faith in Christ. James was the first of the apostles to die for Christ at the command of King Herod in the Book of Acts. John, the brother of James, was dipped in a vat of hot oil and sent to the island of Pergamos in exile for being a Christian. All these men suffered for being a follower of Jesus. Jesus must have known these men would love Him unto death, and that is why He chose them to be granted a remarkable *Supernatural Security Clearance.*

The Apostle John was known as *John the Beloved* because it is recorded in the Book of John that Jesus loved him. John wrote five books of the New Testament and was greatly used by God to spread the Gospel after Jesus ascended into Heaven. The Apostle John had a very intimate relationship with Jesus and even leaned on Jesus' bosom at the Last Supper of Christ. John displayed the love it takes to be close to God and be entrusted with a *Supernatural Security Clearance.*

Now I want to look at three top secret and highly classified events that Jesus only allowed Peter, James, and John to be a witness to:

1. The Raising of Jairus's Daughter from the Dead

2. The Mount of Transfiguration

3. The Garden of Gethsemane

The Raising of Jairus's Daughter from the Dead

Jairus, who was the ruler of the synagogue by the sea of Galilee, came to Jesus and requested if He would heal his daughter. The daughter of Jairus was at the point of death, and Jairus believed that Jesus could heal her by Him laying hands on her. Jesus agreed to go with Jairus to heal his daughter, but along the way, a messenger came and told Jairus not to trouble the Master anymore because his daughter died. At this point, Jesus immediately turns to Jairus and says, "Be not afraid, only believe."

This situation was dire because Jairus' daughter was now dead, and it was going to take *great faith* to raise her from the dead. From this point on, Jesus only allows Peter, James, and John to come with Him to Jairus' house. He only allowed them in because they demonstrated that they had great faith. When Jesus gets to the house, He tells everyone that the girl is not dead but asleep. All these people laugh at Jesus because they know she is dead.

Once Jesus clears the house of these people, He only allows Peter, James, John, Jairus, and his wife to enter the room where their daughter was lying. Jesus then raised the young girl from the dead. Let's read this story, starting when Jairus finds out that his daughter has died.

> **Mark 5:35-43 (KJV)**
> 35 **While he yet spake, there came from the ruler of the synagogue's house certain which said, Thy daughter is dead: why troublest thou the Master any further?**
> 36 As soon as Jesus heard the word that was spoken, he saith unto the ruler of the synagogue, **Be not afraid, only believe.**

37 **And he suffered no man to follow him, save Peter, and James, and John the brother of James.**

38 And he cometh to the house of the ruler of the synagogue, and seeth the tumult, and them that wept and wailed greatly.

39 And when he was come in, he saith unto them, Why make ye this ado, and weep? the damsel is not dead, but sleepeth.

40 And they laughed him to scorn. **But when he had put them all out, he taketh the father and the mother of the damsel, and them that were with him, and entereth in where the damsel was lying.**

41 **And he took the damsel by the hand, and said unto her, Talitha cumi; which is, being interpreted, Damsel, I say unto thee, arise.**

42 And straightway the damsel arose, and walked; for she was of the age of twelve years. And they were astonished with a great astonishment.

43 And he charged them straitly that no man should know it; and commanded that something should be given her to eat.

Peter, James, and John were close to Jesus and possessed great faith. Jesus trusted these three men to stand with Him in faith and believe God for a miracle. Not everyone has this type of faith, but this kind of faith pleases God.

Hebrews 11:6 (KJV)

6 **But without faith it is impossible to please him:** for he that cometh to God must believe that he is, and that he is a rewarder of them that diligently seek him.

These men were operating in a high level of faith which granted them access to Jesus and a *Supernatural Security Clearance.* It takes faith to operate in a *Supernatural Security Clearance,* and it takes faith to get close to God.

The Mount of Transfiguration

The Mount of Transfiguration was the most top-secret event in the life and ministry of Jesus. The Mount of Transfiguration is where Jesus was transfigured into His glorious body on a mountain top. Moses and Elijah showed up on the mountain while Jesus was in His transfigured body to discuss His death and crucifixion. The Father also showed up in a cloud and spoke from Heaven.

> **Luke 9:28-36 (KJV)**
>
> 28 And it came to pass about an eight days after these sayings, **he took Peter and John and James, and went up into a mountain to pray.**
>
> 29 **And as he prayed, the fashion of his countenance was altered, and his raiment was white and glistering.**
>
> 30 **And, behold, there talked with him two men, which were Moses and Elias:**
>
> 31 Who appeared in glory, and spake of his decease which he should accomplish at Jerusalem.
>
> 32 But Peter and they that were with him were heavy with sleep: and when they were awake, they saw his glory, and the two men that stood with him.
>
> 33 And it came to pass, as they departed from him, Peter said unto Jesus, Master, it is good for us to be here: and let us make three tabernacles; one for thee, and one for Moses, and one for Elias: not knowing what he said.
>
> 34 While he thus spake, there came a cloud, and overshadowed them: and they feared as they entered into the cloud.
>
> 35 And there came a voice out of the cloud, saying, This is my beloved Son: hear him.
>
> 36 And when the voice was past, Jesus was found alone. **And they kept it close, and told no man in those days any of those things which they had seen.**

This was such a sacred and secret event that Jesus only allowed Peter, James, and John to be with Him. One important thing to note is that Jesus came to the earth to die on a cross to save humanity, but Jesus dying on the cross was a top-secret and highly classified mission. Jesus did not want His secret mission of dying on the cross to be known to everyone. Jesus, however, trusted Peter, James, and John with this top-secret classified information.

> **Mark 9:9-10 (KJV)**
> 9 And as they came down from the mountain, **he charged them that they should tell no man what things they had seen, till the Son of man were risen from the dead.**
> 10 **And they kept that saying with themselves, questioning one with another what the rising from the dead should mean.**

Peter, James, and John were trusted with this information and told no one. They did not fully understand this secret, but they still did not tell anyone about Jesus rising from the dead. The question must be asked, why was the knowledge of Jesus rising from the dead top-secret information? The reason it was top-secret information is that Jesus was going to take back all authority and power from the devil in His death and resurrection. Jesus would take back ownership of the earth from the devil and restore humanity back in fellowship with God and save them from going to hell. Jesus took back what the first Adam lost in his disobedience to God in the Garden of Eden.

If the devil or the religious leaders knew why Jesus was going to the cross, they would not have crucified Him. This mission was top-secret, and Jesus trusted Peter, James, and John with this confidential information. They had *Supernatural Security Clearances* because they were trustworthy. Jesus was on a top-secret mission from God, and only a trusted few could know about it.

1 Corinthians 2:7-8 (KJV)

7 But we speak the wisdom of God in a mystery, even the hidden wisdom, which God ordained before the world unto our glory:

8 Which none of the princes of this world knew: for had they known it, they would not have crucified the Lord of glory.

Now that Jesus has died, risen again, and taken His rightful ownership of the world, it is no longer a secret. However, before Jesus went to the cross, it was the greatest secret in world history, and this knowledge could be trusted with Peter, James, and John. These men loved Jesus and were faithful to Him, and that is why they were granted an extraordinary *Supernatural Security Clearance.*

The Garden of Gethsemane

The Garden of Gethsemane is located at the bottom of the Mount of Olives near Jerusalem. Jesus spent His final hours in the Garden of Gethsemane praying to the Father about Him going to the cross. It was a sacred moment because people still did not know the secret mission of Christ. The top-secret mission of Christ was to die on a cross, rise again and save all of humanity. If the devil or any religious leader knew about Christ's secret mission, they would not have crucified Him. Thus, He would not be able to redeem all of humanity and take back the authority and power of the earth from the devil.

This mission was so secret that Jesus only revealed it to Peter, James, and John. So, when Jesus came to Gethsemane to pray to His Father, He only brought these three trustworthy disciples.

Mark 14:32-42 (KJV)

32 **And they came to a place which was named Gethsemane:** and he saith to his disciples, Sit ye here, while I shall pray.

33 **And he taketh with him Peter and James and John,** and began to be sore amazed, and to be very heavy;

34 And saith unto them, My soul is exceeding sorrowful unto death: tarry ye here, and watch.

35 And he went forward a little, and fell on the ground, and prayed that, if it were possible, the hour might pass from him.

36 And he said, Abba, Father, all things are possible unto thee; take away this cup from me: nevertheless not what I will, but what thou wilt.

37 And he cometh, and findeth them sleeping, and saith unto Peter, Simon, sleepest thou? couldest not thou watch one hour?

38 Watch ye and pray, lest ye enter into temptation. The spirit truly is ready, but the flesh is weak.

39 And again he went away, and prayed, and spake the same words.

40 And when he returned, he found them asleep again, (for their eyes were heavy,) neither wist they what to answer him.

41 And he cometh the third time, and saith unto them, Sleep on now, and take your rest: it is enough, the hour is come; behold, the Son of man is betrayed into the hands of sinners.

42 Rise up, let us go; lo, he that betrayeth me is at hand.

Peter, James, and John were with Jesus in His final hours before His crucifixion. The Garden of Gethsemane was a *Secret Place* for Jesus to go to, and not everyone knew where Jesus went at night when He was in Jerusalem. Therefore, the religious leaders needed Judas Iscariot to betray Jesus by giving up the secret location of where Jesus went at night to capture Him.

John 18:1-12 (KJV)
1 **When Jesus had spoken these words, he went forth with his disciples over the brook Cedron, where was a garden, into the which he entered, and his disciples.**
2 **And Judas also, which betrayed him, knew the place: for Jesus ofttimes resorted thither with his disciples.**
3 Judas then, having received a band of men and officers from the chief priests and Pharisees, cometh thither with lanterns and torches and weapons.
4 Jesus therefore, knowing all things that should come upon him, went forth, and said unto them, Whom seek ye?
5 They answered him, Jesus of Nazareth. Jesus saith unto them, I am he. **And Judas also, which betrayed him, stood with them.**
6 As soon then as he had said unto them, I am he, they went backward, and fell to the ground.
7 Then asked he them again, Whom seek ye? And they said, Jesus of Nazareth.
8 Jesus answered, I have told you that I am he: if therefore ye seek me, let these go their way:
9 That the saying might be fulfilled, which he spake, Of them which thou gavest me have I lost none.
10 Then Simon Peter having a sword drew it, and smote the high priest's servant, and cut off his right ear. The servant's name was Malchus.
11 Then said Jesus unto Peter, Put up thy sword into the sheath: the cup which my Father hath given me, shall I not drink it?
12 Then the band and the captain and officers of the Jews took Jesus, and bound him,

In his fierce loyalty to Christ, Peter cut off one of the High Priest's servants' ear, which Jesus immediately healed. Judas betrayed Jesus, but Jesus had His most trusted companions next to Him when they came to capture Him. Jesus trusted Peter, James, and John in His most critical moments before going to the cross.

From the history of the Bible, we know Jesus completed His mission. He rose from the dead to defeat the devil, regained back the lost authority of the earth, took back the keys of hell and death from the devil, and died for the right of humankind to be saved. After His resurrection, He sent His three most trusted apostles, Peter, James, John, and His other disciples, to preach the message of the Gospel to the entire world. The secret message of the cross was now placed in the hands of Peter, James, and John to preach openly to the whole world. The ones who were first given the secret message of the cross were now the ones entrusted with their *Supernatural Security Clearances* to preach this message to all the nations.

In conclusion, God is looking for trustworthy disciples like Peter, James, and John that He can give *Supernatural Security Clearances.* If you are willing to believe and pay the price as they did, then you could also be granted access to God and be close to Jesus. Many people are called, but few are chosen to get close to God. God calls many people, but few take God up on His call. If you are willing to pay the price, you can be chosen to get close to God.

CHAPTER 12
THE LORD IS WITH YOU WHILE YOU ARE WITH HIM

The Lord is with you is a term used by God when He is anointing someone to be a king, priest, judge, apostle, prophet, evangelist, pastor, or teacher. God also used this term in the Bible for any anointed man or woman of God who He sent to fulfill a mission. If the Lord was with someone, they were blessed, made prosperous, feared by their enemies, and promoted to a place of great honor and authority. This chapter will reveal what is required to have **the Lord be with you** and how this applies to *Supernatural Security Clearances.*

God made sure that whoever He was sending with an anointing always had conscious knowledge that He was with them. God also wanted them to know that the unseen God would make Himself known in whatever problem or enemy they faced. Just because we cannot see God with our naked eye does not mean He is not there, and He cannot make His presence known. God will make Himself known either by a prophetic word, dream, vision, gift of the Spirit, Divine provision, or a miraculous deliverance from an enemy.

It is important to note that as much as God revealed to people He anointed and sent on missions that He was with them, God wanted to know if they were with Him. The anointed man or woman of God that He was with had a responsibility to prove they were with God also. Here are some of the requirements found in the Bible that were placed on people to have God be with them:

1. They had to love the Lord with all their heart, soul, mind, and strength (Mark 12:29-30)

2. They had to be in Covenant with the Lord (Matthew 26:27-29)

3. They had to Cleave to the Lord (Deuteronomy 13:14)

4. They had to follow Christ (1 Corinthians 11:1)

5. They had to do that which was right before the Lord (1 Kings 11:38)

6. They had to remove hypocritical Christians living in sin from their life (1 Corinthians 5:11-13)

7. They had to obey all the commands of Christ (Matthew 28:19-20)

8. They had to take up their cross daily (Luke 9:23)

9. They had to put off the old man (Ephesians 4:20-22)

10. They had to put on the new man (Colossians 3:8-10)

11. They had to be led by the Spirit (Romans 8:14)

12. They had to walk in the Spirit and not fulfill the lusts of the flesh (Galatians 5:16-26)

13. They had to remove all idols from their life (1 John 5:21)

Many people want God to be with them but are they with God? We cannot expect God to be with us if we are unwilling to show and do what it takes to be with God. God is faithful to keep His Word and deliver His people, but they must be with Him and obey His Word. How can someone expect God to fulfill His Word in their life if they are not keeping His Word? The Lord is with you while you are with Him, but if you forsake the Lord, He will forsake you.

2 Chronicles 15:1-2 (KJV)

1 And the Spirit of God came upon Azariah the son of Oded:
2 And he went out to meet Asa, and said unto him, Hear ye me, Asa, and all Judah and Benjamin; **The Lord is with you, while ye be with him; and if ye seek him, he will be found of you; but if ye forsake him, he will forsake you.**

This may seem harsh to some people, but it is Biblical truth. Fair is fair; God will treat you like you treat Him. This is a truth that is not often preached, and it is also a reason we do not see many people working in the anointing or having a *Supernatural Security Clearance.* God's Word is filled with examples of men and women God was with and not with. It is also filled with the wisdom of God and how to have God be with you. If you obey and listen to the wisdom of God, He will be with you, but if you do not listen to the wisdom of God, He will not be with you in your time of need.

Proverbs 1:20-33 (KJV)

20 **Wisdom crieth without; she uttereth her voice in the streets:**
21 She crieth in the chief place of concourse, in the openings of the gates: in the city she uttereth her words, saying,
22 How long, ye simple ones, will ye love simplicity? and the scorners delight in their scorning, and fools hate knowledge?

23 **Turn you at my reproof: behold, I will pour out my spirit unto you, I will make known my words unto you.**

24 **Because I have called, and ye refused; I have stretched out my hand, and no man regarded;**

25 **But ye have set at nought all my counsel, and would none of my reproof:**

26 **I also will laugh at your calamity; I will mock when your fear cometh;**

27 When your fear cometh as desolation, and your destruction cometh as a whirlwind; when distress and anguish cometh upon you.

28 **Then shall they call upon me, but I will not answer; they shall seek me early, but they shall not find me:**

29 **For that they hated knowledge, and did not choose the fear of the Lord:**

30 **They would none of my counsel: they despised all my reproof.**

31 **Therefore shall they eat of the fruit of their own way, and be filled with their own devices.**

32 For the turning away of the simple shall slay them, and the prosperity of fools shall destroy them.

33 **But whoso hearkeneth unto me shall dwell safely, and shall be quiet from fear of evil.**

God speaks to His children and reveals wisdom to them in how they should live. Those who listen to His wisdom are blessed and can be granted a *Supernatural Security Clearance.* Those who do not listen to God's wisdom cannot expect God to listen to them in their time of need. God will treat you the same way you treat Him. If you honor Him and obey His Word, He will honor you and listen to your prayers in your time of need. If you dishonor Him and do not listen to the wisdom of His Word, He will not honor you and listen to your prayers in your time of need.

It is empowering when you fully understand this truth about God being with you if you are with Him. What I mean by empowering is that now you know the secret to having God be with you. When you come to terms with this secret aspect of God, you can start to walk in a strong faith in knowing that God will answer your prayers if you obey the wisdom of His Word and truly show God you are with Him. If you show God you are with Him, He will show you He is with you.

Everything in God is conditional on how we respond and obey Him. None of God's promises come without conditions. When we meet all of God's conditions, we will see God respond to us miraculously. Be careful of any preaching that offers you all of God's blessings without you having to do anything. God's grace is free, but we must respond correctly to His grace to receive His free gifts.

> **Jude 1:4 (KJV)**
> 4 For there are certain men crept in unawares, who were before of old ordained to this condemnation, **ungodly men, turning the grace of our God into lasciviousness, and denying the only Lord God, and our Lord Jesus Christ.**

Now that we can see that we must be with God for Him to be with us, let us look at the benefits of God being with us. When a man or woman of God knew God was with them, they had bold confidence to face whatever came their way, knowing they were not alone. They knew God was always ready to help them in whatever they needed to succeed and accomplish their mission. If they did all that God spoke, He became an enemy to their enemies and an adversary to their adversaries.

Exodus 23:22 (KJV)

22 **But if thou shalt indeed obey his voice, and do all that I speak; then I will be an enemy unto thine enemies, and an adversary unto thine adversaries.**

God tells His children not to fear because there is nothing to fear when God is with you. If you obey God and His Word, you do not need to fear anything. You can walk in strength and courage when you obey God and show Him you are with Him as He is with you, knowing that God is on your side.

Joshua 1:7-9 (KJV)

7 **Only be thou strong and very courageous, that thou mayest observe to do according to all the law, which Moses my servant commanded thee: turn not from it to the right hand or to the left, that thou mayest prosper withersoever thou goest.**

8 This Book of the law shall not depart out of thy mouth; but thou shalt meditate therein day and night, that thou mayest observe to do according to all that is written therein: for then thou shalt make thy way prosperous, and then thou shalt have good success.

9 **Have not I commanded thee? Be strong and of a good courage; be not afraid, neither be thou dismayed: for the Lord thy God is with thee whithersoever thou goest.**

It is important to note that it did not always mean people would have no problems, tough trials, or enemies to face when God was with someone. God being with them meant He would be a very present help in the time of trouble and help deliver them from whatever enemy or trial they were facing. In many cases, the problem, tough trial, or the enemy they were facing was the very thing God used to promote them to remarkable success. ***THE ATTACK BROUGHT THE BLESSING!***

God also ensured that the enemies of the person He was with knew He was with them. Fear would strike their enemies when they knew God was with them. The unseen God would make His presence known, and their enemies would be afraid of them.

> **2 Chronicles 14:14 (KJV)**
> 14 And they smote all the cities round about Gerar; **for the fear of the Lord came upon them:** and they spoiled all the cities; for there was exceeding much spoil in them.

> **2 Chronicles 17:10 (KJV)**
> 10 **And the fear of the Lord fell upon all the kingdoms of the lands that were round about Judah, so that they made no war against Jehoshaphat.**

> **2 Chronicles 20:29 (KJV)**
> 29 **And the fear of God was on all the kingdoms of those countries, when they had heard that the Lord fought against the enemies of Israel.**

When God is with you, you do not need anything or anyone else because you and God are the majority. God becomes your answer to your every prayer when He is with you. The bottom line is you are special to God, and He will be with you if you will be with Him. God wants to know that He is as special to you as you are to Him and that you are with Him as much as He is with you.

One of the names given to Jesus is **Emmanuel,** which means *God With Us.*

> **Matthew 1:23 (KJV)**
> 23 Behold, a virgin shall be with child, and shall bring forth a son, and they shall call His Name **Emmanuel, which being interpreted is, God with us.**

The Father was with Jesus and anointed Him because Jesus kept the Father's Commandments and proved He was with the Father as much as the Father was with Him.

John 15:10 (KJV)

10 If ye keep my Commandments, **ye shall abide in my love;** even as I have kept my Father's Commandments, **and abide in his love.**

Acts 10:38 (KJV)

38 **How God anointed Jesus of Nazareth with the Holy Ghost and with power:** who went about doing good, and healing all that were oppressed of the devil; **for God was with him.**

One of the most significant passages of Scriptures that reveal the truth of God being with someone if they are with Him is found in 2 Chronicles 15. This passage of Scripture tells the story of King Asa, a powerful king of Israel who loved the Lord. After king Asa defeated a large army, a prophet came to him and prophesied that the Lord would be with him if he were with Him. The prophet also prophesied God would forsake him if King Asa forsook the Lord. Let's read this account together and understand what it meant to be with the Lord in the Old Testament.

2 Chronicles 15:1-19 (KJV)

1 And the Spirit of God came upon Azariah the son of Oded:
2 And he went out to meet Asa, and said unto him, Hear ye me, Asa, and all Judah and Benjamin; **The Lord is with you, while ye be with him; and if ye seek him, he will be found of you; but if ye forsake him, he will forsake you.**
3 Now for a long season Israel hath been without the true God, and without a teaching priest, and without law.
4 But when they in their trouble did turn unto the Lord God of Israel, and sought him, he was found of them.

5 And in those times there was no peace to him that went out, nor to him that came in, but great vexations were upon all the inhabitants of the countries.

6 And nation was destroyed of nation, and city of city: for God did vex them with all adversity.

7 Be ye strong therefore, and let not your hands be weak: for your work shall be rewarded.

8 **And when Asa heard these words, and the prophecy of Oded the prophet, he took courage, and put away the abominable idols out of all the land of Judah and Benjamin, and out of the cities which he had taken from mount Ephraim, and renewed the altar of the Lord, that was before the porch of the Lord.**

9 And he gathered all Judah and Benjamin, and the strangers with them out of Ephraim and Manasseh, and out of Simeon: for they fell to him out of Israel in abundance, **when they saw that the Lord his God was with him.**

10 So they gathered themselves together at Jerusalem in the third month, in the fifteenth year of the reign of Asa.

11 And they offered unto the Lord the same time, of the spoil which they had brought, seven hundred oxen and seven thousand sheep.

12 **And they entered into a covenant to seek the Lord God of their fathers with all their heart and with all their soul;**

13 **That whosoever would not seek the Lord God of Israel should be put to death, whether small or great, whether man or woman.**

14 And they sware unto the Lord with a loud voice, and with shouting, and with trumpets, and with cornets.

15 **And all Judah rejoiced at the oath: for they had sworn with all their heart, and sought him with their whole desire; and he was found of them:** and the Lord gave them rest round about.

16 And also concerning Maachah the mother of Asa the king, he removed her from being queen, because she had made an idol in a grove: and Asa cut down her idol, and stamped it, and burnt it at the brook Kidron.

17 But the high places were not taken away out of Israel: nevertheless the heart of Asa was perfect all his days.

18 And he brought into the house of God the things that his father had dedicated, and that he himself had dedicated, silver, and gold, and vessels.

19 And there was no more war unto the five and thirtieth year of the reign of Asa.

When King Asa heard the prophetic Word of God, he responded by making bold moves with all of Judah to show they were with the Lord. When people saw the Lord was with Asa, they came to him from all over. All of Judah made a public oath to God, and they sought Him with their whole desire, and God was found of them. They even went as far as to say they would kill anyone who did not seek the Lord. These people put God first in their lives and took their commitment to Him seriously.

There are many stories in the Bible where God said He was with someone. Here is a list of people God said He would be with in the Bible:

1. Isaac

2. Jacob

3. Joseph

4. Moses

5. Joshua

6. Gideon

7. Samuel

8. David

9. Solomon

10. Hezekiah

11. Asa

12. Jehoshaphat

13. Jeremiah

14. Mary

15. Jesus

16. Christians

ISAAC

Genesis 26:1-4 (KJV)

1 And there was a famine in the land, beside the first famine that was in the days of Abraham. And Isaac went unto Abimelech king of the Philistines unto Gerar.

2 And the Lord appeared unto him, and said, Go not down into Egypt; dwell in the land which I shall tell thee of:

3 Sojourn in this land, **and I will be with thee,** and will bless thee; for unto thee, and unto thy seed, I will give all these countries, and I will perform the oath which I sware unto Abraham thy father;

4 And I will make thy seed to multiply as the stars of heaven, and will give unto thy seed all these countries; and in thy seed shall all the nations of the earth be blessed;

JACOB

Genesis 26:23-24 (KJV)

23 And he went up from thence to Beersheba.

24 And the Lord appeared unto him the same night, and said, I am the God of Abraham thy father: fear not, **for I am with thee,** and will bless thee, and multiply thy seed for my servant Abraham's sake.

JOSEPH

Genesis 39:1-2 (KJV)

1 And Joseph was brought down to Egypt; and Potiphar, an officer of Pharaoh, captain of the guard, an Egyptian, bought him of the hands of the Ishmeelites, which had brought him down thither.

2 **And the Lord was with Joseph,** and he was a prosperous man; and he was in the house of his master the Egyptian.

MOSES

Exodus 3:11-12 (KJV)

11 And Moses said unto God, Who am I, that I should go unto Pharaoh, and that I should bring forth the children of Israel out of Egypt?

12 And he said, **Certainly I will be with thee;** and this shall be a token unto thee, that I have sent thee: When thou hast brought forth the people out of Egypt, ye shall serve God upon this mountain.

JOSHUA

Deuteronomy 31:7-8 (KJV)

7 And Moses called unto Joshua, and said unto him in the sight of all Israel, Be strong and of a good courage: for thou must go with this people unto the land which the Lord hath

sworn unto their fathers to give them; and thou shalt cause them to inherit it.

8 **And the Lord, he it is that doth go before thee; he will be with thee, he will not fail thee, neither forsake thee:** fear not, neither be dismayed.

Joshua 1:1-9 (KJV)

1 Now after the death of Moses the servant of the Lord it came to pass, that the Lord spake unto Joshua the son of Nun, Moses' minister, saying,

2 Moses my servant is dead; now therefore arise, go over this Jordan, thou, and all this people, unto the land which I do give to them, even to the children of Israel.

3 Every place that the sole of your foot shall tread upon, that have I given unto you, as I said unto Moses.

4 From the wilderness and this Lebanon even unto the great river, the river Euphrates, all the land of the Hittites, and unto the great sea toward the going down of the sun, shall be your coast.

5 There shall not any man be able to stand before thee all the days of thy life: **as I was with Moses, so I will be with thee: I will not fail thee, nor forsake thee.**

6 Be strong and of a good courage: for unto this people shalt thou divide for an inheritance the land, which I sware unto their fathers to give them.

7 Only be thou strong and very courageous, that thou mayest observe to do according to all the law, which Moses my servant commanded thee: turn not from it to the right hand or to the left, that thou mayest prosper withersoever thou goest.

8 This Book of the law shall not depart out of thy mouth; but thou shalt meditate therein day and night, that thou mayest observe to do according to all that is written therein: for then

thou shalt make thy way prosperous, and then thou shalt have good success.

9 Have not I commanded thee? Be strong and of a good courage; be not afraid, neither be thou dismayed: **for the Lord thy God is with thee whithersoever thou goest.**

GIDEON

Judges 6:11-16 (KJV)

11 And there came an angel of the Lord, and sat under an oak which was in Ophrah, that pertained unto Joash the Abiezrite: and his son Gideon threshed wheat by the winepress, to hide it from the Midianites.

12 And the angel of the Lord appeared unto him, and said unto him, **The Lord is with thee, thou mighty man of valour.**

13 And Gideon said unto him, Oh my Lord, **if the Lord be with us, why then is all this befallen us?** and where be all his miracles which our fathers told us of, saying, Did not the Lord bring us up from Egypt? but now the Lord hath forsaken us, and delivered us into the hands of the Midianites.

14 And the Lord looked upon him, and said, Go in this thy might, and thou shalt save Israel from the hand of the Midianites: have not I sent thee?

15 And he said unto him, Oh my Lord, wherewith shall I save Israel? behold, my family is poor in Manasseh, and I am the least in my father's house.

16 And the Lord said unto him, **Surely I will be with thee,** and thou shalt smite the Midianites as one man.

SAMUEL

1 Samuel 3:19-21 (KJV)

19 And Samuel grew, **and the Lord was with him,** and did let none of His Words fall to the ground.

20 And all Israel from Dan even to Beersheba knew that Samuel was established to be a prophet of the Lord.

21 And the Lord appeared again in Shiloh: for the Lord revealed himself to Samuel in Shiloh by the word of the Lord.

DAVID

1 Samuel 18:10-14 (KJV)

10 And it came to pass on the morrow, that the evil spirit from God came upon Saul, and he prophesied in the midst of the house: and David played with his hand, as at other times: and there was a javelin in Saul's hand.

11 And Saul cast the javelin; for he said, I will smite David even to the wall with it. And David avoided out of his presence twice.

12 **And Saul was afraid of David, because the Lord was with him,** and was departed from Saul.

13 Therefore Saul removed him from him, and made him his captain over a thousand; and he went out and came in before the people.

14 And David behaved himself wisely in all his ways; **and the Lord was with him.**

SOLOMON

2 Chronicles 1:1 (KJV)

1 And Solomon the son of David was strengthened in his kingdom, **and the Lord his God was with him,** and magnified him exceedingly.

HEZEKIAH

2 Kings 18:1-7 (KJV)

1 Now it came to pass in the third year of Hoshea son of Elah king of Israel, that Hezekiah the son of Ahaz king of Judah began to reign.

2 Twenty and five years old was he when he began to reign; and he reigned twenty and nine years in Jerusalem. His mother's name also was Abi, the daughter of Zachariah.

3 And he did that which was right in the sight of the Lord, according to all that David his father did.

4 He removed the high places, and brake the images, and cut down the groves, and brake in pieces the brasen serpent that Moses had made: for unto those days the children of Israel did burn incense to it: and he called it Nehushtan.

5 He trusted in the Lord God of Israel; so that after him was none like him among all the kings of Judah, nor any that were before him.

6 For he clave to the Lord, and departed not from following him, but kept his Commandments, which the Lord commanded Moses.

7 **And the Lord was with him;** and he prospered whithersoever he went forth: and he rebelled against the king of Assyria, and served him not.

ASA

2 Chronicles 15:1-8 (KJV)

1 And the Spirit of God came upon Azariah the son of Oded:

2 And he went out to meet Asa, and said unto him, Hear ye me, Asa, and all Judah and Benjamin; **The Lord is with you, while ye be with him; and if ye seek him, he will be found of you; but if ye forsake him, he will forsake you.**

3 Now for a long season Israel hath been without the true God, and without a teaching priest, and without law.

4 But when they in their trouble did turn unto the Lord God of Israel, and sought him, he was found of them.

5 And in those times there was no peace to him that went out, nor to him that came in, but great vexations were upon all the inhabitants of the countries.

6 And nation was destroyed of nation, and city of city: for God did vex them with all adversity.

7 Be ye strong therefore, and let not your hands be weak: for your work shall be rewarded.

8 And when Asa heard these words, and the prophecy of Oded the prophet, he took courage, and put away the abominable idols out of all the land of Judah and Benjamin, and out of the cities which he had taken from mount Ephraim, and renewed the altar of the Lord, that was before the porch of the Lord.

JEHOSHAPHAT

2 Chronicles 17:1-6 (KJV)

1 And Jehoshaphat his son reigned in his stead, and strengthened himself against Israel.

2 And he placed forces in all the fenced cities of Judah, and set garrisons in the land of Judah, and in the cities of Ephraim, which Asa his father had taken.

3 **And the Lord was with Jehoshaphat, because he walked in the first ways of his father David,** and sought not unto Baalim;

4 But sought to the Lord God of his father, and walked in his Commandments, and not after the doings of Israel.

5 Therefore the Lord stablished the kingdom in his hand; and all Judah brought to Jehoshaphat presents; and he had riches and honour in abundance.

6 And his heart was lifted up in the ways of the Lord: moreover he took away the high places and groves out of Judah.

JEREMIAH

Jeremiah 1:4-10 (KJV)

4 Then the word of the Lord came unto me, saying,

5 Before I formed thee in the belly I knew thee; and before thou camest forth out of the womb I sanctified thee, and I ordained thee a prophet unto the nations.

6 Then said I, Ah, Lord God! behold, I cannot speak: for I am a child.

7 But the Lord said unto me, Say not, I am a child: for thou shalt go to all that I shall send thee, and whatsoever I command thee thou shalt speak.

8 Be not afraid of their faces: **for I am with thee to deliver thee, saith the Lord.**

9 Then the Lord put forth his hand, and touched my mouth. And the Lord said unto me, Behold, I have put my words in thy mouth.

10 See, I have this day set thee over the nations and over the kingdoms, to root out, and to pull down, and to destroy, and to throw down, to build, and to plant.

MARY

Luke 1:26-33 (KJV)

26 And in the sixth month the angel Gabriel was sent from God unto a city of Galilee, named Nazareth,

27 To a virgin espoused to a man whose name was Joseph, of the house of David; and the virgin's name was Mary.

28 And the angel came in unto her, and said, Hail, thou that art highly favoured, **the Lord is with thee:** blessed art thou among women.

29 And when she saw him, she was troubled at his saying, and cast in her mind what manner of salutation this should be.

30 And the angel said unto her, Fear not, Mary: for thou hast found favour with God.

31 And, behold, thou shalt conceive in thy womb, and bring forth a son, and shalt call His Name Jesus.

32 He shall be great, and shall be called the Son of the Highest: and the Lord God shall give unto him the throne of his father David:

33 And he shall reign over the house of Jacob for ever; and of his kingdom there shall be no end.

JESUS

Matthew 1:21-23 (KJV)

21 And she shall bring forth a son, and thou shalt call His Name Jesus: for he shall save his people from their sins.

22 Now all this was done, that it might be fulfilled which was spoken of the Lord by the prophet, saying,

23 Behold, a virgin shall be with child, and shall bring forth a son, **and they shall call His Name Emmanuel, which being interpreted is, God with us.**

Acts 10:38 (KJV)

38 How God anointed Jesus of Nazareth with the Holy Ghost and with power: who went about doing good, and healing all that were oppressed of the devil; **for God was with him.**

CHRISTIANS

Matthew 28:18-20 (KJV)

18 And Jesus came and spake unto them, saying, All power is given unto me in heaven and in earth.

19 Go ye therefore, and teach all nations, baptizing them in the Name of the Father, and of the Son, and of the Holy Ghost:

20 Teaching them to observe all things whatsoever I have commanded you: **and, lo, I am with you always, even unto the end of the world. Amen.**

Acts 11:19-21 (KJV)

> 19 Now they which were scattered abroad upon the persecution that arose about Stephen travelled as far as Phenice, and Cyprus, and Antioch, preaching the word to none but unto the Jews only.
>
> 20 And some of them were men of Cyprus and Cyrene, which, when they were come to Antioch, spake unto the Grecians, preaching the Lord Jesus.
>
> 21 **And the hand of the Lord was with them:** and a great number believed, and turned unto the Lord.

Supernatural Security Clearances are given to those with the Lord, and who love Him with all their heart, mind, soul, and strength. If you show that you love God and are committed to obeying His Word, He will honor you and grant you access to His Heavenly Kingdom. God will set you on high and be with you in trouble when you call upon His Name.

Psalm 91:14-16 (KJV)

> 14 Because he hath set his love upon me, therefore will I deliver him: I will set him on high, because he hath known my name.
>
> 15 He shall call upon me, and I will answer him: **I will be with him in trouble;** I will deliver him, and honour him.
>
> 16 With long life will I satisfy him, and shew him my salvation.

When God says He is with someone, this does not mean He is close to them watching what is happening in their life. God is not an innocent bystander watching you in your life troubles when He says He is with you. When God says He is with someone, He is not only near them and watching what is happening in their life, but promises to help them in their time of need. If you are with God and He is with you, you can call upon Him, and He will answer your prayers.

Jeremiah 23:23 (KJV)

> 23 **Am I a God at hand, saith the Lord, and not a God afar off?**

Jeremiah 29:11-13 (KJV)

> 11 For I know the thoughts that I think toward you, saith the Lord, thoughts of peace, and not of evil, to give you an expected end.
>
> 12 **Then shall ye call upon me, and ye shall go and pray unto me, and I will hearken unto you.**
>
> 13 **And ye shall seek me, and find me, when ye shall search for me with all your heart.**

Jeremiah 33:3 (KJV)

> 3 **Call unto me, and I will answer thee, and show thee great and mighty things, which thou knowest not.**

God is a refuge and a very present help in times of trouble.

Psalm 46:1 (KJV)

> 1 **God is our refuge and strength, a very present help in trouble.**

When Jesus walked upon the earth, He revealed that He was **Emmanuel**, God with us. As you read the four Gospels, you can see Jesus helping people in their time of need. When people died, He raised them from the dead. When people were sick, He healed them. If demons were tormenting them, He cast out the demons. He also healed people who were blind and those who could not walk. Jesus was with people and delivered them in their time of need. Jesus was with these people because they repented of their sins and called upon God to help them. The preaching of the Gospel is the good news that God will be there to help you if you repent and call upon the Name of the Lord.

Matthew 4:23-24 (KJV)

> 23 And Jesus went about all Galilee, teaching in their synagogues, **and preaching the Gospel of the kingdom**, and healing all manner of sickness and all manner of disease among the people.
>
> 24 And his fame went throughout all Syria: and they brought unto him all sick people that were taken with divers diseases and torments, and those which were possessed with devils, and those which were lunatick, and those that had the palsy; **and he healed them.**

God the Father, by His Spirit, was there to help people through the ministry of Jesus Christ. We can see God helping people and being there for His people throughout the Bible. We can also see Him not being there for people who rejected Him and His Word. God is with those who are with Him, and He is not there for those who are not with Him. However, God may not be with someone when they are not with Him, but if they repent of their wicked ways and call upon Him, He promises to be there for them, but they must repent of their rebellion and lack of commitment to God.

In conclusion, God wants to show you He is with you and will grant you a *Supernatural Security Clearance,* but you must show Him that you are with Him. If you show God you are with Him as much as He is with you, He will show up in your life repeatedly in a powerful way. God will also make your enemies His enemies. When you are with God, you do not need to fear anything because God will be there for you in your time of need. If the Lord is with someone, they are one of the most blessed, favored, respected, honored, and feared people on the planet.

CHAPTER 13
THE CHARGE OF THE LORD

Every *Supernatural Security Clearance* comes with a charge from the Lord. The charge of the Lord is a mandate, responsibility, duty, personal burden, and assignment placed on someone God raises in a position of authority that He sends on a mission. When someone is given a charge from the Lord, they are being entrusted with a responsibility to safeguard holy items, protect sacred places, keep the commands of God, preach the Word of God, watch over God's people, and defeat God's enemies. Anointed Leaders in both the Old and New Testaments were commanded to keep the charge of the Lord. In this chapter, we will discover people in the Bible that were given a *Supernatural Security Clearance* to keep the charge of the Lord.

In the Old Testament, the charge of the Lord was given to someone God anointed to be a prophet, priest, judge, or king. Different charges of the Lord were commanded by God depending upon what they were called to do. In the New Testament, charges of the Lord concerned preaching God's Word, protecting God's people, and fulfilling the *High Calling* of God.

Once the charge of the Lord was placed upon someone, they would be blessed if they kept it, but there were consequences if they did not keep the charge of the Lord. If someone did not keep the charge of the Lord, they would be punished, which could also include a penalty of death. A charge from the Lord is not to be taken lightly. Keeping the charge of the Lord is a sacred high calling that comes with great responsibility.

Here is a list of some of the people God gave a charge to in the Bible:

1. Adam and Eve

2. Abraham

3. Jacob

4. Moses and Aaron

5. Levites

6. Kohathites

7. Aaron and His Sons

8. Judges

9. Joshua

10. Solomon

11. Angels

12. Joshua, the High Priest

13. The Church of Thessalonica

14. Timothy

15. The Rich

Adam and Eve

Adam and Eve were the first of humankind to receive a charge from the Lord. They were charged with keeping the Garden of Eden and not eating from the Tree of Knowledge of Good and Evil. They ended up eating from the Tree of Knowledge of Good and Evil. The death process began, and they spiritually died when they ate from the Tree of Knowledge of Good and Evil. They also physically died years later, but they were originally created to live forever.

Genesis 2:15-17 (KJV)

15 And the Lord God took the man, and put him into the garden of Eden to dress it and to keep it.

16 And the Lord God commanded the man, saying, Of every tree of the garden thou mayest freely eat:

17 **But of the tree of the knowledge of good and evil, thou shalt not eat of it: for in the day that thou eatest thereof thou shalt surely die.**

Adam was given the authority over the whole earth as the first created man. He relinquished his authority to the devil when he ate of the Tree of the Knowledge of Good and Evil. Adam was supposed to protect and father the earth with the help of God. When he disobeyed God's charge to not eat of the Tree of the Knowledge of Good and Evil, he exposed the entire world to the evil forces of the devil. Adam did not protect the world when he disobeyed God and ate from the Tree of the Knowledge of Good and Evil. Because Adam did not keep the charge of the Lord, he lost his *Supernatural Security Clearance,* was kicked out of the Garden, and eventually died. Adam also brought many curses upon himself and the entire world.

Genesis 3:9-19 (KJV)

9 And the Lord God called unto Adam, and said unto him, Where art thou?

10 And he said, I heard thy voice in the garden, and I was afraid, because I was naked; and I hid myself.

11 And he said, Who told thee that thou wast naked? **Hast thou eaten of the tree, whereof I commanded thee that thou shouldest not eat?**

12 And the man said, The woman whom thou gavest to be with me, she gave me of the tree, and I did eat.

13 And the Lord God said unto the woman, What is this that thou hast done? And the woman said, The serpent beguiled me, and I did eat.

14 And the Lord God said unto the serpent, Because thou hast done this, thou art cursed above all cattle, and above every beast of the field; upon thy belly shalt thou go, and dust shalt thou eat all the days of thy life:

15 And I will put enmity between thee and the woman, and between thy seed and her seed; it shall bruise thy head, and thou shalt bruise his heel.

16 Unto the woman he said, I will greatly multiply thy sorrow and thy conception; in sorrow thou shalt bring forth children; and thy desire shall be to thy husband, and he shall rule over thee.

17 **And unto Adam he said, Because thou hast hearkened unto the voice of thy wife, and hast eaten of the tree, of which I commanded thee, saying, Thou shalt not eat of it: cursed is the ground for thy sake; in sorrow shalt thou eat of it all the days of thy life;**

18 **Thorns also and thistles shall it bring forth to thee; and thou shalt eat the herb of the field;**

19 In the sweat of thy face shalt thou eat bread, till thou return unto the ground; for out of it wast thou taken: for dust thou art, and unto dust shalt thou return.

Adam was kicked out of the Garden of Eden, so he could not partake of the Tree of Life and live forever.

Genesis 3:22-24 (KJV)

22 And the Lord God said, Behold, the man is become as one of us, to know good and evil: and now, lest he put forth his hand, and take also of the tree of life, and eat, and live for ever:

23 Therefore the Lord God sent him forth from the garden of Eden, to till the ground from whence he was taken.

24 **So he drove out the man; and he placed at the east of the garden of Eden Cherubims, and a flaming sword which turned every way, to keep the way of the tree of life.**

Abraham

Abraham was another man that God entrusted with a charge from the Lord. Abraham is known as the father of faith. Abraham obeyed God to leave his family and homeland to go to an unknown land. Abraham obeyed the voice of the Lord, not knowing where he was going. Abraham was also called the friend of God and had great faith in God. Abraham was obedient and willing to obey God and offer his son Isaac as a sacrifice on an altar when commanded by God. He believed God could raise his son from the dead if he did this; however, this was just a test, and God ended up not having Abraham offer up his son, but a ram instead. Abraham showed his willingness to obey God in anything He commanded him to do, and he is an excellent example of a man who kept the charge of the Lord.

Genesis 26:5 (KJV)

5 Because that Abraham obeyed my voice, and **kept my charge**, my Commandments, my statutes, and my laws.

Jacob

Jacob, the grandson of Abraham, was given a charge from his father Isaac not to take any wife of the daughters of Canaan. Jacob was sent to his uncle Laban to find a wife. Jacob ended up marrying two of Laban's daughters and became the father of the twelve tribes of Israel. Jacob kept his charge and was faithful to God.

Genesis 28:1-7 (KJV)

1 And Isaac called Jacob, and blessed him, **and charged him,** and said unto him, Thou shalt not take a wife of the daughters of Canaan.

2 Arise, go to Padanaram, to the house of Bethuel thy mother's father; and take thee a wife from thence of the daughers of Laban thy mother's brother.

3 And God Almighty bless thee, and make thee fruitful, and multiply thee, that thou mayest be a multitude of people;

4 And give thee the blessing of Abraham, to thee, and to thy seed with thee; that thou mayest inherit the land wherein thou art a stranger, which God gave unto Abraham.

5 And Isaac sent away Jacob: and he went to Padanaram unto Laban, son of Bethuel the Syrian, the brother of Rebekah, Jacob's and Esau's mother.

6 When Esau saw that Isaac had blessed Jacob, and sent him away to Padanaram, to take him a wife from thence; **and that as he blessed him he gave him a charge, saying, Thou shalt not take a wife of the daughers of Canaan;**

7 And that Jacob obeyed his father and his mother, and was gone to Padanaram;

Moses and Aaron

Moses and Aaron were given a charge of the Lord to bring the children of Israel out of Egypt. God used Moses and Aaron to bring down ten plagues upon the land of Egypt when Pharoah refused to let the people of God go. Moses and Aaron remained faithful to God, fulfilled their charge, and successfully brought the children of Israel out of the land of Egypt. The charge of the Lord was also given to Pharaoh to let God's people go, and he kept disobeying God. God ended up killing his firstborn son because he was not keeping the charge of the Lord. Death comes upon those who do not keep the charge of the Lord.

> **Exodus 6:13 (KJV)**
> 13 **And the Lord spake unto Moses and unto Aaron, and gave them a charge unto the children of Israel, and unto Pharaoh king of Egypt, to bring the children of Israel out of the land of Egypt.**

Levites

The Levites were given a charge from the Lord to guard and protect the Tabernacle of Moses. They pitched their tents around the Tabernacle and were charged to guard it and ensure no stranger came near it. Any stranger who came near the Tabernacle of Moses was put to death. God's Tabernacle had to be guarded and protected. The Levites were given a *Supernatural Security Clearance* and charged to protect and keep the Tabernacle of Moses.

> **Numbers 1:47-54 (KJV)**
> 47 But the Levites after the tribe of their fathers were not numbered among them.
> 48 For the Lord had spoken unto Moses, saying,
> 49 Only thou shalt not number the tribe of Levi, neither take the sum of them among the children of Israel:

50 **But thou shalt appoint the Levites over the tabernacle of testimony, and over all the vessels thereof, and over all things that belong to it: they shall bear the tabernacle, and all the vessels thereof; and they shall minister unto it, and shall encamp round about the tabernacle.**

51 And when the tabernacle setteth forward, the Levites shall take it down: and when the tabernacle is to be pitched, the Levites shall set it up: **and the stranger that cometh nigh shall be put to death.**

52 And the children of Israel shall pitch their tents, every man by his own camp, and every man by his own standard, throughout their hosts.

53 But the Levites shall pitch round about the tabernacle of testimony, that there be no wrath upon the congregation of the children of Israel: **and the Levites shall keep the charge of the tabernacle of testimony.**

54 And the children of Israel did according to all that the Lord commanded Moses, so did they.

Kohathites

The Levitical family of the Kohathites was given a charge of the Lord to maintain and protect the Ark of the Covenant, Table of Shewbread, Golden Candlestick, Altars, Vessels of the Sanctuary, The Hanging, and all the services in the Tabernacle of Moses.

Numbers 3:29-31 (KJV)

29 The families of the sons of Kohath shall pitch on the side of the tabernacle southward.

30 And the chief of the house of the father of the families of the Kohathites shall be Elizaphan the son of Uzziel.

31 **And their charge shall be the ark, and the table, and the candlestick, and the altars, and the vessels of the sanctuary**

wherewith they minister, and the hanging, and all the service thereof.

Aaron and His Sons

Aaron and his sons were given a charge to be chief over the Levites and oversee those that kept the charge of the Lord concerning the Tabernacle of Moses.

Numbers 3:32 (KJV)

32 And Eleazar the son of Aaron the priest shall be chief over the chief of the Levites, **and have the oversight of them that keep the charge of the sanctuary.**

Judges

Moses gave a charge to appointed judges to judge righteously and not have any respect of persons in judgment. They were charged to hear all cases, small and great, and not to fear men's faces because the judgment was of God.

Deuteronomy 1:16-18 (KJV)

16 **And I charged your judges at that time,** saying, Hear the causes between your brethren, and judge righteously between every man and his brother, and the stranger that is with him.

17 Ye shall not respect persons in judgment; but ye shall hear the small as well as the great; ye shall not be afraid of the face of man; for the judgment is God's: and the cause that is too hard for you, bring it unto me, and I will hear it.

18 And I commanded you at that time all the things which ye should do.

Joshua

Moses gave a charge to Joshua, his minister before he was commissioned to lead the children of Israel into the Promised Land after Moses died. Joshua was charged to be strong and have courage while bringing the children of Israel into the Promised Land.

> ### Deuteronomy 31:14-15 (KJV)
> 14 And the Lord said unto Moses, Behold, thy days approach that thou must die: **call Joshua,** and present yourselves in the tabernacle of the congregation, **that I may give him a charge.** And Moses and Joshua went, and presented themselves in the tabernacle of the congregation.
> 15 And the Lord appeared in the tabernacle in a pillar of a cloud: and the pillar of the cloud stood over the door of the tabernacle.

> ### Deuteronomy 31:23 (KJV)
> 23 **And he gave Joshua the son of Nun a charge,** and said, Be strong and of a good courage: for thou shalt bring the children of Israel into the land which I sware unto them: and I will be with thee.

Solomon

King David gave a command to his son Solomon to keep the charge of the Lord. King David said that if Solomon kept the charge of the Lord and continued in God's Word, He would prosper him in everything he did. The Lord also promised that if David's children kept the charge of the Lord, God would keep an offspring of David on the throne. We know through Biblical history that many of David's royal offspring failed to keep the charge of the Lord, but Jesus was faithful to keep the charge of the Lord and will sit on the throne of David throughout all eternity in His kingdom.

1 Kings 2:1-4 (KJV)

> 1 Now the days of David drew nigh that he should die; **and he charged Solomon his son,** saying,
>
> 2 I go the way of all the earth: be thou strong therefore, and shew thyself a man;
>
> 3 **And keep the charge of the Lord thy God,** to walk in his ways, to keep his statutes, and his Commandments, and his judgments, and his testimonies, as it is written in the law of Moses, that thou mayest prosper in all that thou doest, and whithersoever thou turnest thyself:
>
> 4 That the Lord may continue His Word which he spake concerning me, saying, If thy children take heed to their way, to walk before me in truth with all their heart and with all their soul, there shall not fail thee (said he) a man on the throne of Israel.

Angels

The angels of God were given a charge from the Lord to protect those who dwell in the *Secret Place* of the Most High.

Psalm 91:1-12 (KJV)

> 1 He that dwelleth in the secret place of the most High shall abide under the shadow of the Almighty.
>
> 2 I will say of the Lord, He is my refuge and my fortress: my God; in him will I trust.
>
> 3 Surely he shall deliver thee from the snare of the fowler, and from the noisome pestilence.
>
> 4 He shall cover thee with his feathers, and under his wings shalt thou trust: his truth shall be thy shield and buckler.
>
> 5 Thou shalt not be afraid for the terror by night; nor for the arrow that flieth by day;
>
> 6 Nor for the pestilence that walketh in darkness; nor for the destruction that wasteth at noonday.

7 A thousand shall fall at thy side, and ten thousand at thy right hand; but it shall not come nigh thee.

8 Only with thine eyes shalt thou behold and see the reward of the wicked.

9 Because thou hast made the Lord, which is my refuge, even the most High, thy habitation;

10 There shall no evil befall thee, neither shall any plague come nigh thy dwelling.

11 **For he shall give his angels charge over thee,** to keep thee in all thy ways.

12 They shall bear thee up in their hands, lest thou dash thy foot against a stone.

Joshua, the High Priest

Joshua, the high priest in the Book of Zechariah, was given a charge of the Lord and was given promises if he walked in God's ways.

Zechariah 3:6-7 (KJV)

6 And the angel of the Lord protested unto Joshua, saying,

7 Thus saith the Lord of hosts; If thou wilt walk in my ways, **and if thou wilt keep my charge,** then thou shalt also judge my house, and shalt also keep my courts, and I will give thee places to walk among these that stand by.

The Church of Thessalonica

The Apostle Paul charged the Church of Thessalonica to walk worthy of God, who called them to His kingdom and glory.

1 Thessalonians 2:11-12 (KJV)

11 As ye know how we exhorted and comforted **and charged every one of you,** as a father doth his children,

12 That ye would walk worthy of God, who hath called you unto his kingdom and glory.

Paul also charged the Church of Thessalonica that his letter was to be read to all the holy brothers in Christ.

1 Thessalonians 5:27 (KJV)

27 **I charge you by the Lord** that this epistle be read unto all the holy brethren.

Timothy

The Apostle Paul charged his son in the faith, Timothy, to war a good warfare by the prophecies that went before him. He was also charged to hold the faith and a good conscience.

1 Timothy 1:18-20 (KJV)

18 **This charge I commit unto thee, son Timothy,** according to the prophecies which went before on thee, that thou by them mightest war a good warfare;

19 Holding faith, and a good conscience; which some having put away concerning faith have made shipwreck:

20 Of whom is Hymenaeus and Alexander; whom I have delivered unto Satan, that they may learn not to blaspheme.

Paul also charged Timothy to preach the Word in season and out of season.

2 Timothy 4:1-5 (KJV)

1 **I charge thee therefore before God, and the Lord Jesus Christ**, who shall judge the quick and the dead at his appearing and his kingdom;

2 **Preach the word; be instant in season, out of season;** reprove, rebuke, exhort with all long suffering and doctrine.

3 For the time will come when they will not endure sound doctrine; but after their own lusts shall they heap to themselves teachers, having itching ears;

4 And they shall turn away their ears from the truth, and shall be turned unto fables.

5 But watch thou in all things, endure afflictions, do the work of an evangelist, make full proof of thy ministry.

The Rich

The rich were charged not to be high-minded or trust in uncertain riches but in the living God. They were also commanded to be rich in good works and give to others.

1 Timothy 6:17-19 (KJV)

17 **Charge them that are rich in this world,** that they be not highminded, nor trust in uncertain riches, but in the living God, who giveth us richly all things to enjoy;

18 That they do good, that they be rich in good works, ready to distribute, willing to communicate;

19 Laying up in store for themselves a good foundation against the time to come, that they may lay hold on eternal life.

From all these examples found in the Scriptures, we can see the charge of the Lord is vital for anyone granted a *Supernatural Security Clearance.* Every *Supernatural Security Clearance* from God comes with a mandate. People in the Bible were not anointed just to do mighty works of the Holy Spirit, but instead, they were anointed to keep the charge of the Lord. The Lord is looking for people He can entrust with this honor. Keeping the charge of the Lord is the highest honor God can bestow upon a man or woman. You must be faithful and diligent to keep the charge of the Lord.

In conclusion, we can see from God's Holy Word the responsibility and importance of keeping the charge of the Lord. God is looking for a mature breed of people of God who can be trusted with His most sacred locations, spiritual weapons, and top secrets. All *Supernatural Security Clearances* come with commands to keep and holy things to guard. Those who are faithful will keep the charge of the Lord and protect the sacred things of God. They will not act irresponsibly with God's kingdom, people, secrets, or treasures. Anyone granted the privilege and opportunity from God to be given a *Supernatural Security Clearance* and charge of the Lord needs to guard it with their life.

CHAPTER 14
THE HIGH CALLING OF GOD

God has a Heavenly *High Calling* for those willing to pay the price to be a part of His kingdom. When Jesus was on the earth, He preached a message of total commitment with tremendous rewards. The stakes could not be higher for anyone seeking to walk in a powerful anointing on this earth, be near God and live forever in His eternal kingdom. Only those who take up their cross daily, deny themselves and live for God will be given a *Supernatural Security Clearance* and granted access to the Heavenly city of Jerusalem.

If you are to access God's *High Calling*, you must be willing to leave everything behind and follow Christ with utter abandonment of self.

Philippians 3:13-15 (KJV)
13 Brethren, I count not myself to have apprehended: but this one thing I do, forgetting those things which are behind, and reaching forth unto those things which are before,
14 **I press toward the mark for the prize of the high calling of God in Christ Jesus.**

15 Let us therefore, as many as be perfect, be thus minded: and if in any thing ye be otherwise minded, God shall reveal even this unto you.

There could be nothing more valuable in this life than serving Christ and being a part of His kingdom. Jesus said the kingdom of God was so valuable that it was like a treasure hidden in a field. The person who found this treasure knew its value and sold everything to buy that field.

Matthew 13:44 (KJV)

44 Again, the kingdom of heaven is like unto treasure hid in a field; the which when a man hath found, he hideth, **and for joy thereof goeth and selleth all that he hath, and buyeth that field.**

Jesus also said that the kingdom of God was like a pearl of great price, and a merchantman, when he found that pearl, he sold everything he had to buy the pearl of great price.

Matthew 13:45-46 (KJV)

45 Again, the kingdom of heaven is like unto a merchant man, seeking goodly pearls:
46 Who, when he had found one pearl of great price, **went and sold all that he had, and bought it.**

These two examples serve as the mentality we should have concerning the kingdom of God. There is nothing more important you could do in this life than to accept Christ into your heart and serve in His kingdom. When Jesus was on this earth, He was on a secret mission to find people who would love God with all their hearts and value Him and His kingdom more than anything else. The disciples of the New Testament knew there was something special about Jesus and left everything to follow Him. Peter, James, and John left their fishing careers at a moment's notice at the beckoning call of Jesus. No one was ever the same when they encountered the Son of God. Jesus left an indelible impression on everyone He met.

Religious leaders hated Him because He opposed everything they stood for. However, the common folk loved Jesus and saw the beauty of who He was and what He was offering them. Jesus was offering people a new chance at life. He was showing people a new way to live, and if they chose this new way to live, He would grant them access to His Heavenly Kingdom. Jesus was also displaying mighty miracles for those who had faith.

Jesus offered people an opportunity to be a part of His mission to reveal His kingdom to others and gain *a Supernatural Security Clearance*. A *Supernatural Security Clearance* not only grants you access to God's Heavenly Kingdom in the future but grants you access to the kingdom of God here and now.

The kingdom of God message was the main message that Jesus preached, and Jesus expected people to abandon everything to be a part of it. Jesus also needed fellow workers to help Him preach His message. This was the *High Calling* of God.

> **Luke 9:59-62 (KJV)**
> 59 And he said unto another, Follow me. But he said, Lord, suffer me first to go and bury my father.
> 60 **Jesus said unto him, Let the dead bury their dead: but go thou and preach the kingdom of God.**
> 61 And another also said, Lord, I will follow thee; but let me first go bid them farewell, which are at home at my house.
> 62 **And Jesus said unto him, No man, having put his hand to the plough, and looking back, is fit for the kingdom of God.**

Jesus knew the value of the kingdom of God and what He was offering people even when they did not fully realize it. It was not every day that people were given the opportunity to be with Jesus and help in spreading the good news of the Gospel. The kingdom of God is an opportunity of a lifetime. Why would anyone choose this life over God's life for them? It does not matter how much money you have; it will never compare to the opportunity that Jesus offers to those who will be a part of His kingdom.

Jesus offered people the opportunity to leave their mundane lives and be a part of His remarkable life and dynamic kingdom. Once a rich young ruler came to Jesus asking what he must do to inherit eternal life. This rich young ruler must have known there was more to this life. Jesus made this rich young ruler an offer to follow Him, but he had to sell all he had and give to the poor to follow Christ.

This rich young ruler foolishly chose his riches rather than accept the *High Calling* that Jesus offered him. Suppose this rich young ruler had taken up the offer of Christ. He may have been chosen to replace Judas Iscariot as one of the twelve apostles. We do not know the destiny in God he would have had, but we do know it would have been far greater than anything this world had to offer.

Mark 10:17-27 (KJV)

17 And when he was gone forth into the way, there came one running, and kneeled to him, and asked him, Good Master, what shall I do that I may inherit eternal life?
18 And Jesus said unto him, Why callest thou me good? there is none good but one, that is, God.
19 Thou knowest the Commandments, Do not commit adultery, Do not kill, Do not steal, Do not bear false witness, Defraud not, Honour thy father and mother.

20 And he answered and said unto him, Master, all these have I observed from my youth.

21 **Then Jesus beholding him loved him, and said unto him, One thing thou lackest: go thy way, sell whatsoever thou hast, and give to the poor, and thou shalt have treasure in heaven: and come, take up the cross, and follow me.**

22 And he was sad at that saying, and went away grieved: for he had great possessions.

23 And Jesus looked round about, and saith unto his disciples, How hardly shall they that have riches enter into the kingdom of God!

24 And the disciples were astonished at His words. But Jesus answereth again, and saith unto them, Children, how hard is it for them that trust in riches to enter into the kingdom of God!

25 It is easier for a camel to go through the eye of a needle, than for a rich man to enter into the kingdom of God.

26 And they were astonished out of measure, saying among themselves, Who then can be saved?

27 And Jesus looking upon them saith, With men it is impossible, but not with God: for with God all things are possible.

This rich young ruler is now dead, and all his possessions belong to someone else or were destroyed through time. What would this rich young ruler give to go back and make a different decision? Jesus offered him treasures in Heaven. This rich young ruler could have been granted a *Supernatural Security Clearance* to walk with Jesus while He was on the earth and then live eternally with God where the true treasures of Heaven are found.

Jesus only came to this earth once to live as a man for 33 years. Jesus' ministry started when He was around thirty, and He died on the cross when He was thirty-three. People only had a few years to make big decisions for God before Jesus went back to Heaven. The rich young ruler only had a short window of time, and he chose his temporary earthly treasures over eternal treasures in Heaven. Still, just because this rich young ruler refused the offer of Christ, there were some like Peter who gave up everything to be with Jesus. Peter is now living in his eternal inheritance with Christ in the Heavenly Kingdom of God.

> **Mark 10:28-31 (KJV)**
> 28 **Then Peter began to say unto him, Lo, we have left all, and have followed thee.**
> 29 And Jesus answered and said, Verily I say unto you, There is no man that hath left house, or brethren, or sisters, or father, or mother, or wife, or children, or lands, for my sake, and the Gospel's,
> 30 But he shall receive an hundredfold now in this time, houses, and brethren, and sisters, and mothers, and children, and lands, with persecutions; and in the world to come eternal life.
> 31 But many that are first shall be last; and the last first.

Jesus will soon return to earth on a white horse to judge the world. You cannot let your opportunity to press into the *High Calling* of God fall by the wayside. *Supernatural Security Clearances* are not easy to come by and will cost you everything to be granted one. God is looking for those who will respond to His golden opportunity to be a part of His kingdom.

God's *High Calling* will come with an assignment for you to do while on this earth. If you are faithful to fulfill that assignment, you will be given your eternal assignment when you die and go to Heaven. The whole goal in this life is to find the will of God and faithfully do whatever God asks you to do. Those who faithfully serve God in this life will hear God say on Judgement Day; *"Well done, good and faithful servant: you have been faithful over a few things, I will make you ruler over many things: enter into the joy of thy Lord."*

Matthew 25:14-30 (KJV)

14 For the kingdom of heaven is as a man travelling into a far country, who called his own servants, and delivered unto them his goods.

15 And unto one he gave five talents, to another two, and to another one; to every man according to his several ability; and straightway took his journey.

16 Then he that had received the five talents went and traded with the same, and made them other five talents.

17 And likewise he that had received two, he also gained other two.

18 But he that had received one went and digged in the earth, and hid his lord's money.

19 After a long time the lord of those servants cometh, and reckoneth with them.

20 And so he that had received five talents came and brought other five talents, saying, Lord, thou deliveredst unto me five talents: behold, I have gained beside them five talents more.

21 **His lord said unto him, Well done, thou good and faithful servant: thou hast been faithful over a few things, I will make thee ruler over many things: enter thou into the joy of thy lord.**

22 He also that had received two talents came and said, Lord, thou deliveredst unto me two talents: behold, I have gained two other talents beside them.

23 **His lord said unto him, Well done, good and faithful servant; thou hast been faithful over a few things, I will make thee ruler over many things: enter thou into the joy of thy lord.**

24 Then he which had received the one talent came and said, Lord, I knew thee that thou art an hard man, reaping where thou hast not sown, and gathering where thou hast not strawed:

25 And I was afraid, and went and hid thy talent in the earth: lo, there thou hast that is thine.

26 His lord answered and said unto him, Thou wicked and slothful servant, thou knewest that I reap where I sowed not, and gather where I have not strawed:

27 Thou oughtest therefore to have put my money to the exchangers, and then at my coming I should have received mine own with usury.

28 Take therefore the talent from him, and give it unto him which hath ten talents.

29 For unto every one that hath shall be given, and he shall have abundance: but from him that hath not shall be taken away even that which he hath.

30 And cast ye the unprofitable servant into outer darkness: there shall be weeping and gnashing of teeth.

God calls different people for different assignments while they are on the earth. It is crucial everyone finds what they are called to do and faithfully serve God while they are on this earth waiting for the return of Christ. God may call you to a five-fold position, or He may call you to serve in a local Church in some capacity. Whatever He calls you to do, remain faithful, and you will be rewarded.

The whole goal in this life is to put God first and be willing to leave anything and anyone behind if God makes you a kingdom offer. Every person that God used in the Bible was living their life until someone walked by and threw a mantle on them, and they left everything to accept God's *High Calling*.

Moses was tending sheep and saw a burning bush. He responded to God, who was talking in the burning bush and became the deliverer of Israel from the hand of Pharoah. David responded to the prophet Samuel, who anointed him to be king. Elisha responded to Elijah when Elijah threw his mantle on him by leaving everything. Peter left his fishing career and followed Christ. The other apostles of Jesus also left everything on a moment's notice to follow Christ.

History is filled with people of God who left everything to follow God and be a part of His kingdom. History is also filled with people who did nothing and did not accept God's offer. Only in eternity will we see those who sacrificed everything, put God first, and followed Him wholeheartedly.

When you look at this life, it is very short compared to eternity. We can only make tough decisions to serve God in this life. Once you are dead, it is over; you no longer have a chance to make big decisions for God. Being a Christian does not mean everything will be easy. It will be challenging, and you might have to be willing to be a martyr for Christ. God is looking for those who are not afraid to serve Him and obey Him. The choice is yours to make. Will you choose the Lord and His **High Calling**, or will you choose your own mundane life?

> **Deuteronomy 30:19 (KJV)**
> 19 I call heaven and earth to record this day against you, **that I have set before you life and death, blessing and cursing: therefore choose life,** that both thou and thy seed may live:

I also want to add that there will be Christians who barely make it into Heaven. I don't want to be one of those Christians, and I hope you don't want to either. I assume everyone reading this book wants something more in their walk with God during this life. In the parable of the sower sows the Word, Jesus revealed that there would be some who received a hundred-fold harvest of the kingdom of God. While others only received thirty or sixty-fold harvests of God's kingdom.

Matthew 13:23 (KJV)

23 But he that received seed into the good ground is he that heareth the word, and understandeth it; **which also beareth fruit, and bringeth forth, some an hundredfold, some sixty, some thirty.**

This parable reveals higher levels at reaching into the *High Calling* of God. God has higher levels of anointing and *Supernatural Security Clearances* in His kingdom. It all depends on people's commitment levels as to what they will attain in this life and be rewarded in the next life. Not everyone will be rewarded the same when they stand before the Judgment Seat of Christ.

2 Corinthians 5:10-11 (KJV)

10 **For we must all appear before the judgment seat of Christ; that every one may receive the things done in his body, according to that he hath done, whether it be good or bad.**
11 Knowing therefore the terror of the Lord, we persuade men; but we are made manifest unto God; and I trust also are made manifest in your consciences.

1 Corinthians 3:11-15 (KJV)

11 For other foundation can no man lay than that is laid, which is Jesus Christ.
12 Now if any man build upon this foundation gold, silver, precious stones, wood, hay, stubble;
13 **Every man's work shall be made manifest: for the day shall declare it, because it shall be revealed by fire; and the fire shall try every man's work of what sort it is.**

14 If any man's work abide which he hath built thereupon, he shall receive a reward.

15 If any man's work shall be burned, he shall suffer loss: but he himself shall be saved; yet so as by fire.

In the next life, Jesus is going to give people different crowns based on what they did in this life. Here is a list of those crowns:

1. Crown of Glory

2. Crown of Knowledge

3. Crown of Righteousness

4. Incorruptible Crown

5. Crown of Rejoicing

6. Crown of Life

Crown of Glory

The Crown of Glory is given to those who listen to wisdom and understanding from God. Those who listen to the wisdom of God become wise and will be crowned with a Crown of Glory. The Crown of Glory is also given to leaders of God's Church who are examples of how the believer should live, and they don't lord their position over God's people. The Lord of hosts is the Crown of Glory.

Proverbs 4:7-9 (KJV)

7 Wisdom is the principal thing; therefore get wisdom: and with all thy getting get understanding.

8 Exalt her, and she shall promote thee: she shall bring thee to honour, when thou dost embrace her.

9 She shall give to thine head an ornament of grace: a **crown of glory** shall she deliver to thee.

Isaiah 28:5-6 (KJV)

5 In that day shall the Lord of hosts be for a **crown of glory**, and for a diadem of beauty, unto the residue of his people,

6 And for a spirit of judgment to him that sitteth in judgment, and for strength to them that turn the battle to the gate.

1 Peter 5:1-4 (KJV)

1 The elders which are among you I exhort, who am also an elder, and a witness of the sufferings of Christ, and also a partaker of the glory that shall be revealed:

2 Feed the flock of God which is among you, taking the oversight thereof, not by constraint, but willingly; not for filthy lucre, but of a ready mind;

3 Neither as being lords over God's heritage, but being examples to the flock.

4 And when the chief Shepherd shall appear, ye shall receive a **crown of glory** that fadeth not away.

Crown of Knowledge

The prudent are crowned with knowledge. The word *prudent* means who is humble and does not flaunt their knowledge and takes no offense at insults. A prudent person takes careful thought of their ways and thinks before taking action. They also see and avoid danger.

Proverbs 14:18 (KJV)

18 The simple inherit folly: **but the prudent are crowned with knowledge.**

Crown of Righteousness

The Crown of Righteousness is given to those who stay faithful to fight the good fight of faith, finish their course and keep the faith just like the Apostle Paul did in his life while serving the Lord before going to Heaven.

2 Timothy 4:7-8 (KJV)

> 7 I have fought a good fight, I have finished my course, I have kept the faith:
>
> 8 Henceforth there is laid up for me a **crown of righteousness**, which the Lord, the righteous judge, shall give me at that day: and not to me only, but unto all them also that love his appearing.

Incorruptible Crown

The Incorruptible Crown is a crown that never fades away. Earthly crowns are corruptible, and will all be destroyed, but an Incorruptible Crown lasts throughout eternity. Those who win in this life by serving the Lord and fulfilling their *High Calling* will be given an Incorruptible Crown.

1 Corinthians 9:24-27 (KJV)

> 24 Know ye not that they which run in a race run all, but one receiveth the prize? So run, that ye may obtain.
>
> 25 And every man that striveth for the mastery is temperate in all things. **Now they do it to obtain a corruptible crown; but we an incorruptible.**
>
> 26 I therefore so run, not as uncertainly; so fight I, not as one that beateth the air:
>
> 27 But I keep under my body, and bring it into subjection: lest that by any means, when I have preached to others, I myself should be a castaway.

Crown of Rejoicing

The Crown of Rejoicing is the people you minister to in this life, and you help them make it into the presence of the Lord when He appears.

1 Thessalonians 2:18-20 (KJV)

18 Wherefore we would have come unto you, even I Paul, once and again; but Satan hindered us.

19 For what is our hope, or joy, or **crown of rejoicing**? Are not even ye in the presence of our Lord Jesus Christ at his coming?

20 For ye are our glory and joy.

Crown of Life

A Crown of Life is given to those who endure and say no to temptation, just like Jesus endured the temptations of the devil in the wilderness. The Crown of Life is also given to those who are faithful unto death during days of tribulation.

James 1:12 (KJV)

12 Blessed is the man that endureth temptation: for when he is tried, he shall receive the **crown of life**, which the Lord hath promised to them that love him.

Revelation 2:9-11 (KJV)

9 I know thy works, and tribulation, and poverty, (but thou art rich) and I know the blasphemy of them which say they are Jews, and are not, but are the synagogue of Satan.

10 Fear none of those things which thou shalt suffer: behold, the devil shall cast some of you into prison, that ye may be tried; and ye shall have tribulation ten days: be thou faithful unto death, **and I will give thee a crown of life.**

11 He that hath an ear, let him hear what the Spirit saith unto the churches; He that overcometh shall not be hurt of the second death.

The Bible also teaches that Jesus is coming quickly and we are to hold on to what we have and not let any man take our crown. The crowns we are to be given must be guarded. Someone can take your crown through deception and lead you astray by sinning against the Lord and following a false Christ.

Revelation 3:11 (KJV)

11 Behold, I come quickly: hold that fast which thou hast, **that no man take thy crown.**

The twenty-four elders in the Book of Revelation cast their crowns before the Throne of God.

Revelation 4:10-11 (KJV)

10 The four and twenty elders fall down before him that sat on the throne, and worship him that liveth for ever and ever, **and cast their crowns before the throne,** saying,
11 Thou art worthy, O Lord, to receive glory and honour and power: for thou hast created all things, and for thy pleasure they are and were created.

As we can see, God has many rewards for those who faithfully serve Him in this life. This life is only a testing ground for those who will live with God forever. God is looking to see those who will give up everything in this life, seek the *High Calling* of God and prepare themselves for the next life. Everything people do in this life is being written in books, and on Judgment Day, those books will be opened and reveal what people chose. Those who accept Christ and make Him their Lord by keeping His Commandments will be written in the Lamb's Book of Life.

Daniel 7:9-10 (KJV)

9 I beheld till the thrones were cast down, and the Ancient of days did sit, whose garment was white as snow, and the hair

of his head like the pure wool: his throne was like the fiery flame, and his wheels as burning fire.

10 A fiery stream issued and came forth from before him: thousand thousands ministered unto him, and ten thousand times ten thousand stood before him: the judgment was set, **and the books were opened.**

Revelation 20:11-15 (KJV)

11 And I saw a great white throne, and him that sat on it, from whose face the earth and the heaven fled away; and there was found no place for them.

12 And I saw the dead, small and great, stand before God; **and the books were opened: and another book was opened, which is the Book of life: and the dead were judged out of those things which were written in the books, according to their works.**

13 And the sea gave up the dead which were in it; and death and hell delivered up the dead which were in them: **and they were judged every man according to their works.**

14 And death and hell were cast into the lake of fire. This is the second death.

15 And whosoever was not found written in the **Book of life** was cast into the lake of fire.

I am writing this book as a warning and a challenge. I am warning those who deny God and forsake the calling to be a follower of Christ. I am also challenging every follower of Christ to press into the *High Calling* of God. What I mean by *High Calling* is the perfect will of God for your life. Do not settle for anything less than all that God has to offer you. He may call you to be a missionary or do something locally where you live. Whatever you do, make sure you pay the price to fulfill your God-given destiny and do the perfect will of God.

Romans 12:1-2 (KJV)

> 1 I beseech you therefore, brethren, by the mercies of God, that ye present your bodies a living sacrifice, holy, acceptable unto God, which is your reasonable service.
> 2 And be not conformed to this world: but be ye transformed by the renewing of your mind, that ye may prove what is that good, and acceptable, **and perfect, will of God.**

Don't settle for anything less than the perfect will of God. Also, do not let anyone deceive you into living a lukewarm Christian life because you will only be vomited out of the mouth of God.

Revelation 3:15-16 (KJV)

> 15 I know thy works, that thou art neither cold nor hot: I would thou wert cold or hot.
> 16 **So then because thou art lukewarm, and neither cold nor hot, I will spue thee out of my mouth.**

There is only one decision to make: one of an all-in, all-the-time commitment to Christ. Your decision will be written down in the Books of Heaven. God is offering His life and kingdom for your mundane life. What will you choose? Choose wisely because this life will be over soon for everyone. No one lives forever in this life. Those who choose to deny themselves and take up their cross daily and follow Christ will be granted an eternal *Supernatural Security Clearance.* This eternal *Supernatural Security Clearance* will grant you access to God, entrance into the Heavenly Jerusalem, and enable you to live eternally with God. You will also be granted access to the Tree of Life and the River of Life.

Revelation 22:1-3 (KJV)

> 1 And he shewed me a pure river of water of life, clear as crystal, proceeding out of the Throne of God and of the Lamb.

2 In the midst of the street of it, and on either side of the river, was there the tree of life, which bare twelve manner of fruits, and yielded her fruit every month: and the leaves of the tree were for the healing of the nations.

3 And there shall be no more curse: but the Throne of God and of the Lamb shall be in it; and his servants shall serve him:

In conclusion, God wants to know where you stand and if you are willing to do what it takes to be granted an eternal *Supernatural Security Clearance.* You can continue living the way you have been living for years or decide to serve God with your whole life. I believe the Spirit of God is talking to you as you read this book. I am talking to someone directly as I write this book. If you obey God and follow Him with your whole life, you will be granted a place to sit at His Heavenly table. Now is the day of Salvation, and today is the day to say yes to God's *High Calling.* There could not be more at stake than answering God's *High Calling*!

CHAPTER 15
DEBRIEFING

This book may be one of the most challenging books you have read in a long time, and it is meant to be. God has done everything in His power to not only create humankind but also to save them. God has also revealed His great love for us. However, just because God loves us, it does not mean He will lower His standards for granting *Supernatural Security Clearances* to just allow people to live with Him throughout all eternity. If we love God with all our hearts by obeying His Word and accepting Jesus as our Lord, we can inherit all that God has to offer.

This book was written to reveal through many Scriptures that God has requirements and they must be met for someone to be given a *Supernatural Security Clearance*. Some teachers of our day have watered down the message of Christ and the Bible. Both the Old and New Testaments are filled with stories and examples of people given and some losing their *Supernatural Security Clearance*. *Supernatural Security Clearances* from God are real and are not handed out to everyone.

Everything about God and His kingdom is sacred, and His eternal treasures will only be given to those who have *Supernatural Security Clearances*. I have gone into painstaking detail to reveal the many aspects of this subject in this book. The subject of *Supernatural Security Clearances* is not to be taken lightly. Your life and future will be determined if you have a *Supernatural Security Clearance*. Those who have one will be granted access to God's Heavenly Kingdom, and those who do not will be destined to go to hell. It is no accident you are reading this book. I believe God is speaking to someone reading this book and offering them clues on how to walk closer with Him and be granted a *Supernatural Security Clearance*.

Heaven and hell are very real places, and what we do in this life will determine where we end up. In writing this book, the Lord revealed to me that there would be many people reading this book who do not know Jesus or have any knowledge of God's *Supernatural Security Clearances*. If this is you, then know that God is reaching out to you and revealing the secret message of His Kingdom! Not everyone is granted to know the mysteries of God's Kingdom. God loves everyone, but not everyone loves God back in return. God also knows the timing of when someone is ready to hear His message and make a choice to serve Him. I believe the fact that you found this book and are reading it today shows that God is reaching out to you.

I made a list of requirements revealed in the Bible for what one must do to enter the kingdom of God, receive answers to prayers, go to Heaven, and be granted a *Supernatural Security Clearance*.

1. Repent of Your Sins

2. Believe in Your Heart that God Raised Jesus from the Dead

3. Confess with Your Mouth that Jesus is Lord

4. Enter the New Covenant and Obey Your Conscience

5. Keep the Commands of Jesus

6. Be Led by the Holy Spirit and Walk in the Holy Spirit

7. Live by Faith

Repent of Your Sins

When Jesus came to this earth, He preached that people must repent for the kingdom of God was at hand.

Matthew 4:17 (KJV)

17 From that time Jesus began to preach, and to say, **Repent: for the kingdom of heaven is at hand.**

The word *repent* means to change one's mind, have a change of heart to God, turn from your sin, and show sorrow for your sins. When someone repents, they feel sorrow and remorse for sinning against God and His Word. A repentant sinner has a change of heart and makes a decision to turn from their sins. At the same moment, they make a decision to serve God and obey His Commandments. Repentance involves a change of heart, mind, and actions. It is not good enough to only feel bad about your sins; you must change your actions also.

Believe in Your Heart that God Raised Jesus from the Dead

Jesus came to this earth, died, and rose again for us to be saved. It is by God's grace we are saved if we believe. Believing what Jesus has done for us plays a big part in our salvation.

Ephesians 2:8-9 (KJV)

8 **For by grace are ye saved through faith;** and that not of yourselves: it is the gift of God:

9 Not of works, lest any man should boast.

Jesus not only taught that men need to repent for the kingdom of God is at hand, but He also preached that they were to believe the Gospel. The Gospel is the good news of Jesus coming to this earth and delivering us from evil by dying on a cross so that we might be saved.

Mark 1:15 (KJV)

15 And saying, The time is fulfilled, and the kingdom of God is at hand: **repent ye, and believe the Gospel.**

Your belief plays a significant role in you getting saved and given authorized Divine access to a *Supernatural Security Clearance.* You must believe that Jesus died on the cross for your sins and that God raised Him from the dead for you to be saved.

Romans 10:6-11 (KJV)

6 But the righteousness which is of faith speaketh on this wise, Say not in thine heart, Who shall ascend into heaven? (that is, to bring Christ down from above:)

7 Or, Who shall descend into the deep? (that is, to bring up Christ again from the dead.)

8 But what saith it? The word is nigh thee, even in thy mouth, and in thy heart: that is, the word of faith, which we preach;

9 That if thou shalt confess with thy mouth the Lord Jesus, **and shalt believe in thine heart that God hath raised him from the dead, thou shalt be saved.**

10 **For with the heart man believeth unto righteousness;** and with the mouth confession is made unto salvation.

> **11 For the scripture saith, Whosoever believeth on him shall not be ashamed.**

It pleases God when we believe what He has done for us through the death, burial, and resurrection of Jesus Christ. To be saved and be granted a *Supernatural Security Clearance,* you must believe that Jesus Christ rose again. Your faith also plays a vital role in your life as a Christian.

> **Habakkuk 2:4 (KJV)**
> 4 Behold, his soul which is lifted up is not upright in him: **but the just shall live by his faith.**

It is only by faith that you can please God.

> **Hebrews 11:6 (KJV)**
> 6 **But without faith it is impossible to please him:** for he that cometh to God must believe that he is, and that he is a rewarder of them that diligently seek him.

Confess with Your Mouth that Jesus is Lord

Your confession plays a vital role in your salvation. It is crucial what comes out of your mouth. The Bible says that death and life are in the power of the tongue. God listens to everything we say, and so does all of creation. We were made in the image of God, who spoke everything into existence with the power of His Words. We can only access salvation by confessing Jesus as our Lord and Savior.

> **Romans 10:6-11 (KJV)**
> 6 But the righteousness which is of faith speaketh on this wise, Say not in thine heart, Who shall ascend into heaven? (that is, to bring Christ down from above:)

> 7 Or, Who shall descend into the deep? (that is, to bring up
> Christ again from the dead.)
> 8 But what saith it? The word is nigh thee, even in thy mouth,
> and in thy heart: that is, the word of faith, which we preach;
> 9 **That if thou shalt confess with thy mouth the Lord Jesus,**
> and shalt believe in thine heart that God hath raised him
> from the dead, thou shalt be saved.
> 10 For with the heart man believeth unto righteousness; **and**
> **with the mouth confession is made unto salvation.**
> 11 For the scripture saith, Whosoever believeth on him shall
> not be ashamed.

If you confess that Jesus is Lord, you will be saved. This confession of Jesus as Lord does not mean you make this statement of Him being your Lord, and nothing in your life changes. To confess Jesus as your Lord means you will obey Him and do the will of the Father. If you do not obey Jesus and do not do the will of the Father, your confession of calling Jesus Lord means nothing.

Matthew 7:21-23 (KJV)

> 21 **Not every one that saith unto me, Lord, Lord, shall enter**
> **into the kingdom of heaven; but he that doeth the will of**
> **my Father which is in heaven.**
> 22 Many will say to me in that day, Lord, Lord, have we not
> prophesied in thy name? and in thy name have cast out
> devils? and in thy name done many wonderful works?
> 23 And then will I profess unto them, I never knew you:
> depart from me, ye that work iniquity.

To become a Christian and obtain a *Supernatural Security Clearance,* Jesus must be your Lord. You cannot be saved if you do not make Jesus your Lord. Every human will proclaim that Jesus is Lord, either by their own choice or by force. You can confess that Jesus is Lord now before you die, or you will be forced to call Him Lord as you are sent to hell. Either way, Jesus will be confessed as Lord by everyone.

> **Philippians 2:5-11 (KJV)**
> 5 Let this mind be in you, which was also in Christ Jesus:
> 6 Who, being in the form of God, thought it not robbery to be equal with God:
> 7 But made himself of no reputation, and took upon him the form of a servant, and was made in the likeness of men:
> 8 And being found in fashion as a man, he humbled himself, and became obedient unto death, even the death of the cross.
> 9 Wherefore God also hath highly exalted him, and given him a name which is above every name:
> 10 That at the name of Jesus every knee should bow, of things in heaven, and things in earth, and things under the earth;
> 11 **And that every tongue should confess that Jesus Christ is Lord, to the glory of God the Father.**

Every knee will bow and every tongue will confess that Jesus is Lord. Some will do it against their will, but God is looking for those who will do it now by their own choice. Jesus paid a heavy price to be the Lord of everything, and we need to honor Him with a life of obedience to His Word.

Enter the New Covenant and Obey Your Conscience

On the night before Jesus died on the cross, He revealed the New Covenant. The Old Covenant was the Law of Moses. Jesus was fulfilling the Law of Moses by dying on the cross, and the blood of Jesus was the *sacrificial atonement* of the New Covenant.

Matthew 26:26-29 (KJV)

26 And as they were eating, Jesus took bread, and blessed it, and brake it, and gave it to the disciples, and said, Take, eat; this is my body.

27 **And he took the cup, and gave thanks, and gave it to them, saying, Drink ye all of it;**

28 **For this is my blood of the new testament, which is shed for many for the remission of sins.**

29 But I say unto you, I will not drink henceforth of this fruit of the vine, until that day when I drink it new with you in my Father's kingdom.

When Jesus died and rose again, He established the New Covenant. The words Covenant and Testament mean the same thing. We can read about this New Covenant in the Book of Jeremiah.

Jeremiah 31:31-34 (KJV)

31 Behold, the days come, saith the Lord, that I will make a new covenant with the house of Israel, and with the house of Judah:

32 Not according to the covenant that I made with their fathers in the day that I took them by the hand to bring them out of the land of Egypt; which my covenant they brake, although I was an husband unto them, saith the Lord:

33 But this shall be the covenant that I will make with the house of Israel; After those days, saith the Lord, I will put my law in their inward parts, and write it in their hearts; and will be their God, and they shall be my people.

34 And they shall teach no more every man his neighbour, and every man his brother, saying, Know the Lord: for they shall all know me, from the least of them unto the greatest of them, saith the Lord: for I will forgive their iniquity, and I will remember their sin no more.

The New Covenant was the writing of the Law of Moses on the hearts of God's chosen people. God said He would write His Laws on the inside of people and that He would be their God and they would be His people. It also says that we can all know the Lord for ourselves and that our sins will be forgiven and not be remembered.

We can read more about the New Covenant in the Book of Hebrews.

Hebrews 10:15-23 (KJV)
> 15 Whereof the Holy Ghost also is a witness to us: for after that he had said before,
> 16 **This is the covenant that I will make with them after those days, saith the Lord, I will put my laws into their hearts, and in their minds will I write them;**
> 17 **And their sins and iniquities will I remember no more.**
> 18 Now where remission of these is, there is no more offering for sin.
> 19 **Having therefore, brethren, boldness to enter into the holiest by the blood of Jesus,**
> 20 By a new and living way, which he hath consecrated for us, through the veil, that is to say, his flesh;
> 21 And having an high priest over the house of God;
> 22 **Let us draw near with a true heart in full assurance of faith, having our hearts sprinkled from an evil conscience, and our bodies washed with pure water.**
> 23 Let us hold fast the profession of our faith without wavering; (for he is faithful that promised;)

When someone confesses and makes Jesus their Lord, Jesus' blood is sprinkled on their heart and evil conscience. At this point, the conscience is washed clean, and the Laws of God are written on their heart. A sign that someone has an authentic salvation experience is they will no longer want to sin. The blood of Jesus revives their dead conscience by His blood, and they want to do the will of God and obey His Laws.

The Laws of God being written on someone's heart is the reviving of the conscience. The newborn believer in Christ wants to obey Jesus. The blood of Jesus changes the heart of the repentant sinner. From this point forward, they need to follow their conscience in all things as they grow in God. There is no way for new believers to know all the Laws of God revealed in the Bible, but they can know God on the inside of them and His Laws by the leading of the Holy Spirit through their conscience.

God will judge the entire world on the Day of Judgment based upon the Laws of God and if they obeyed their conscience.

> **Romans 2:11-16 (KJV)**
> 11 For there is no respect of persons with God.
> 12 For as many as have sinned without law shall also perish without law: and as many as have sinned in the law shall be judged by the law;
> 13 (For not the hearers of the law are just before God, but the doers of the law shall be justified.
> 14 **For when the Gentiles, which have not the law, do by nature the things contained in the law, these, having not the law, are a law unto themselves:**
> 15 **Which shew the work of the law written in their hearts, their conscience also bearing witness, and their thoughts the mean while accusing or else excusing one another;)**
> 16 **In the day when God shall judge the secrets of men by Jesus Christ according to my Gospel.**

Your conscience is not always right, but it is never right to go against it. Your conscience is not always right because it may still be learning the Laws of God; until then, you must follow it. You may not know all the

Laws of God, but you can know if your heart and conscience are telling you that something you are about to do is right or wrong. If you always obey your conscience, you will remain in right standing with God. Your conscience will grow as you learn more of God's Word, but until then, by obeying your conscience, you are pleasing God. Anyone seeking a *Supernatural Security Clearance* from God must obey their conscience.

Keep the Commands of Jesus

When Jesus sent out His disciples to preach the Gospel after His death, burial, and resurrection, He gave them a charge. Let's read this charge found in the Gospel of Matthew.

> **Matthew 28:18-20 (KJV)**
> 18 And Jesus came and spake unto them, saying, All power is given unto me in heaven and in earth.
> 19 **Go ye therefore, and teach all nations, baptizing them in the Name of the Father, and of the Son, and of the Holy Ghost:**
> 20 **Teaching them to observe all things whatsoever I have commanded you:** and, lo, I am with you always, even unto the end of the world. Amen.

This passage of Scripture is called the Great Commission. Jesus commissioned His disciples to go into all the world and preach the Gospel. Here is a list of what He told them to do:

1. Go

2. Teach all nations

3. Baptizing them in the Name of the Father, Son, and Holy Spirit

4. Teaching them to observe everything He commanded them

The Great Commission was not about sending out the disciples to just get people saved. Jesus sent them out to baptize people, which represented them coming into a new life, but most importantly, He sent them to teach people to observe everything He commanded them. A big part of the Gospel is keeping the teachings and Commandments of Christ.

Moses, in the Law, prophesied that God would send a **Prophet** and that God would require of us everything He spoke.

> **Deuteronomy 18:15-19 (KJV)**
> 15 **The Lord thy God will raise up unto thee a Prophet from the midst of thee,** of thy brethren, like unto me; unto him ye shall hearken;
> 16 According to all that thou desiredst of the Lord thy God in Horeb in the day of the assembly, saying, Let me not hear again the voice of the Lord my God, neither let me see this great fire any more, that I die not.
> 17 And the Lord said unto me, They have well spoken that which they have spoken.
> 18 **I will raise them up a Prophet from among their brethren, like unto thee, and will put my words in his mouth; and he shall speak unto them all that I shall command him.**
> 19 **And it shall come to pass, that whosoever will not hearken unto my words which he shall speak in my name, I will require it of him.**

Jesus was the **Prophet** to come, and He spoke the Words of God. Jesus taught in His teachings that He would not judge us on Judgement Day, but the Words He was speaking would judge people on that day.

John 12:47-50 (KJV)

> 47 **And if any man hear my words, and believe not, I judge him not:** for I came not to judge the world, but to save the world.
>
> 48 **He that rejecteth me, and receiveth not my words, hath one that judgeth him: the word that I have spoken, the same shall judge him in the last day.**
>
> 49 **For I have not spoken of myself; but the Father which sent me, he gave me a commandment, what I should say, and what I should speak.**
>
> 50 And I know that his commandment is life everlasting: **whatsoever I speak therefore, even as the Father said unto me, so I speak.**

Every red letter you see in your Bible where Jesus spoke is of utmost importance. You must read, study, and obey everything Jesus taught to be saved. Your very life depends upon how you respond to the Words of Christ. You will be judged by everything Jesus spoke. Everything Jesus spoke came from the heart of Father God. Jesus said you were only His disciple if you continued in His Word, and you would know the truth.

John 8:30-32 (KJV)

> 30 As he spake these words, many believed on him.
>
> 31 Then said Jesus to those Jews which believed on him, **If ye continue in my word, then are ye my disciples indeed;**
>
> 32 **And ye shall know the truth, and the truth shall make you free.**

To gain access to God and His kingdom, you must adhere to and obey all the Words of Christ. *Supernatural Security Clearances* will only be handed out to those who continue to observe all that Jesus commanded and taught.

Be Led by the Spirit and Walk in the Holy Spirit

When someone accepts Christ and makes Him their Lord, they become a son of God.

John 1:12 (KJV)

12 **But as many as received him, to them gave he power to become the sons of God, even to them that believe on His Name:**

Jesus revealed to Nicodemus that for someone to enter the kingdom of God, they must be born again. When someone is born again, they become a son of God.

John 3:1-8 (KJV)

1 There was a man of the Pharisees, named Nicodemus, a ruler of the Jews:

2 The same came to Jesus by night, and said unto him, Rabbi, we know that thou art a teacher come from God: for no man can do these miracles that thou doest, except God be with him.

3 Jesus answered and said unto him, Verily, verily, I say unto thee, **Except a man be born again, he cannot see the kingdom of God.**

4 Nicodemus saith unto him, How can a man be born when he is old? can he enter the second time into his mother's womb, and be born?

5 Jesus answered, Verily, verily, I say unto thee, **Except a man be born of water and of the Spirit, he cannot enter into the kingdom of God.**

6 **That which is born of the flesh is flesh; and that which is born of the Spirit is spirit.**

7 Marvel not that I said unto thee, Ye must be born again.

8 The wind bloweth where it listeth, and thou hearest the sound thereof, but canst not tell whence it cometh, and whither it goeth: so is every one that is born of the Spirit.

When someone accepts Christ, they are born of the Spirit, and from this point forward, the Spirit leads them. Being led by the Spirit is a sign you are a son of God.

Romans 8:14 (KJV)

14 **For as many as are led by the Spirit of God, they are the sons of God.**

The Spirit led even Jesus, who is The Son of God.

Luke 4:1 (KJV)

1 **And Jesus being full of the Holy Ghost returned from Jordan, and was led by the Spirit into the wilderness,**

To be led by the Spirit, we must walk in the Spirit. Walking in the Spirit means we do not obey the lust of the flesh. Walking in the Spirit also means we bear the fruit of the Spirit in our lives.

Galatians 5:16-25 (KJV)

16 **This I say then, Walk in the Spirit, and ye shall not fulfil the lust of the flesh.**

17 For the flesh lusteth against the Spirit, and the Spirit against the flesh: and these are contrary the one to the other: so that ye cannot do the things that ye would.

18 **But if ye be led of the Spirit, ye are not under the law.**

19 Now the works of the flesh are manifest, which are these; Adultery, fornication, uncleanness, lasciviousness,

20 Idolatry, witchcraft, hatred, variance, emulations, wrath, strife, seditions, heresies,

21 Envyings, murders, drunkenness, revellings, and such like: of the which I tell you before, as I have also told you in time past, that they which do such things shall not inherit the kingdom of God.

22 But the fruit of the Spirit is love, joy, peace, longsuffering, gentleness, goodness, faith,

23 Meekness, temperance: against such there is no law.

24 And they that are Christ's have crucified the flesh with the affections and lusts.

25 **If we live in the Spirit, let us also walk in the Spirit.**

To gain access into God's kingdom and become a son of God, you must walk in the Spirit and not fulfill the lust of the flesh. If you fulfill the lusts of the flesh, you are not a true son of God. Jesus died and rose again that we might become the sons of God, but we must be led by the Spirit to become the children of God. If you are given a *Supernatural Security Clearance,* you must walk in the Spirit and be led by the Spirit.

Live by Faith

Faith plays a vital role and gets into every aspect of a believer's life. God has done everything for us. He created us, sent Jesus to die for our sins, prepared a place for us in Heaven, and provided for every need we would have on earth. God's main requirement is for His children to believe Him. All the promises of God are waiting to be fulfilled for the man or woman who will believe God for them. Christians are called to live by faith in every area of their life, and you cannot operate in a *Supernatural Security Clearance* without faith.

Romans 1:16-17 (KJV)

> 16 For I am not ashamed of the Gospel of Christ: for it is the power of God unto salvation to every one that believeth; to the Jew first, and also to the Greek.
>
> 17 For therein is the righteousness of God revealed from faith to faith: as it is written, **The just shall live by faith.**

True Biblical faith involves believing God and what His Word says without any wavering, doubt, or unbelief. A believer takes God at His Word without seeing with their naked eye. They have the eye of faith that can see into the unseen world and believe that God is, and He is a rewarder of those who diligently seek Him. They know by faith they have the answer, even if they cannot see it. Faith is a knowing deep in the heart that God is there with you and ready to help you in your time of need.

Hebrews 11:6 (KJV)

> 6 **But without faith it is impossible to please him: for he that cometh to God must believe that he is, and that he is a rewarder of them that diligently seek him.**

We cannot see God with our naked eye at this time, but we know He is there by faith. Faith can see the unseen God with the eye of faith. We not only can see God by faith, but we also believe and trust God for all our needs. We trust and believe God with our faith that He will not let us down. Our faith allows us to trust in God with all our hearts. Although we cannot see Him, we can sense His presence and trust in His Word, knowing He will be there for us and not let us down.

God has made many promises in His Word, and by faith, we can receive and inherit all of them. But we must be diligent in staying in His Word and remaining faithful while God works everything out in our favor.

Hebrews 6:12 (KJV)

12 **That ye be not slothful, but followers of them who through faith and patience inherit the promises.**

Our faith can believe God, even when odds are stacked against us. Sometimes we go through challenging times in life, but we believe we will overcome every situation we face by faith in God. Faith never doubts God in tough times and never blames God for the hard times. We know that Jesus is inherently good and works all things out for our good to those who love Him and are called according to His purpose.

Romans 8:28 (KJV)

28 **And we know that all things work together for good to them that love God, to them who are the called according to his purpose.**

Jesus did many miracles during His ministry on the earth, but He always pointed to people's faith who received a miracle.

Matthew 15:28 (KJV)

28 Then Jesus answered and said unto her, **O woman, great is thy faith: be it unto thee even as thou wilt.** And her daughter was made whole from that very hour.

Mark 5:34 (KJV)

34 And he said unto her, Daughter, **thy faith hath made thee whole**; go in peace, and be whole of thy plague.

Luke 7:50 (KJV)

50 And he said to the woman, **Thy faith hath saved thee**; go in peace.

Luke 18:42 (KJV)

42 And Jesus said unto him, Receive thy sight: **thy faith hath saved thee.**

Our faith is particularly important to Jesus. Jesus is the *Author* and *Finisher* of our faith.

> **Hebrews 12:2 (KJV)**
> **2 Looking unto Jesus the author and finisher of our faith;** who for the joy that was set before him endured the cross, despising the shame, and is set down at the right hand of the Throne of God.

Our faith is more precious than gold which perishes, and it will be our faith that will praise and honor Jesus when He appears. Although we do not see God now, we love Him and have joy unspeakable, knowing God is with us and for us.

> **1 Peter 1:7-8 (KJV)**
> **7 That the trial of your faith, being much more precious than of gold that perisheth,** though it be tried with fire, might be found unto praise and honour and glory at the appearing of Jesus Christ:
> **8 Whom having not seen, ye love; in whom, though now ye see him not, yet believing, ye rejoice with joy unspeakable and full of glory:**

We as Christians live by faith, walk by faith and please God with our faith. You please God when you believe God and take Him at His Word, even when the situation seems impossible. God wants His children to know He can work miracles and pull you out of any pit if you believe Him. God's power works best in challenging situations where you need a miracle. God loves working miracles for His children that believe in Him.

As we come near the end of this book and understand what it takes to obtain a *Supernatural Security Clearance,* it is essential to understand what we must do to meet the requirements to receive a *Supernatural Security Clearance* from God. I know that everyone who reads this book may not be a Christian, and God has brought this book to you so you can see what it takes to enter the *High Calling* of God.

God is calling many people to Himself in these last days, and He is looking for those who answer His call. If you do not know Jesus as your personal Savior, today is your day of salvation. What you must do to be saved is believe God raised Jesus from the dead and confess that Jesus is your Lord. Here is a prayer you can pray now:

Father in Heaven, I humbly come to you and repent of my sins. I believe in my heart that you raised Jesus from the dead, and with my mouth I confess Jesus as my Lord. I commit to loving you and obeying your Commandments. I give you the reigns of my life, and I ask you to lead me by your Spirit. I thank you for everything you have done for me. In Jesus' Name, Amen!

This is a simple prayer you can pray to God, and He will hear you. Call out to God, and He will be with you in your time of need.

I also understand that many believers reading this book seek a deeper walk with God. This book was not written to reveal all the secrets of God to you. This book was written to show you the deeper commitments God is looking for before He begins to reveal His deeper secrets to you. You can go from hearing the parables of Jesus to being explained the parables of Jesus if you will commit your whole life to God so you can receive a *Supernatural Security Clearance*.

God has desired to give you a *Supernatural Security Clearance*, but He needs you to make the commitment it will take to walk in the requirements of having one. God will not give out a *Supernatural*

Security Clearance to those too immature to handle it. You must be ready to walk in the demands a *Supernatural Security Clearance* will place upon your life. You may have to sit under *tutors* and *governors* until you mature and prepare for God's *High Calling.* Tutors and governors refer to mature spiritual leaders in the body of Christ.

> **Galatians 4:1-2 (KJV)**
> 1 Now I say, That the heir, as long as he is a child, differeth nothing from a servant, though he be lord of all;
> 2 **But is under tutors and governors until the time appointed of the father.**

In conclusion, *Supernatural Security Clearances* are very real. The term *Supernatural Security Clearance* may not be in the Bible, but the truth of what the term stands for can be found all over the Bible. God's Spirit led me to use this term so people could take what they understand in the natural about security clearances and apply it to the Bible. God always takes what people know to help them understand things they do not know. Now you know what a *Supernatural Security Clearance* is from the many Scriptural stories and truths found in this book. God is looking for people who will answer His call, take up His mantle and meet the requirements of being found worthy to obtain a *Supernatural Security Clearance.*

ABOUT THE AUTHOR

Vince Baker was born in Southern California and lived on 17 acres just north of Sacramento. As a child, Vince was raised as a Southern Baptist. Vince was always drawn to the Lord and even said he wanted to be a preacher at a young age.

Vince's life was uneventful until one day he encountered God while driving in his car at the age of 17. God manifested Himself to Vince in such a powerful way that his life would never be the same. After this experience, Vince dedicated his life to the Lord and became a Christian. In that same month, Vince received a book from his Christian Grandma called *"The Secret of His Power."* This book was about a famous miracle-working Evangelist named Smith Wigglesworth. God used his testimony to prepare Vince for ministry. God also used the testimony of Smith to talk to Vince about things He wanted to do through him in his later years.

Vince decided to go to a Christian High School his senior year. He met a seasoned Evangelist at this high school, who took different Churches to feed the poor and evangelize. Vince found out he lived near the Evangelist and started traveling with him. During this time, Vince became his right-hand man and saw many amazing miracles on the streets through this ministry. This ministry was called to train the Church on how to evangelize with power. Vince was able to travel up and down the West Coast ministering to the homeless and helpless while equipping the Church. Vince has a big heart when it comes to the poor, homeless, and hurting people.

Within a short time, Vince heard from God to go to Bible College. Through confirmation from God and a miracle of his tuition paid for, Vince started to study the Bible more deeply at this Bible College. The training and foundation in the Scriptures Vince received were priceless. Vince ended up graduating as the Valedictorian from this Bible College.

After Bible College, Vince started ministering to kids at a Christian school, taught Sunday School, and functioned in the local Church. Vince later moved into full-time ministry and was an assistant Pastor at another local Church for five years during the 90's.

As an assistant pastor, Vince visited a Church where the Prophet Kim Clement was ministering. Prophet Kim Clement pulled Vince out of the crowd and prophesied over him. In that prophecy, God spoke to Vince through Kim Clement that he would use him and that he needed to prepare himself.

Vince later worked in the marketplace, where he is the CEO and part-owner of Agora Advantage. God called Vince to the marketplace, but Vince knew that he would be called back into full-time ministry later in life. Agora Advantage has been a fantastic opportunity where Vince grew in many ways. Vince knew that Agora was where he was supposed to be. He was voted in as the CEO of Agora Advantage on the Day of Pentecost as a sign from God.

As Vince started nearing the prophesied time that God would bring him back into full-time ministry, he began seeking the Lord more deeply. During this time, Vince had another unforgettable encounter with God regarding the Ark of the Covenant. God gave Vince a vision of four men carrying the Ark of the Covenant into a large Church. The Holy Spirit spoke to Vince and said, "Wherever you read Ark of the Covenant in the Old Testament think Holy Spirit. Wherever you read Holy Spirit in the New Testament think Ark of the Covenant. Put the two together and you will know Me." Vince went and studied these two subjects everyplace he could find them in the Bible, and he received tremendous insight into understanding the Holy Spirit.

God also revealed to Vince a prophetic way to study the Bible from this experience. Vince went on to spend years in the Word of God, with the Holy Spirit studying different subjects of the Bible. At the leading of the Holy Spirit, Vince researched every place a word or phrase was found, from the Old and New Testaments. Vince has currently done over 400 of these studies, some of which took over a month to complete. The revelations that came out of these studies were life changing. Vince wrote all these teachings and revelations down, which make up a lot of the truths he writes about in his books and messages. When you study a subject everywhere it is found in the Bible you can understand the full counsel of God on the subject. Vince also received many dreams and visitations from God during this time.

Vince has a unique calling where he can preach, teach, prophecy, move in the gifts of the Spirit, bring healing, and perform miracles by the power of the Holy Spirit. Vince is called to help the body of Christ come into their destiny and *High Calling*.

Currently, Vince resides in Northern California with his wife Eunice and their two dogs enjoying the blessings of God.

INVITE VINCE TO SPEAK

Visit

www.VinceBakerMinistries.com

ADDITIONAL BOOK BY
<u>VINCE BAKER</u>

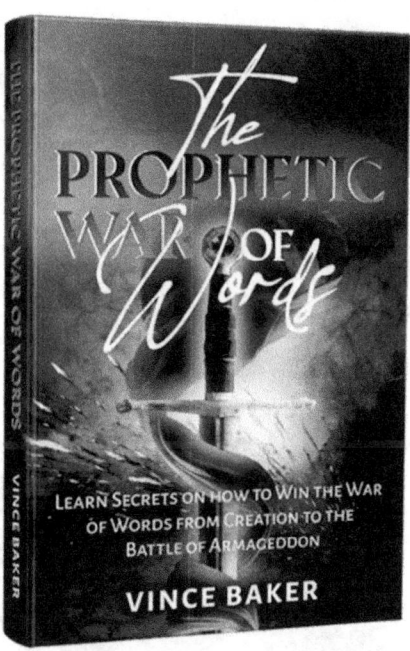

www.amazon.com/author/vincebaker
www.VinceBakerMinistries.com

ADDITIONAL BOOK BY
VINCE BAKER

www.amazon.com/author/vincebaker

www.VinceBakerMinistries.com

ADDITIONAL BOOK BY
<u>VINCE BAKER</u>

www.amazon.com/author/vincebaker

www.VinceBakerMinistries.com

ADDITIONAL BOOK BY
<u>VINCE BAKER</u>

ADDITIONAL BOOK BY
<u>VINCE BAKER</u>

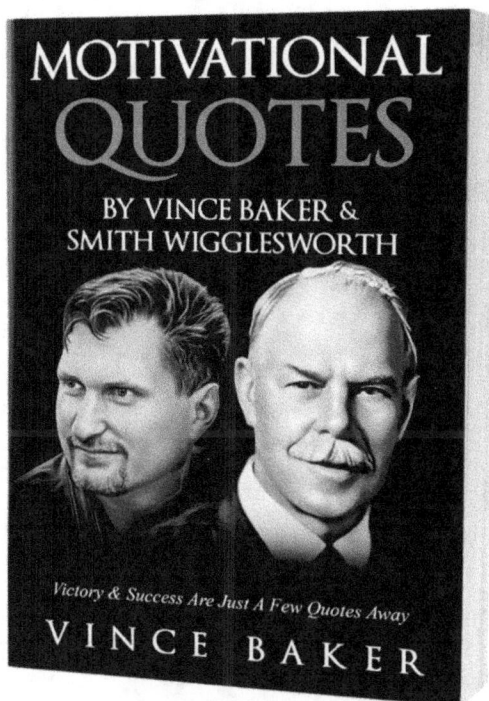

www.amazon.com/author/vincebaker

www.VinceBakerMinistries.com